Gower in History

Myth, People, Landscape

Paul Ferris

Armanaleg
Books

ISBN 978-0-9562332-0-2

Designed, printed and bound by Y Lolfa Cyf., Talybont, Ceredigion

Armanaleg Books
PO Box 177, Hay on Wye, HR3 5XZ

CONTENTS

For Mary

ACKNOWLEDGEMENTS

For information and advice I am indebted to:

Michael Gibbs. John Vivian Hughes. Richard Morris. The Gower Society, in particular Malcolm and Ruth Ridge, and Bernard Morris (editor, *Gower* journal). Crofton Black. Gradon Carter (formerly of the Defence Science and Technology Laboratory, Porton Down). Marilyn Jones (Swansea Reference Library). Professor Jim Kennedy (Director, Oxford University Museum of Natural History.) The Methuen-Campbells: David, Joanna (Martin), Lucinda, Oona and Thomas. National Library of Wales. National Museum of Wales (Mark Redknap, Medieval Archaeology and Numismatics; Tom Sharpe, Palaeontology.)

Jennifer Arthure. Rosalind Caird (Hereford Library). Bernice Cardy. Jeff Childs. Rodney Cooper. Fred Cowley. Susan J. Davies. Mari Evans. Gloria Ferris. Jonathan Ferris. Gerald Gabb. Jessica Glauert. Jonathan Gray. Canon Joe Griffin. Edward Harris. Emily Hewitt. Chris Howes. Debbie and Peter Lloyd. John Lucas. T.F.G. Higham. Sally and Peter Lyne. Feargus G. MacIntyre. Edward Martin. Penny Matthews. Hugh Morgan. Lindsay and Valerie Morgan. Mary Morgan. Professor Prys Morgan. Professor Richard Rathbone. Benita Afan Rees (Llanelli Historical Society). Harvey Rees. Alan Richards. Ann Roberts. Michael Rush. Garethe El Tawab (Royal Institution of South Wales). Jeff Towns (Dylans Book Store). Jeff Walden (BBC Archives). Gwen Watkins. Canon Peter Williams.

Joseph P. Clancy's creative translations of Welsh medieval verse (Chapter 2) are from *Medieval Welsh Poems* (2003), The Four Courts Press. Dublin. Nigel Jenkins' poem 'Oxwich' (Chapter 6) is from *Gower* (1972). The three lines of R.S. Thomas's poem 'Welsh Border Blues' (Chapter 7) are from *The Bread of Truth*, Rupert Hart-Davis (1963). Vernon Watkins' poem 'Ballad of the

Equinox' (Chapter 11) is from *The Collected Poems of Vernon Watkins*, Golgonooza Press (1968).

In Chapter 12, passages from *Kilvert's Diary, 1870-1879* (ed. William Plomer), published by Cape, are reprinted by permission of Random House Group. In Chapter 4, an extract from Dylan Thomas's story 'Extraordinary Little Cough' in *Portrait of the Artist as a Young Dog* is reprinted by permission of Dent.

PICTURE SOURCES

My thanks are due to: Peter and Sally Lyne (photograph of Rev. J.D. Davies). Lady Avebury (Dylan Thomas and Pamela Hansford Johnson at Caswell). Estate of R.L.T. Lucas (wreck of the *Cleveland*). J.V. Hughes (C.R.M. Talbot and Emily Talbot). Thomas Methuen-Campbell (Lady Blythswood). Chris Elphick (wreck of the *City of Bristol*). *South Wales Evening Post* (Prince Charles and Stone).

Other pictures: Death Ray Matthews: E.H.G. Barwell, *The Death Ray Man*. Swansea Sands: T.U.C. 'Souvenir' (1901). Paviland Cave sketch: William Buckland, *Reliquiae Diluvianae*.

Remaining photographs are the author's.

The illustration at pages 188-9, 'Swansea Bay, from Mumbles, June 5 1944,' is from a drawing by Rod Cooper, based on the author's notes made at the time.

Some of Gower's anglicised place-names have always had a Welsh-language equivalent, and more have acquired one in recent times. I have used whichever form comes naturally. The Carmarthenshire town across the estuary, formerly known as 'Llanelly,' now spells itself 'Llanelli.' For most of the period covered by this book, the 'y' version prevailed. I use both, unsystematically.

INTRODUCTION

THE GOWER PENINSULA lies off South Wales, west of Swansea, and runs parallel to the inner coastline, from which it is separated by an estuary. It is about fourteen miles long – depending on where you start measuring at the Swansea end – a rocky appendage, like something left over from a design that hasn't quite worked. Mumbles Pier, in Swansea Bay, to Worms Head is fourteen and a half miles. Most people call it 'Gower.' Some say 'the Gower,' from the Welsh-language form, 'Y Gwyr.' This annoys the 'Gower' brigade.

Gower is not on the way to anywhere, which made it remote. In its time it has been home to prehistoric people, to incomers who arrived with swords (a few brought bibles), to Cornish traders, Devonshire farmers, Carmarthenshire fishermen, London escapers. Its minority of Welsh-speaking Welsh are still there, just. Every weekday, cars take hundreds from the peninsula to work in Swansea and beyond. Every year, visitors arrive for a day or a fortnight. But Gower, with its huge bays and green moors, survives as a place apart. On a summer afternoon the car parks glitter with hot roofs. On a winter morning a gull screams above Oxwich churchyard, and along the shoreline one man throws a stick for one dog.

Gower's classic historian is a 19th century clergyman, John D. Davies, of Llanmadoc, who was uneasy with formal history, and worked best when he recorded what he saw and heard. In the four volumes of *West Gower*, published between 1877 and 1894, gossip and memory were part of his stock-in-trade. He is remembered for his curiosity, not his learning. Stories of wrecked treasure appearing on the coast, not long before his time, appealed to him: he touched the coins himself. He believed in ghosts, and heard a boy scream in terror when (he thought) the phantom of a drowned sailor came and peered into the church. Lady Wilkinson, one of Gower's grander inhabitants in the 19th century, told Davies a story she heard from 'an old man in Rhossili village,' that once, when Viking raiders landed at the northern end of the bay and attacked Llangennith, villagers from Rhossili, down at the other end, went and set fire to the invaders' boats. Davies makes no comment on this thousand-year memory, he simply passes it on. Stories, in his day, were still handed down by word of mouth; they were history as entertainment.

Everyone's book is their own, but more than once, Davies's has been in my thoughts as I wrote this one. It is mostly a narrative of episodes and individuals that between them tell a wider story. A troublesome Welshman is hanged by a Norman overlord and apparently comes back to life (1290). A child in a legend, born of incest, goes to sea in a basket and becomes a saint (first recorded 1400s). Men in armour fight over a barrel of figs (1557). An eccentric professor finds a woman's skeleton in a cave and makes her into a Romanesque fantasy (1823); her red bones had been there almost thirty thousand years, but the professor was not to know that. A herd of pigs and two men swim ashore from a nightmare of a wreck (1840). A bomb filled with anthrax is dropped on a beach, not by accident, two miles from a Gower village and three or four from the Carmarthenshire town of Llanelli (1942). Dylan Thomas declines to bathe in the sea (1950). A family with a long history adapts to a new age. A man with a grudge removes a five-ton monument that Prince Charles is about to unveil.

And always, in the background, are the poor, the dispossessed and the ordinary, and they are here too.

PAUL FERRIS
Boughrood, Powys, 2009

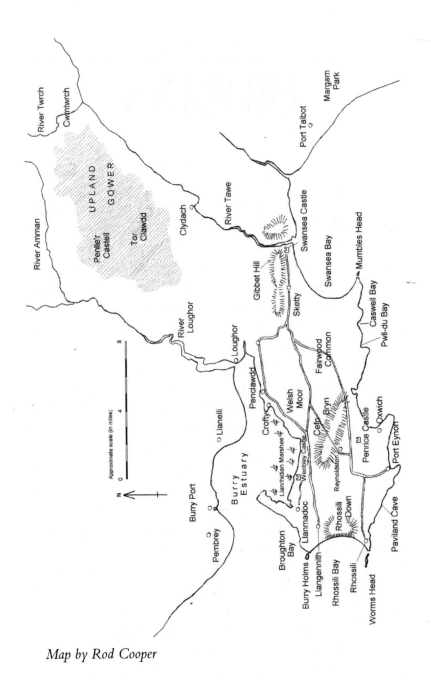

Map by Rod Cooper

CHAPTER 1

ORIGINS

L LANMADOC, a village in a corner of the Gower peninsula, in South Wales, straggles along the road and ends with a small church, after which there is nothing but fields, sand dunes and the sea. The church seems an afterthought, although it was there before the village, built by or for the Normans, who brought their own brand of muscular Christianity when they invaded. If ancient churches were rare, any one of them might attract tourists curious to see what a building put up seven hundred years ago looked like. But the place and its functions are taken for granted; there are seventeen working churches and some ruins in the peninsula, most of them ancient. Llanmadoc's has bleached stone, a steep roof, a little tower with battlements, and a churchyard where not all the gravestones are standing up straight.

I was there on a cold, dark weekday for research purposes. I used to know the village because it was on the way to the Whitford sands, but I had never bothered with the church. In the 19th century, Llanmadoc (and the linked parish of Cheriton) had a rector, John D. Davies (1831-1911) who wrote a famous history of Gower; famous in Gower, anyway. For someone thinking of writing a book about the territory, Davies's parish was a place to start.

Madoc was a little known Celtic saint with Irish connections. The church has been there since the 13th century although the legend says that Madoc's original church, probably wooden, was centuries earlier, in the sixth. Christianity took root in Wales long before the Normans, beginning when the Roman garrisons still clung to Britain, and monks came from France or Ireland as missionaries. The building faces the weather in two directions, west and north. An adjacent line of trees on the north side must have been planted as a windbreak. Beyond it, a mile or two away, depending on the state of the tide, is a blue line of estuary water, looking harmless enough, as though it has never drowned anyone. Sailors are buried in the churchyard. It is not a safe coast, and there have been disasters.

Llanmadoc is at the north-west corner of the Gower peninsula, whose southern edge of cliffs extends fourteen miles down the Bristol Channel from Swansea; turns to make the beautiful blunt end of the peninsula, Rhossili Bay; then goes back on itself to the east, along a narrowing estuary with marshes instead of beaches and headlands, though it does have cliffs here and there. Llanmadoc, roughly speaking, is where the turn to the east occurs.

The church, the smallest in Gower, was unlocked. A thief (looking for what? A silver candlestick? A laptop in the vestry?) would be deterred, they hope, by a notice in the porch:

> Protected property warning. To assist police, the property in the church has been coded with the Alpha Dot Security Marking System. THIEVES BEWARE – YOU WILL BE CAUGHT.

> Ecclesiastical Insurance Group

13

The only person inside the church was a woman, working at a deep windowsill to one side of the door, rubbing a sheet of paper laid on a slab of stone. She was using what looked like a wax crayon. She didn't look up.

Gower is no longer remote countryside, though loneliness can be found. Tourists are implored to visit and spend money each summer, and commuters live there all year. Before cars and proper roads, Gower was a dead-end. For most of its history the place was remote, of interest to outsiders only for its grain, its woodlands and its fish. These natural assets were enough to die for, and many did, over time. Intermittent conflict with the English is part of Welsh history, and Gower, a finite scrap of land with its own geographic identity, has provided a small theatre for history to happen in. Old blood-and-vengeance stories survive in Welsh manuscripts, and the peninsula is the setting for at least one of them, which has wolves feeding on the corpses of five hundred and sixteen English – soldiers, settlers or both – ambushed by a Welsh prince's men on a moor in eastern Gower. You wonder who counted them. It was New Year's Day, 1136. There would have been enough Englishmen to feel safe. The unsettling thing about history is that we know what was going to happen to people next, and they did not. Our past was still their future.

In later centuries, travellers rode or were conveyed into Gower out of curiosity, some of them romantics who wanted lakes and mountains, and found instead bare cliffs and moorland. Sand dunes were not much admired at the time. Also there was a lack of gentlemen's residences and the polite society that went with them. The place mouldered quietly. The first event in the second millennium to draw attention to Llanmadoc and Cheriton may have been the arrival in 1860 of the rector who wrote the book, John David Davies. To begin with he was not popular, being suspected of dangerous Roman Catholic tendencies. His father was himself a Gower clergyman, but Davies senior was an uncontroversial figure, married to a tea merchant's daughter. The new man, wifeless, was thought to be over-fond of ritual, going against the grain of plainer Christians. Such things mattered in 1860. 'Away with popish processions!' and 'Smash the candles and candlesticks to atoms!' said letters in the Swansea newspaper, the *Cambrian*.

Later his parishioners calmed down and grew fond of him. J.D. Davies was not as extreme as the low-church lobby made out. Under the robes and the Roman-style biretta, a sort of Italian mortar-board that he wore around the village, he had a nervous disposition that may have softened the image. He kept biscuits in his pocket to placate angry dogs. Mr Davies believed in ghosts, and even saw one in broad daylight. Best of all, he was curious about the small world he lived in, and the stories that clung to it.

By now he would have been long forgotten – he died in 1911 – but for his book, which ran to four volumes, published between 1877 and 1894, *A History of West Gower*. Only Volume 1 used that title. Having set out to write a comprehensive work, he prudently turned Vols. 2, 3 and 4 into more random collections of 'Historical Notices,' presented parish by parish. The work meanders in a creative sort of way, full of anecdote and observation, mixed in with long extracts from old documents, valuable if the reader is that way inclined, though otherwise hard going. But no well-informed writer had previously seen the place so closely and so fondly. The faded leather-bound books, one thick and three thin, which he published himself in Swansea, Gower's metropolis, have the authority of a man who made the most of the freedom to research and write that a rural living offered. Anyone lucky enough to find a set will pay about six hundred pounds for it. Every worthwhile guide and history since Davies has drawn on *West Gower*. He is the patron saint of Gower writing.

Davies knew the value of the strange and unusual. He thought it worth recording, for example, the ancient penalty of an earlier day, inflicted on those who offended the faith or the clergyman, which must have been the same thing. That time, probably the late 18th century, was not as far back in his past as he is in ours. The offender had to do penance in public: stand wrapped in a sheet, a watered-down version of wearing sackcloth and having ashes sprinkled on one's shaven head. It was embarrassing but not painful. The evidence came to light when he was having Llanmadoc church rebuilt, at his own expense, because he found the place dirty and ill-kept, 'meaner than the meanest hovel in the village.' In the process the builders found a hole in a wall that would have held the base of a staircase to a gallery above, the 'Rood Loft' that had once stretched across the church. The 'Rood' was the Crucifix, together with religious statues, displayed high in the air to impress and instruct the congregation. Someone must have torn it down as too ritualistic, unless it just collapsed.

Davies's story was prompted by the hole, not the loft.

> An aged man, Christopher Lewis, who died in his 90th year, and was formerly the parish clerk, told me that the entrance to the Rood Loft was called by the old people of his remembrance 'The Pillory Hole,' and that offenders against the Church were made to do penance by standing in this hole, clothed in a white sheet, during service time. There are many instances of persons having been made to undergo the discipline of public penance, standing openly in church, until comparatively recent times.

Without stretching dates too far, the tale, if one can trust oral history and Mr Lewis, reaches back to a memory of the late 18th century, well over two hundred years before our present.

A wooden plaque in the Church lists incumbents since 1649. Average turnover from then till 1860, when J.D.D. went there, was a new clergyman every twenty-four years. He lasted a record fifty-one. Since 1911, when he died, the average stay has been nine years.

The woman was still at work by the window. She was stencilling the letters incised in a piece of sandstone, a couple of feet long. J.D. Davies found it in the wall of the Old Rectory when it was being repaired in 1861, and had it moved into the church, where it now sits as one of the oldest artefacts in the country to have left a message behind – a sixth-century Celtic gravestone with Roman undertones that some builder short of material a thousand years later had found a use for, and shoved in the wall of the house, where Davies noticed and rescued it. The incomplete Roman capitals are thought to commemorate '[A]dvectus, son of Guanus. He lies here,' wherever 'here' was originally. Llanmadoc Church is protected by a preservation order, but Advectus's gravestone has an extra one of its own.

At the west end of the church, where the tower is, a rope hangs down from a single bell, and you can see a cubbyhole behind a curtain, which has to serve as a vestry. A door feels private but a curtain is half-hearted. Not that there is anything to see except a spare surplice, hanging neatly inside a travelling bag. At the other end of the church is an oak altar carved by Davies and a tablet on the wall to one of his predecessors. 'Underneath lie the remains of W.L. Knight, Clark, who died Jany 2 1795, Aged 74 Having been 22 Years Rector of the Parish Also'

There is nothing after the 'Also'.

West Gower devotes a page to Mr Watkin Knight that he would not have cared for. He was a large man. Davies comes straight out with it. He was fat. He was so fat that when he died, the coffin had to be manoeuvred through a bedroom window and lowered by ropes. Davies says nothing about his predecessor's good works or theology; instead we get a story about a corpse.

Should a human skeleton ever be dug up on Llanmadoc hill, within an earthwork called 'the Bulwark' – it is still marked as such on the Ordnance Survey maps – Davies says he knows how it got there. A servant girl at Watkin Knight's rectory had trouble lighting the fire one morning; smoke came back into the kitchen. 'There must be a man in the chimney,' she said, not seriously, but when they looked, there was, stuck fast and quite dead. They got him out on the thatched roof, and, as instructed by Mr Knight, threw him down without ceremony and carted him off to be buried on the hill, since he was a potential thief, or even murderer, not fit to lie in Christian ground. 'I had this account from Mrs Anne Button, since deceased,' wrote Davies. One wonders, might the miscreant have been the servant girl's lover? Mrs Button informed Davies that 'when she was a little girl, it was a common custom among the young people to go on Sundays to visit [the grave],' a curious form of entertainment if there was no story behind the story.

A subsequent rectory, a few yards away across a grass track, looks big enough for an hotel. When Davies tired of the old 'parsonage house,' he had it rebuilt on the same site and gave it six or more bedrooms on two upstairs floors, rather more than a bachelor might need. Its steep roof and overhanging eaves make it look mildly Alpine, a style that produced a pretty fable about a holiday in Switzerland, and a romance there that inspired the design, and all those bedrooms. Davies used a Swansea architect with a taste for Swiss buildings, that was all. A lifelong bachelor, he may have fancied leaving a large rectory for his successors and their children, though he had to take out an ecclesiastical mortgage to finance it. Now the house is in private ownership, and the present rector lives elsewhere.

Davies was a resourceful man. He built himself boats and sailed them in the puzzling waters of the estuary that flanks Gower on the north, which are more dangerous than they seem. A disaster nearby in the nineteenth century, off Broughton Bay, destroyed sixteen ships or more in one night off Llanmadoc. Davies was foreman of the inquest jury on the drowned that sat in a Llanmadoc pub, the Farmers Arms, although the account of the disaster in Vol. 2 doesn't mention his role. It hasn't been a pub for thirty years and is now a holiday cottage, advertised on the net as a three-and-a-half-hour drive from London.

Some of the sailors lost at Broughton are buried in the churchyard; no one seems to know exactly where, except that they used to be under a tree that was chopped down long ago. Graves of drowned sailors are not uncommon in Gower. But the geography of shipwrecks is different here. Instead of the coves and cliffs of the south coast, facing the Bristol Channel and deep water, the Ordnance map has miles of 'Mud and Sand' at low tide, with what used to be an industrial coastline beyond, four miles away, the estuary soon dwindling and becoming a river.

Lost ports and industries are over there, and Gower would have been drawn into that coal-and-iron world around Llanelli, but for river and soft sand that let tides wear away the coast to make the Burry Estuary.

The river is the Loughor, the anglicised version of Llwchwr, a name beyond Saxon tongues. The name also belongs to a small town at the head of the estuary. The Englishman John Capgrave, a literary monk of the fifteenth century, publicised the place by including a local hermit in his collection of saints' lives, St Cennydd. This is the saint whose name is commemorated in Llangennith (in Welsh, Llangenydd), a village on the other side of the hill from Llanmadoc. Davies printed the legend, both in Capgrave's original Latin and in translation, in his Vol. 3; a moral fantasy, with good coming out of evil. It concerns a deformed child – his leg was 'stuck to his thigh' – who is born one Christmas when King Arthur is holding a court near Loughor. The mother is the 'very lovely' daughter of Dihocus, prince of Brittany. We are not told her name. She gives birth in a tent a mile from Arthur's palace, and is evidently being kept out of the way. As the translation puts it, she had 'conceived a son by a most unnatural sin.' At this point Davies censors the story – 'I need scarcely remind those who are acquainted with the Latin tongue, that a literal translation of the text in this place was hardly possible.'

The father was the problem. Dr Crofton Black has translated the passage (2007). 'Dihocus ... having been often allured by illicit love, burnt keenly with the flames. At last, with the demons instigating, [his daughter] knew him, and in the first approach she yielded a pregnancy.' The baby was deformed – 'the leg stuck to the very thigh and he was not able to erect it in any way, this signifying that just as [the leg] which is below the thigh was sticking to the thigh, so the daughter who was under her father had been carnally yoked to her father.'

Incest out of the way. Davies can resume the story in English.

'By the command of the Prince' the boy is put in a wicker cradle and launched into the river near Loughor. This would have been the end of him, except that heavenly powers intervened. The raft drifted down the estuary to the west, evidently on an ebb tide, for seven or eight miles, cleared the land and turned to head south by east across Rhossili Bay for another five miles, ending up at the half-tide island of Worms Head, which seems to be the destination Capgrave had in mind. There is no sand, so the raft would have been deposited on rocks (low tide only), at which point sea birds lifted the child to safety on the Worm, supplied a bed of feathers and expelled serpents and reptiles. Finally an angel brought a brass bell shaped like a woman's breast which delivered milk and was known ('to this day,' says Davies) as 'the Titty bell.' Even natural functions were taken care of – 'the secretions which childhood naturally discharges in its retirements, he never did, for he was fed with a most subtile food, which had no secretion.' Inevitably, the infant became the man who became the saint, a holy cripple. Capgrave lived in a Northumbrian monastery and can hardly have visited the Burry Estuary. The tale has a few fragments of local geography, so perhaps someone who knew the place passed on the information to help the fable.

Llangennith, across the hill from Llanmadoc, keeps up the St Cennydd legend. Once a year they hoist a wooden seagull to the top of the church tower in memory of the birds who rescued the saint. A small priory was established there by the 13th century, and local place-names – 'College Farm,' 'College Mill' – may indicate the site. Church or priory had an out-station on the Burry Holms, the half-tide island at the northern end of Rhossili Bay, where the remains of a 12th century church and other buildings have been excavated. This, too, gets commemorated. The vicar of Llangennith, Canon Peter Williams, is also the rector of Llanmadoc, which would have baffled J.D. Davies. Williams holds a service on the Burry Holms every August, when the tides are right. It's a two-mile walk from the village. A few dozen attend, if it's a fine day. The vicar, like Davies, is an Anglo-Catholic, which would have pleased the old boy, and even owns a biretta. But he keeps it in a bag and doesn't wear it.

I have never lived in my own house in Gower, but I often had reasons to be there. I remember walking on Cefn Bryn, the ridge down the middle of the peninsula, at eight o'clock in the morning, shortly after my daughter was born, looking across the marshes and sandbars that Cennydd would have passed on his way to the Worms Head. The thin sound of works hooters – Wales still had some works then – came over the water from Llanelli, announcing the start of the day shift. That industrial coastline on the other side, very close but safely remote, made Gower seem a distant place, too good to last. We all create our own mythology. Gower became part of mine.

CHAPTER 2

HANGED MAN

THE FIRST ordinary person in Gower's history who says anything to us from the distant past lived in Llanridian seven hundred years ago. His name was Gwilym ap Rhys, William the son of Rees. He had a nickname, Gwilym Cragh, 'Scabby William,' suggesting scars from smallpox or injury; perhaps hinting at something in his character as well.

At that distance in time, personal histories have gone, except in the case of rulers and warriors, often the same people. A few poets, patronised by Celtic high-society as far back as the Dark Ages, have left hints of themselves in their verse. Names survive here and there in documents. Gower had an Anglo-Norman family called Mansel that probably arrived from France soon after the Conquest and settled there, later becoming rich and powerful. Its local descendants, no longer called Mansel, still have a few drops of the blood in their veins. The name first appears in 1201, when a John Mansel witnesses a legal document. Of John himself, nothing is known. Centuries passed before the Mansels began to make history.

So to be able to look directly at a particular man, born in humble circumstances in a Gower village about sixty years after John Mansel signed the document, is unheard of. But there he is, Llanrhidian's Gwilym, speaking Welsh, making a nuisance of himself, being unlucky and then lucky. How his story has survived is another story in itself.

Cragh sounds a difficult man. There was a criminal edge on him, and he left enough of his life behind to make the basis of an unpopular novel, or a dark docu-drama for television that would be guaranteed to give offence. The tale has become better known in recent years, but is not yet absorbed into the literature of Gower. It is an unquiet memory, a scream from the past.

Llanrhidian, which is another village on the estuary coast, is three or four miles to the east of J.D. Davies's Llanmadoc, in the general direction of Swansea. In Cragh's time that part of the peninsula, towards the north-east, would not have been penetrated by English voices, a process that was already under way a few miles to the south, on the other side of Cefn Bryn.

Cragh's horizon was the great grey bath of the estuary, emptying and filling. He lived more than half a million tides ago. Perhaps he scraped cockles from the sand and fished as well as farmed. Land in north Gower is acid and less fruitful than on the south side, but Cragh owned a little of it, maybe a field or two. Unfortunately for all concerned, his 'lord' took the land away. Impoverished, he went to live with his family. No wife or child is mentioned. Nor do we know why the land was taken.

His 'lord' was William de Breos II. Fighting men of that family (sometimes 'de Braose' or 'de Briouze') had been part of the Conqueror's invasion force two centuries earlier. To begin with they seized or were granted land in the south of England; then, like others, they extended their range. Marauding barons could police the undefined border with the region in the west that would later be called Wales, where the natives came down from the hills and made trouble; at the same time the barons could line their pockets and flatter their egos by exploiting the local economy and setting themselves up as absolute rulers. No 'Wales' existed as such, except as a group of small kingdoms with a common language. Central government in London was far away, and the Welsh Marches, the border lands, were open for exploitation by Anglo-Norman warlords.

The de Breoses were a clever, violent family, even for an era when being clever and violent was the way to get on, although seven centuries later, popular history has forgiven them. A Street and an Avenue in Swansea bear their name, Porthcawl has a Drive, and a few small houses in Hay-on-Wye have been given the hopeful-sounding address of 'De Breos Court.'

The Anglo-Norman lord and the Welsh farmer lived in interesting times. Wales itself was periodically invaded by English armies, who found the region difficult to control. The Welsh were the original inhabitants of the British Isles; they *were* the British, the Britons. Fading away to the west as the Saxon pressure grew, they never amounted to a political nation as such, remaining a scattered population with a common language, their rulers, who lived in style, always quarrelling among themselves over who owned what. Blood-feuds festered between kings and princes of tiny sub-kingdoms; at least one ruler blinded and emasculated his own relatives. They were desperate men with saving graces, among them poetry.

Some of it was personal and romantic:

> I had a girl who concurred one day;
> I had two, the more is their praise;
> I had three and four with good fortune;
> I had five of them, fair their white flesh;
> I had six with no shying from sin.
> A bright girl from a white fort was mine;
> I had seven, with earnest effort;
> I had eight as reward, prize for praise I sang –
> Best for teeth to guard tongue

Most of it was not:

> I saw savage troops and stiff red corpses,
> It was left to the wolves, their burial.
> I saw their ruin, three hundred dead;
> I saw, battle over, bowels on thorns...

Away from their northern terrain the Welsh were vulnerable; lowland South Wales was open to outsiders, and Gower was soon discovered by Anglo-Normans, probing into the west. The incomers built castles and colonised it with ploughs and ploughmen, dispossessing the inhabitants.

William Cragh's ancestors would have seen violence before, created from within, Welsh on Welsh. 'And then Gower was ravaged by Einion ab Owain,' says the Red Book of Hergest, describing events of the year 970, a century before the Normans were ever heard of. Welsh warriors were always ravaging.

The changes now were permanent. The 'lordship' of Gower, though sixty miles west of the English border, came to resemble the Welsh Marches, a self-contained piece of real estate, with Welsh and English living side by side for ever. Even before the Normans there were incomers from the West Country. Trading across the Bristol Channel has a long history; sailors meet local women and decide to stay. Port Eynon in Gower is twenty-five miles due north of Bull Point in Devon, a day's sail.

The geography of Gower is confusing. The name is taken to mean the peninsula west of Swansea, which is the part the Normans colonised, but historically it was joined to what is now the city, and beyond it a long tongue of land, much of it hilly and barren, that reaches further to the north of central Swansea than Rhossili does to the west. These forgotten uplands were once a hunting ground for the Welsh aristocracy and their Norman successors. Originally both Gowers were part of a Welsh kingdom to the west, Ystrad Tywi. When the Normans moved in, they used the same boundaries of rivers and sea to create an administrative region, with a Norman lord to run it: the lordship of Gower.

Long after the Conquest the dispossessed kept trying to win Ystrad Tywi back to the lost cause of Welsh separatism. They failed, leaving traces of hostility between 'Welsh' and 'English.' This was less true of Upland Gower, a comparative wilderness, where Welsh remained the principal language, and is still widely spoken. In the peninsula, where the two cultures were side by side, hostility persisted for centuries, though in the end it meant nothing. As early as 1386, the record, written in Latin, of a manorial court sitting at Pennard, south Gower, has the likes of 'Llew ap Jevan' and 'Jevan ap Traharn' co-existing with 'Maud Fox' and 'Richard Baker.'

Gwilym Cragh, Scabby William, would have had other ideas about co-existence. He was not a peaceable member of society; if he had been, we would never have heard of him. He was either a criminal or a political rebel, or more likely a bit of both. A wanted man, he was captured in November 1290, taken to Swansea Castle, and brought before the Norman overlord, William de Breos II, who controlled the district. It was de Breos's eldest son, another William, already well on the way to being even more unsavoury than his father, whose men did the capturing. No doubt it was de Breos's bailiffs who had dispossessed the Welshman of his land. In one version of Cragh's story he is a notorious brigand who has killed thirteen men, which seems a lot of death even for a medieval career in robbery with violence. In another he is a rebel against King Edward I, a patriot dreaming of a free Welsh nation, possibly with a personal motive because an English baron had nicked his fields.

West Wales was full of patriots (or terrorists) who rebelled, burnt castles and ambushed the king's men. Not long before, in 1287, they had been on the rampage in the Gower area. Cragh was a dangerous nuisance.

Barons far from London were little kings. Among the powers they gave themselves was the right of 'pit and gallows,' which meant they could execute felons, drowning the women and hanging the men. De Breos sentenced Cragh to hang. Under Welsh law the condemned man's family in Llanrhidian might have purchased his life and freedom. They tried to do this, offering a hundred cows, above the going rate. The offer was refused; de

Breos wanted him dead. Cragh was consigned to a dungeon with a dozen others to await execution.

That should have been the end of the story. As far as posterity is concerned, there would not have been a story to end. The crimes and punishment of a minor criminal in medieval Wales would have been of no consequence, and a summary trial at Swansea castle left no records. Cragh should have vanished without trace. It was what happened after they hanged him that matters.

At dawn on a Monday morning Cragh was taken out to be executed. Something supernatural was said to have occurred in the cell that night, but for the moment the usual routines were in place. Medieval communities did their hanging outside the town itself, and at Swansea the chosen site was on a hill to the north-west, within sight of the castle. Cragh had to walk there, hands tied and a rope already round his neck, guarded by armed horsemen under the command of John of Baggeham, de Breos's steward, the head of his household staff. Some of Cragh's family had been forced to come from Llanrhidian to walk with him: Gruffydd Foel, Dafydd ap Gruffydd, Ithel Fychan. They were told they had to hang him themselves. Baggeham was there to see they did it properly.

The journey from castle to place of execution, along a track that would one day be the High Street, then veering left towards the high ground, could have taken an hour, a stumbling procession, past onlookers, in winter mud. Swansea grew up around its castle, near the mouth of the River Tawe. Inland is a long ridge, a few hundred feet high, that runs from west to east, parallel to the shore, overlooking the town. Most of it is now covered in houses, but near its eastern extremity the nineteenth-century terraces stop short of the hilltop. Above Portia Terrace and Wordsworth Street, names chosen to give the place a bit of class, is the scrubland where executions took place.

Today the small houses are neat and respectable but the district has a touch of the sinister. You reach it up a steep, busy road called Mount Pleasant, which begins not far from the city centre, and climbs past houses and a block of educational buildings, on a site that formerly contained the Grammar School, where Dylan Thomas failed to profit from his education in the 1920s. Farther up the hill is a range of brown Victorian buildings that have been hollowed out for agreeable apartments, but was once, wonderful irony, the Workhouse, where the starving poor paid for sustenance with hard labour.

The site of the old Slaughterhouse, later made to sound more genteel as the 'Abattoir,' was lower down. Around the side of the hill was – still is – a Jewish Cemetery, another facility that in unenlightened times would have been kept at a distance. And then there is that scrubland at the top.

The north-south streets up there are so steep, they are fitted with hand-rails to help pedestrians. The last street-name before open ground is North Hill Road, running east-west. It was Gibbet Hill Road till early in the twentieth century, when the town council decided that 'Gibbet' gave the wrong message. A trace of folk-memory survives. An elderly man in a suit, buying his morning paper in the corner shop, opposite a Congregational chapel the size of a cinema, built 1867, said. 'They used to hang people up here. Dad told me.'

Steep tracks lead up behind the houses to grass, bushes and panoramas of the city, the empty docks, the bay, the Mumbles Head, the Bristol Channel and the distant blue edge of England.

A school is nearby, the 'Round School,' a Swansea landmark. The castle ruins, hard to pick out in the urban clutter, are rather more than half a mile away in line of sight. The execution was said to have been witnessed by people at the castle, which might have been possible in cleaner air, with the gallows outlined on the skyline.

Swansea Bay from Gibbet Hill

Nowadays the sky above the hill is full of seagulls, which would have had better things to do in medieval Wales. Gibbet Hill, which nobody calls Gibbet Hill any more, is a feeding ground, strewn with rubbish, much of it edible. Dozens of plastic takeaway boxes have been shredded by birds or dogs to resemble the skeletons of fish. Gulls swoop down, screaming, hoping the latest visitors have brought something nice. Broken televisions, mattresses, bottles, old pyjamas, sanitary towels and burst bin-bags of domestic sludge are strewn about in the sea-breeze. Gibbet Hill is not, after all, sinister. Just squalid, or it was on July 16 2007.

The scaffold that awaited Gwilym ap Rhys, alias Gwilym Cragh, consisted of a crossbeam between two posts, with room to hang more than one at a time. Cragh was not alone. There was a second condemned man, of whom we know nothing except that he was called Trahearn ap Hywel, and was a Welsh nobleman of some kind. The Trahearns were or had been a family of note in North and Mid Wales. Perhaps they had a history of rebellion, and Trahearn and Cragh were seen as part of the same conspiracy.

From the start, it was not a normal execution. Cragh was hanged first. Ithel Fychan put the rope around his kinsman's neck, and the prisoner was made to climb a ladder that was then pulled away. In the twelfth century and for a long time afterwards, the victim might strangle slowly, depending where the slip-knot of the noose was placed in relation to the throat. Medieval society lacked the later refinement, if that's the word, of a trapdoor that opens and a drop that breaks the neck and kills in seconds.

After Cragh, Trahearn. For some reason, presumably because he refused to mount the ladder, Trahearn had to be hauled up. He was heavily built and struggling as he was hoisted. Then the crossbeam broke. Apparently the de Breoses were watching from the castle and saw the two men fall to the ground. Both were said to have been dead already, but on de Breos's instructions, Cragh was re-hanged, just in case, and left there till sunset.

Cragh, or Cragh's corpse, was not finished with. De Breos had a wife, Lady Mary. Before the executions she had asked her husband to spare both men. Merciful women who intervene to save the condemned are not uncommon in medieval tales. But de Breos would have needed to be in very merciful mood to accede. Cragh was probably a political rebel. It was only three years since the Welsh had been ravaging in the area. The town was attacked in summer 1287 by raiders from West Wales who damaged the castle and briefly seized its counterpart at Oystermouth, at the other end of Swansea Bay. The times were not right for clemency, and one wonders why Lady Mary was so active on behalf of her husband's enemy. She was William's third wife, born about 1255 into a titled family from Yorkshire, so in 1290 she was still comparatively young. William de Breos, about sixty-six, was elderly. Mary seems to have been a tough-minded woman, insisting that her children by de Breos were provided for at the expense, where necessary, of their older half-brothers; always a recipe for family dissent.

When Cragh was pronounced dead, she asked to have custody of the body, so that she could have it buried the next day. This time de Breos said yes.

The Cragh story now becomes science-fiction. John of

Baggeham, who had been in charge of the execution, cut down the dead man, and the corpse was taken to the house of a local citizen, Thomas Matthews, where people crowded in and saw it lying on the floor. Why it went there, and not to a church, was never explained. That evening, Lady Mary sent a woman from the castle to 'measure' the body. This popular religious procedure was used to invoke the aid of a particular saint on behalf of someone in need. A thread was used to measure the length, sometimes the width, of the person concerned, after which a candle of the same length as the thread was made, and dedicated to the chosen saint. A maid called Marie did the measuring and took the thread back to the castle. John of Baggeham was at the house as well. So, at some point, was William de Breos Jnr, Mary's stepson. The corpse was described: the face blackened and bloody, eyes out of their sockets, tongue and neck swollen grotesquely.

The saint Lady Mary was appealing to was not actually a saint. He was a former Bishop of Hereford, Thomas Canteloup, a dominant figure in his diocese, who had died eight years before the Cragh affair. By the early 1290s he was already being credited with miracles performed from the afterlife, and a movement was under way to have him canonised. Saints were useful to cathedrals. They brought pilgrims, prestige and income, and Hereford already had a popular shrine to Thomas Canteloup. The late bishop was a saint-in-waiting.

What was about to happen advanced Canteloup's cause and gave the story the legs to carry it, and Cragh, into the 21st century. At some time that night, perhaps near dawn, the dead man moved his foot and came back to life. No one who gave evidence saw it happen. It was some time before Cragh could speak. Food was sent round from the castle, broth and almond puree. It was a miracle.

It took a week or two for him to recover. Then he and the de Breoses, husband and wife, went on a pilgrimage to pray at

Canteloup's unofficial shrine and thank him for performing this miracle of reviving a dead Welsh terrorist. Swansea to Hereford along their likely route – across Mynydd y Gwair and the hills of Upland Gower – would have meant a journey of seventy or eighty miles. Cragh is said to have walked on his bare feet; presumably the de Breoses kept their shoes on, and had horses on standby. It took them three days. We are not told where they slept overnight. On arrival at Hereford the de Breoses donated the hangman's rope to the cathedral, together with a model, in wax, of a hanging man.

The event, perhaps, changed them all. It was, or it came to be presented as, a notable religious experience. But could it be proved? Seventeen years later, when the cathedral authorities in Hereford were pressing to have their late bishop made a saint, they had to convince officials of the Roman Catholic Church that Canteloup's miracles were genuine. A three-man papal commission, consisting of two bishops and a tax collector, investigated the claims in 1307. They were offered two hundred and four Canteloup miracles, and chose to investigate seventeen. One of them was the case of the hanged man.

The commissioners were careful men. They began by making an inventory of the offerings that had been left at the unofficial shrine. The north transept of the cathedral must have been like a religious outpatients' department, permanently occupied by the sick and infirm, waiting to be cured by the grace of the late bishop. The offerings included 170 ships in silver and 41 in wax, 129 images of men or their limbs in silver, 1,424 men-and-limbs in wax, 116 gold and silver rings, 38 garments of gold-thread and silk, 97 nightgowns and 108 crutches. There doesn't seem to be a noose or a hanged man in wax on the list.

Then the commissioners turned to the reported miracles. In the case of the complicated Cragh affair, they heard nine witnesses – three in London, the rest in Hereford. A legal secretariat was there to summarise the evidence, which was given in English, French and in one case Welsh, and record it in Latin. This is how we know about Gwilym ap Rhys of Llanrhidian. The documents can still be read, if you happen to read medieval Latin, in the Vatican archives, with Cragh-alias-Gwilym's life-story written into the permanent record of the Roman church.

The events as described by the witnesses, eight men and a woman, were not as clear-cut as I have made them sound. There were many contradictions, hardly surprising after seventeen years. The evidence was riddled with hearsay. The general opinion at the time, c. 1290, was that Cragh had been properly hanged and came back to life. But scientific evidence of death was not available then. One unsettling observation emerged to the effect that Cragh, when hanged, lost control of his bowels and bladder, which meant that he was definitely dead; although the commissioners would have known that terror can have the same effect.

The process of hanging was scrutinised. Questions were asked about the nature of the knot in the noose, and where it was placed in relation to the throat, which would have had implications for a slower or a quicker death. The witnesses included three freemen of Swansea; two priests, one of them on the de Breos staff; John of Baggeham, in charge of the execution squad; together with Lady Mary de Breos, and her ominous son, who had succeeded his father long before 1307, and was now William de Breos III. The ninth witness was the hanged man, William Cragh.

He was hardly expected. When the Canteloup hearings began in London, de Breos III said that Cragh had died of natural causes a few years before the hearings of 1307. But when the inquiry moved to Hereford later in the year, the Welshman appeared and told his story.

Since, on the day of the hanging, he was dead, or absent in some way, for most of the time, this was not much help. The last thing he remembered hearing was the roar of the crowd as Trahearn was hanged. What he did recall, in some detail, was what happened the night before, in the dungeons of Swansea Castle. A woman in white covered in jewels appeared, along with a 'lordly figure' called St Thomas. A ladder appeared as well, and Cragh was told he could climb it, as could the other prisoners in the dungeon, except Trahearn – the woman in white, whom he took to be the Virgin Mary, said, 'You should leave him.' All the rest, said Cragh, were pardoned and set free.

The tax collector and two bishops would have known that magic ladders and jewels were not going to help the cause of sainthood. What mattered was the fact that although 'everyone' knew that Cragh had come back to life, nobody could be found who had seen it with his own eyes. When the time came for the case of Canteloup to be formally submitted, and details of miracles that had passed the test went off to Rome, William Cragh's was among them. But at some late stage in the procedure it was dropped, and played no further part. They had better miracles. In due course the bishop became a saint, of whom Hereford Cathedral continues to be proud. His shrine, red-lit, has Post-it notes on a board, seeking the saint's intercession, but no silver ships or wax men.

What really happened to William Cragh? If there was trickery, as there must have been, Lady Mary was complicit. Her stepson, too, and her husband. Professor Robert Bartlett, in his deft book about the case (2004), makes a mock apology for his 'dry objective history' and says that were it a novel or a film, Lady Mary's close personal interest in Cragh could be explained by a love affair between lady of the manor and wild Welsh rebel.

Fiction aside, piety, more powerful in their society than ours, might seem a motive, except that the man to be saved was an early version of the terrorist threat to society. Was Lady Mary pious enough to plead for the life of someone who threatened life at Swansea Castle? I think her motive was less spiritual than that. The Canteloups were related to the de Breoses. I came across the connection while searching de Breos histories on the net. It was not a close relationship. Thomas Canteloup had an older brother, yet another William. William Canteloup had married a de Breos heiress, Eva, a daughter of the violent 'Black William' de Breos, hated by the Welsh, with good reason. She died about 1255, thirty-five years before the Hanged Man episode. Her inheritance passed to William Canteloup.

The Canteloups and the Gower de Breoses were no more than distant cousins, but the relationship could have given Lady Mary an interest in seeing Thomas Canteloup canonised. Other writers, I soon discovered, knew about the Canteloup-de Breos connection, and attached little importance to it. But women are the social fixers in families. I imagine Mary de Breos arranged matters so that Cragh was not hanged properly.

William de Breos must have been involved, if only by looking the other way. John of Baggeham, in charge both of the execution and the corpse, was doing as he was told. My guess is that William Jnr., who provided first-hand evidence that what lay on the floor of Thomas Matthews' house was a corpse, was the one who gave the instructions. He could have had reasons for assisting his stepmother, and organising the deception on her behalf. His father did not have long to live – he died soon after the Cragh affair, and may already have been ill, with Lady Mary assuring him that his compliance would help make Canteloup a saint, and do the baron no end of good in the afterlife. William Jnr. knew that he would soon have to deal with a difficult widow, so a good relationship was prudent. A sexual ingredient, even, is possible. She was in her mid-thirties, he was in his mid-twenties. It would make a bleaker scenario for a novel than a love-affair between Lady Mary and Cragh. But it might have happened.

As far as Welsh Gower was concerned, the story would have been widely known. Everyone in Llanrhidian must have heard it over the years. Had it survived the centuries as a Gower folk-tale, J.D. Davies could have used it in his book. As with St Cennydd and the basket, it was a good yarn with a religious message, but Cragh's story would have been in Welsh, which is not the Gower language of record. And his account, no doubt told for the rest of his life to anyone who listened, may have ruined itself in the telling. It was too good to be true.

CHAPTER 3

RED LADY

Abstract: Goats Hole is a cave in a Carboniferous limestone sea-cliff of the Gower Peninsula, approx. 14 metres above mean sea-level. Dr Buckland, of Oxford University – clergyman, geologist and eccentric – found part of a human skeleton there in 1823, and the site became (and remains) world-famous. Buckland's interest was in the bones of animals, not people. But the skeleton amused him, and he hinted that she must have been a witch and prostitute who found the cave convenient for her trade: earthworks above the cliff meant that soldiers might have lived there during the Roman occupation of Britain. The truth was more interesting – scientifically, anyway.

THE CAVE is on Gower's south coast, roughly midway between Port Eynon Point and the Rhossili headland. It is not easy to access. The main Swansea to Rhossili road is about a mile distant. A footpath from Pilton Green follows the western boundary of Paviland Farm, which identifies the cave for most people, who prefer 'Paviland' to the original 'Goats Hole.' At the coast the path descends into a deep, steep-sided gully, Foxhole Slade, and ends in a rocky inlet and the edge of the ocean; a straight line to the south-west would reach land at Venezuela or thereabouts, four thousand miles away.

Goats Hole is immediately on the right of the gully, when facing the sea. It is a wide cleft, tilted a little to one side, three or four metres across at the entrance. It narrows at the top, ten metres higher up the cliff. Visitors reach it by scrambling up the rocks, which are uncovered for two and a half hours either side of low water. It extends for about 18 metres, the roof getting lower towards the back, and finally closing off the cave. Anyone caught by the incoming tide is safe enough there, but has a seven-hour wait before they can get out again. The only other route is the face of the cliff, which is dangerous.

Romans, or Romanised Celts using their money, found their way to it, and left behind, perhaps for luck, a coin or two of the 3rd century Emperor Carausius. Why would anyone bother to visit such a place, apart from seeing the local witch? Someone always does. Holes and corners of the countryside get explored out of curiosity and on the principle that you never know what you'll find.

In the early 19th century, 'everyone,' meaning the locals – farmers, farm labourers, quarrymen, fishermen – knew the cave was there, along with other caves nearby. They knew that old bones, large ones, could be found in it. But bones were less interesting than coins. Even antiquarians found coins significant. Bones were just bones.

In the summer of 1822, two young professional men, a doctor and a curate, went exploring at Goats Hole, and found two elephants' teeth and part of a long tusk. One of the explorers was Daniel Davies, a local doctor, the first the peninsula ever had. He had been there six years, living at Prospect Cottage in the central village of Reynoldston, where the local GP had his practice (not in Prospect Cottage) until the second half of the 20th century. Daniel would marry the following year. His companion, the curate, was the Rev. John Davies, of Port Eynon, who had married the year before. One of his sons would be the Rev. J.D. Davies of Llanmadoc, who wrote *West Gower*. Wales has many Davieses; the curate and the surgeon were not related.

Having found teeth and tusk, they reburied them in the floor of the cave. In itself, it was not much of a discovery. It mattered only because an early geologist, William Buckland, was busy looking for bones in caverns. Dr Buckland, not yet forty, was vigorous, clever and theatrical. Examining the preserved heart of a French king, he was said to have eaten it. His geological ideas were revolutionary, but he was also a clergyman, and he had to respect the Biblical scheme of things. Treading carefully, he developed a novel theory about the early days of life on Earth, when the divine Flood or Deluge more or less wiped out the human race. At the heart of it was the disposition of animal bones – why and how they were found in caverns.

The two Davieses seem to have known nothing about Buckland, or not to have made a connection between him and the Paviland bones. The Port Eynon curate was friendly with the Talbot family, who lived at Penrice Castle – which was a house, built forty or so years earlier, in the shadow of Norman ruins – and owned most of Gower. The Rev. Davies had canvassed votes for the head of the family in the 1818 general election, which saw him elected to Parliament. But if Davies told the Talbots anything about bones, no word of it reached Buckland, although the Talbots had known him for years.

Some of the family had a serious interest in natural history. Science then was kinder to amateurs, and they were drawn into Buckland's grand design of an early Britain, in which bones of alien species – tigers, elephants, bears, rhinoceri – occurred in such puzzling quantity. The only possible explanation had always been that the Deluge floated their corpses north from the Tropics and left them to decay. On the contrary, said Buckland, they were living here all the time. He found remains of hyenas, another alien breed, inside caves, together with splintered bones that suggested the hyenas had been eating bears and tigers. At first these ideas were seen as eccentric. There were Buckland jokes and satires. He pressed ahead. To his friends as well as his enemies, Buckland had a slightly demented air, always in a hurry, rushing about the country in his coach, furthering the New Geology. The Bible, of course, had to be true. But the Biblical record, he felt, could safely be interpreted for the modern world by a man like himself.

In 1821, the year before the two Davieses went to Paviland, one of the Talbot daughters with a keen interest in natural history, Mary Theresa, sent Buckland some teeth and bones which had been at the house since they were found in a quarry at Crawley Rocks, near Penrice Castle, about 30 years earlier, in 1792. Rhinoceros and hyena were among the animals represented. Mary Theresa, who had kept the relics in her collection, was twenty-seven and unmarried. As the senior spinster she was 'Miss Talbot,' and would remain so. She had the time and energy for Buckland's enthusiasms.

On November 26 1821 he wrote to thank her for lending him the bones, and dwelt on his theories about God and the Flood, as yet unannounced. In Yorkshire, at Kirby Moorside, a cave had been discovered. Buckland gave her a preview. It was 'entirely paved' with the bones and teeth of exotic creatures, including hyenas, which 'we know' – he meant, which he knew – 'to have been the Antediluvian inhabitants of the Country. I hope you will get some Converts to this theory of mine or supply a better. In Gower also your specimens shew there once lived Bears or Hyenas, but the teeth do not prove which, & contemporaneously with them Herds of Elephants & Rhinoceros's browsed in the woods of Nicholston & on the summit of Cefn Bryn...'

Gower was able to share these scientific excitements. Another interested party, when the time came, would be Lewis Weston Dillwyn, industrialist and leading citizen of Swansea. The family were Quakers, with American connections. In 1902 Dillwyn was sent from London to Swansea to manage the local pottery, purchased for him by his father. But he was not much interested in commerce. His heart was in natural history. He was a Fellow of the Royal Society. Sea-shells and plants were his specialties, and he liked the idea of decorating Swansea-ware made at the pottery with flowers that he was fond of. He delighted in rare birds, which, as was customary at the time, he shot on sight.

Buckland was Dillwyn's friend. So were numerous scientific celebrities, their names scattered through Dillwyn's diary whenever he visited London. He attends a party given by Sir Humphry Davy. He dines with Dr Wollaston the physicist. He spends an evening with Sir Joseph Banks, who takes him to the Royal Mint next day to see a new apparatus for engraving bank notes. At the British Museum he bumps into Buckland and they spend hours together at the College of Surgeons.

In December 1822, the story of the two Davieses and the Paviland cave, which had been simmering since the summer, came to the boil. Dillwyn was busy over the Christmas period with his scientific friends. He lived on his estate to the north of Swansea, at Penllergaer, which, to the annoyance of the Welsh, he insisted on spelling 'Penllergare.' Wollaston and Davy were there, and on Christmas Day they all went to a copperworks 'to witness an Experiment.' But around that time, Dillwyn heard about the bones at Paviland. Previously the two Davieses seem to have kept their find to themselves. Perhaps Dillwyn, who worried about his health, had occasion to consult Davies the doctor, and heard it from him. Or Davies the curate could have met him in someone's drawing room over a seasonal sherry.

However he came to hear, Dillwyn sent the news to Buckland, and on Christmas Eve Buckland wrote to his friends the Talbots, who would know what was going on in their peninsula. He addressed the letter to Lady Mary Cole, widow of T.M. Talbot, former head of the family; she was now married to Sir Christopher Cole. Buckland must have thought the matter too important to be dealt with by a daughter.

> Pray oblige me by a line to say whether there really has or has not been a Discovery of a New Cave full of Bones in your

neighbourhood. Mr Dillwyn in his short letter alludes to it as a thing notorious to me & as if understanding that I was coming into Glamorganshire immediately to examine it, whereas I know nothing at all about the Matter & never heard of it but by Mr Dillwyn's letter, & Mr Talbot [C.R.M. Talbot, Lady Mary's son and heir, aged nineteen] whom I saw just before He left Oxford said he believes it is so but could give me no Particulars. I begged him to ask you to send me up a few of the best marked teeth & Bones in a Box by the Mail...

On Boxing Day, Dillwyn was at Penrice Castle. Was this because of the bone cave, or was it a social visit, already planned? Penrice was the only place for miles with intellectual pretensions and the wealth to indulge them, the rooms glowing with candles and oil-lamps in the long winter nights, ready to welcome the guests who came splashing along roads of mud.

Dillwyn had taken Davy with him to Penrice, and a clergyman friend, J.M. Traherne. Next day some of them went to Paviland. Dillwyn wrote in his diary:

John Traherne, Miss Talbot & I spent most of the Day at a Cavern which has been discovered on the Coast about 6 Miles W. Of Penrice, & we there found the Bones of Elephants &c.

On the 28th he and Miss Talbot went back to the cave, and 'brought away a great quantity of Bones.' On both occasions no doubt they had workmen to do the digging: manual labourers, picks and shovels at the ready, were taken for granted. A sample was sent off to Buckland from Penrice. By New Year's Eve, three days later, he had written thanking Miss Talbot 'for sending me up the Tooth' – postal delivery-times between Penrice and England are much the same after two centuries – although he was 'extremely vexed' not to have been present for 'the opening of your very interesting new Cave at Paviland.' A string of detailed questions about the interior followed, and Buckland said he would be there as soon as possible. (In his best-known work, *Reliquae Diluvianae*, 'Relics of the Flood,' he wrote that he went 'immediately,' but in fact it took him another three weeks). 'Meantime,' he concluded, 'pray have the Mouth closed up again to prevent total destruction.' The cliffs, like most of Gower, belonged to the Talbots, so the cave was their property.

Buckland arrived in the third week of January, 1823. Dillwyn expected him in the evening, but he was there just after breakfast on the 18th, which was a Saturday. John Traherne was with him. 'We [were] engaged together Geologically nearly all day,' recorded Dillwyn. On Sunday morning they went to church, and in the afternoon Buckland and Traherne travelled to Penrice Castle, ready for action on Monday.

'Engaged Geologically' on Saturday presumably meant they went to Paviland. Low water that afternoon was 3.40, so the cave would have been accessible from about 1.10 p.m. The tide was over the rocks again by early evening: by that time, in any case, the winter daylight had gone.

On the Monday, January 20, Dillwyn had business in Swansea, but in the afternoon he went, with his wife and elder son, John, to visit Penrice yet again. His diary says only that they arrived soon after 4 o'clock. It was John, aged twelve, writing a dutiful letter to his brother Lewis, aged eight, who was the first person to record the Red Lady: 'Soon Sir C. Cole, Mr Traherne and Miss Talbot returned from having left Mr Buckland there and saying that they had found a human skeleton & which we suppose was the skeleton of a murdered person.' (It was only half a skeleton, the left side, and it lacked a skull.)

Next morning, Tuesday January 21, John was called into the library 'to see Mr Buckland off on a second visit to the cave.' Low tide was 5.43 a.m., so by 8.15 the passage was closed. Buckland can't have been hurrying off to visit the cave before dawn. Perhaps the skeleton had been left for safe-keeping at a cottage in the vicinity, inside one of the blue bags that he used for his fossils, rather than risk bringing it back after dark on frosty roads; the

Goats Hole from Buckland's *Reliquae Diluvianae*

weather had turned cold. It can't have been at Penrice overnight or surely John Dillwyn would have begged to see the murdered man with his own eyes. His father's diary makes no mention of skeletons. The entry of January 21 says, 'Went with Miss Talbot & John Traherne to meet Buckland who had gone early, at Goat Cave near Paviland, & from thence we went together to look at the Hounds Hole & Deborah Cave – We all got back to dine at Penrice.' Hounds and Deborah are caves close to Paviland.

The following day, Wednesday January 22, Buckland and others went to an Oxwich cave, at Great Tor, and visited Pennard Castle, after which he and Traherne 'proceeded in their Chaise homeward.' The visit was over. It is an odd episode. Buckland is generally assumed to have spent several days, even a week, in the cave. He did not. He was there on three days, the Saturday, the Monday and the Tuesday. Given the tides and the short daylight, the longest he could have stayed altogether was six or seven hours – unless they were using local boatmen to row them there, an option dismissed by those who know what that rocky coast is like in winter seas. By today's exacting standards it was a geological smash-and-grab raid, a tribute to Buckland's energy. But questions linger.

The skeleton was found a short distance inside the cave, on the left going in, under six inches of earth. Although storm water blows in, the ground slopes upward from the entrance, and once inside, Goats Hole seems unaffected by weather. The grave's light covering, and the fact that only part of the skeleton – and no skull – was left, suggests that creatures or humans or both had disturbed it before.

Even with an enthusiastic work-force to dig up the cave-floor – in the days before cautious examination, inch-by-inch, became good practice – they were lucky to have found the remains so quickly. Is it conceivable that Buckland was discreetly led to the discovery? Dillwyn and Miss Talbot might have come across it first. No honourable person would have been eager to plunder the cave, property of 'Earl Talbot' – as Buckland, erring on the side of obsequiousness, called him in *Reliquiae Diluvianae* (corrected, in an Errata slip, to 'C.M. Talbot, Esq.')

When the two Davieses uncovered their elephant's teeth and piece of tusk, they were careful to put them back where they found them. If Dillwyn and Miss Talbot unearthed what looked like human remains, they – or she – might have thought that it was the Talbots' famous friend who deserved the credit, since but for him the cave would not have been properly investigated in the first place. It is the kind of speculation that Buckland might have made, head on one side to indicate that it might be a joke but it might be serious.

In purely scientific terms, as Buckland understood them, the skeleton was a non-event. These were not ancient bones on which an avant-garde geologist could pin speculation about the world before and after the divine Deluge (which Buckland believed in.) They threatened to be an embarrassment, since humans were not supposed to have lived in northern Europe before the Flood. Animals were in order; people were not. So the Goats Hole skeleton had to be comparatively recent. When *Reliquiae Diluvianae* was published in 1823, Chapter 7, 'Cave of Paviland,' needed a page and a half to list the animal remains. One line at the end, 'Man. Portion of a female skeleton, clearly postdiluvian,' had to suffice for the human bones.

At first, as young John Dillwyn said in his letter, it was thought that the remains might have been those of a 'murdered person,' a Customs officer killed by smugglers. But Buckland thought of a better story. Writing to Lady Mary at Penrice on February 15 he said it wasn't an exciseman after all but 'a Woman, whose History wd. Afford ample Matter for a Romance to be entitled the Red Woman or the Witch of Paviland, for some such Personage she must have been.' This idea was incorporated in *Reliquiae Diluvianae*. Red ochre, which occurs naturally in local rocks, covered the bones, which were, and still are, 'a dark brick-red colour.' He didn't suggest, as was later established, that the colouring was artificially added to the remains, or had been contained in some covering material. But he took account of the small sea-shells and fragments of ivory beside the skeleton. Plainly it was a woman, buried with her ornaments and toys.

The Rev. Buckland had found an acceptable explanation, wrapped up in a good story. The bones were old, but not as old as the Flood. At the top of the cliff were earthworks – the Ordnance map still marks them, in Old English type, as 'Fort,' and the site, like others in Gower, is now identified as an Iron Age enclosure. The term in 1823 was 'British camp.' Buckland used his imagination:

> The circumstance of the remains of a British camp existing on the hill immediately above this cave, seems to throw much light on the character and date of the woman under consideration; and whatever may have been her occupation, the vicinity of a camp would afford

a motive for residence, as well as the means of subsistence, in what is now so exposed and uninviting a solitude.

The idea that she was a witch as well as a tart occurred to him because among the Goats Hole bones was the shoulder-blade of a sheep, used in necromancy. In his February 15 letter to Lady Mary Cole he said that 'the Blade Bone of Mutton gives grounds for a Conjecture wh. Favours the Theory that she was a Dealer in Witchcraft.'

Buckland used a jovial manner to cover his tracks. He lectured at the university with a smile, so that extravagant statements could later be dismissed as humorous asides. He was a practical joker all his life. There is a story that when he died, the grave-diggers found he had chosen a burial-plot where an outcrop of rock lay a few inches below the surface, and explosives had to be used to make room for him. It isn't true, but storytellers thought it should be.

All this is ancient history. Others went to Goats Hole and dug there, over decades. Early in the 20th century the geologist W.J. Sollas realised that the remains were far older than Buckland and his contemporaries could have grasped. Buckland had been right the first time, before his private romance intervened. The bones were those of a young man. But the popular epithet, Red Lady of Paviland – red with the ceremonial ochre that someone had flung over her, metaphorically red with the blushes of a fallen woman – is too attractive to change. She is sometimes given quotation marks to suggest that although 'Red Lady' is wrong, she is best left alone.

The early residents of the cave – who may have been visitors rather than permanent inhabitants – left behind, among other things, at least five thousand 'lithics,' stone fragments resulting from human activity. But the skeleton is unique. It was recognised long ago as being more than 20,000 years old. Scientific reassessment of both skeleton and cave is still in progress. The literature is written for specialists ('Samples of bone gelatine >30kD MW were lyophilized and combusted using a CHN elemental analyzer...') The paper that this comes from – Jacobi and Higham, 2007 – has pushed the Red Lady even farther back in time, to 29,000 years before the present. This, it is said, makes him an afterthought in the history of the cave. Its use as a burial-place may have been long after it was used for living in. This conclusion, like so many, raises new questions in the course of answering old ones. Why bury him there at all? What was his status, in what kind of society?

The Paviland inquiry has come a long way since Buckland's dream-woman, but she still flickers in the imagination, a reminder of unreachable lives and stories. More is known about her than Buckland could have imagined. The Red Person was aged between twenty-five and thirty; he received a ceremonial burial at least 29,000 years ago, in a cave which looked out on a broad valley threaded with the river Severn; the sea was sixty or seventy miles to the west. His height was about five feet eight inches (1.73 metres), his weight around 11 and a half stone (73kg). The bones contain evidence that he and his contemporaries ate quantities of fish, very likely salmon from the Severn.

The broken skeleton and the fragments found beside it – pierced periwinkles, ivory rods that could have been magic wands – are locked away in Oxford's Museum of Natural History. A display cabinet in the main hall contains replicas. In 2007 I applied to see the originals, and was welcomed, but not before I was asked a precautionary question about any interest I might have, as a Welsh person, in wanting Oxford's treasures returned to Gower; the museum is uneasily aware that the newly vocal Welsh nation is starting to ask for her back, a request of the Elgin Marbles kind. Cardiff and Swansea would both like to get their hands on her. There has been talk of an 'interpretive visitor centre' near Goats Hole.

Or the cliffs could stay as they are, their caves hard to get at, the Red Lady no more than a presence in the dark; explained and classified, yet scarcely explained at all.

CHAPTER 4

BAY

THE BRISTOL CHANNEL, narrowing from west to east, makes a funnel for tides and the prevailing south-westerly winds, which move in the same direction and collide with Gower. There are tales of professional wreckers with lanterns luring mariners on to the rocks, but it was only the poor making the most of Acts of God – the free barrels, boxes or entire cargoes, whatever came out of the boiling green sea. Nowhere in peninsula Gower is more than two and a half miles from salt-water. Wrecks were part of the local economy, and the legalities about who owned what were less important than who got there first. Port Eynon, where the bay is shallow and there is no safe anchorage, had a popular prayer: 'Oh Lord, let there not be wrecks. But since we know there must be wrecks, let them be here, not Rhossili.'

On a winter Sunday in 1898 the Rector of Rhossili, the Rev. John Lucas, left his house to walk up to the church and take morning service. At that time the rectory was below the hill, just above the beach itself; well-placed for the clergyman, who was Vicar of Llangennith as well as Rector of Rhossili. Later inhabitants had problems. Dylan Thomas once toyed with living in it; the National Trust owns it now and rents it to visitors; when it was unoccupied, in the nineteen-fifties, a man I used to know sheltered in it with his girlfriend during a rainstorm, and they made love on the bare floorboards.

The Rev. Lucas faced a walk of nearly a mile to reach the church, across fields and then up a steep path to the village, a

51

couple of hundred feet above. As he came out of his back gate he saw 'an *immense crowd*, a long long procession of people' coming towards him down the path. He described it in a letter to his son. For a moment he was bewildered; then he saw the rocket-launching rescue apparatus being taken in the same direction. A 'steamer' (in 1898 it was still commonplace to point out that it wasn't a sailing ship), the *Marshal Keith*, Dieppe to Llanelly, had run aground on a sandbank in the estuary, and the able-bodied population of Rhossili was on its way to scour the shore. The vessel floated off on the next tide. But it had been worth a try.

Rhossili Bay itself is a leading recipient of wrecks. This has not stopped non-mariners, bemused by its spaciousness, proposing it as a safe haven, a harbour of refuge with a tug on permanent standby. It is more of a death trap. Facing west and the weather, its shore-line runs north to south for three and a half miles of pure sand, curving slightly inward, between rocks at either end. This smooth bed is subject to surf that can pound hulls to pieces. In World War 2, attempts were made to fix anti-invasion obstacles in the sand: long lines of wooden posts, later steel girders. Neither survived.

Serious wrecks are infrequent now, but when ships were small and numerous, casualties were taken for granted. The Bristol Channel's gales and currents made it notorious. The frequent death of strangers in the sea was a matter for respect, not grief. This is from a Register of Burials at Port Eynon:

> On Saturday morning, January 27 1883, the S.S. Agnes Jack from Cagliari was wrecked off Port Eynon Point, and every man drowned. On April 9 the body of Mr Watkins, chief mate, was found [...]

> On the 6th-7th of February 1883, the French schooner 'Surprise,' from Paimpol, was wrecked on Overton cliffs, and the crew drowned. After the Rector had received the bodies at the Church-gate on Saturday the 10th, and had preceded 2 of them to the grave-

side, a messenger arrived from Swansea acquainting him that the bodies would be fetched away on Monday morning for interment in the Roman Catholic cemetery. Subsequently the coffins were placed in the Church porch, where they remained over Sunday.

East of Milford Haven the Bristol Channel no longer sees much commercial traffic, apart from a few container ships, oil tankers and ore-carriers. Swansea Bay, once alive with shipping, is empty most of the time.

Rhossili is still there, mouth open to swallow ships if there were any. The half-buried ribs of ancient wood, high up the beach, that visitors see as they walk down from the village, belonged to a sailing vessel with a cargo of timber, the *Helvetia*, and have been there since 1887, when she was blown to the west from outside the Mumbles and then, improbably, blown back into Rhossili. A local entrepreneur bought the wreck because he knew it had a valuable copper keel, but the hull settled in the sand and the copper must still be there.

Towards the other, northern end of the bay, a piece of black lopsided machinery sticks up from the sea at low water, the

remains of the *City of Bristol*'s beam-engine. She was a paddle-driven steamer, Waterford in Ireland to Bristol, John Stacey commander, aground November 17 1840. Those were the early days of short-sea crossings by ships with engines, which were the latest thing, better able to keep to a time-table; though that didn't happen with the *City of Bristol*.

For its day it was a 'fine and powerful steam vessel' – a smart ship, made of wood, 210 tons, thirteen years old, recently given a new boiler and keel. Captain Stacey was carrying several hundred pigs, fifteen bullocks, some barrels of grain, one hundred and twenty flitches of bacon, and a few passengers – perhaps five, perhaps seven – people sufficiently well-off to use the 1840 equivalent of first-class air travel; one of them was a woman. There were more crew than passengers – the commander, first and second mates, six seamen, some engineers, one cook, one carpenter, a couple of stewards and a stewardess.

The ship left Waterford on a Tuesday morning. It was delayed by gales, returned to harbour, tried again that evening, and by Wednesday morning it was off the Pembrokeshire coast, still in bad weather. The ship crawled up the Bristol Channel, land never far away on the left. As the light faded, Capt. Stacey decided to spend the night anchored on the edge of Rhossili Bay, north of Worms Head.

By early evening they still hadn't reached the anchorage. Heavy rain was falling. The sun had set at 4.22. Stacey's intended course was to the Worm, but at some point he began to steer to the left of it. Perhaps he had seen disturbed white water ahead of him shining in the dark, and thought it was sea breaking over the Helwick sands, a notorious bank south of the Gower coast. In fact he was looking at the white of breakers on the Worms Head. By changing course to the left, away from the Worm and deep water, he ran too far inside the bay.

The error must have been something like that. A survivor, a seaman called William Poole, told the inquest what happened.

> The vessel was steered for the head. About a quarter after six o'clock we observed land on our larboard quarter [the Burry Holms, the

half-tide island at the north end of the bay], and immediately afterwards land on our starboard [the Rhossili headland], and the vessel struck. After she struck every endeavour was made by the captain and crew to get her off and to keep her head to the sea, and the engines were kept working, but their power was counteracted by the power of the sea, and she turned broadside towards the sea, which then ran quite over her. All on board came on deck soon after she struck [...] The sea was running too high to use the boats, and we stayed by the vessel in the hope that she would hold together until the tide left her. We knew we were near the shore from hearing the people. The cook, James Cromwell, was the first person washed away, and the stewardess soon after...

Villagers had come on to the beach and were able to hear 'the cries of the unfortunate persons.' The nearest settlement was Llangennith, a mile or two away, beyond the dunes, but farms were nearer and eyes were always watching the bay, even – especially – on a wild night. There were no such things as lifejackets; it would be another decade before a mariner invented 'cork vests' for lifeboatmen. After two or three hours the ship began to break up. Demented pigs, racing about the deck, added to the nightmare. Captain Stacey, his first mate and three seamen were saving themselves, up in the rigging of the foremast. When it collapsed, the officers and two of the seamen drowned. The third was William Poole. He found himself on the paddle-box, then fell into the water, close to a plank. With its help he swam ashore. At 8 o'clock the tide had turned and was coming in.

Poole, who was a sea-pilot by profession, and the ship's carpenter were the only survivors, together with seventy determined pigs and three cattle. The usual inquest was held at the usual place, a pub – the Kings Head in Llangennith – and reached the usual conclusion, expressed in fine Biblical language that dwelt on 'the force and violence of the wind and waves' and the persons who were 'accidentally, casually and by misfortune thrown into the sea, and in the waters thereof were then and there suffocated and drowned.'

Poole said that when he reached the shore, uninjured, 'I was so exhausted that I could not rise, and I should have perished in the surf if the persons on shore had not assisted me.' For days the sands were littered with the dead, animal and human. The body of 'a gentleman in a frock-coat and boots' was found, two gold sovereigns in his pocket.

The harrowing end of the *City of Bristol* seems to have guaranteed that none of the locals availed themselves of personal property. The *Cambrian* felt it had to offer congratulations:

> In connexion with this lamentable occurrence, it is due to the inhabitants of the lower district of Gower to state, that their conduct, both as respects the property and the two survivors, has been most praiseworthy. For several days property to a considerable amount, and some of which might easily have been taken away, lay on the beach, and yet not an article of the slightest use to the owners was removed.

Afterwards there was talk of putting a lighthouse on Worms Head. In the end the authorities decided to mark the Helwick Sands, and kept a lightship there for a hundred and fifty years, until lightships went out of fashion in the late 20th century.

The family of William Poole still remember their ancestor's deliverance, and refer to it on a web blog. This suggests he was saved by holding on to the tail of a cow. People dwell on miracles of survival. Why him? Why Poole? He had a keepsake at home, a 'caul,' the fragment of membrane sometimes found on the face of a new-born child. A caul was seen as a charm against death by drowning, a belief that was still held in Gower as late as 1955. The family legend says the caul helped save him. It may have been true in a different way. He believed in the power of the relic and so he tried harder.

★

Down the other end of the bay from the *City of Bristol*, near the *Helvetia* and the headland, there is, or was, a wreck with treasure in it. This has contributed to the local economy more than once, but, not surprisingly, details are lacking. The treasure seems to consist of silver dollars, half-dollars and pieces of eight, which have been in the sand, assuming any of them are left, for upwards of three hundred years. The assumption, based on not very much except the coins themselves, is that a Spanish vessel was wrecked at Rhossili in the mid-seventeenth century, and from time to time rises up like an apparition, remaining just long enough to excite the population before returning to the dark.

One way into the history is Davies's *West Gower*, Vol. 3 (1885), which quotes George Holland of Cwm Ivy, within Davies's parish of Llanmadoc. Holland had died in 1862 at the age of eighty-six. He once told the rector that as a boy, he heard 'an old carpenter' tell him that 'there was plenty of money on Rhossili sands, only dig for it.' If Davies has his dates right, Holland was born in 1776. Boys in harsh places grew up quickly, so 'as a boy' means before 1790. If the 'old carpenter' heard the tale as a child, from a man of eighty, he would have been reaching back to memories of the early 1700s.

In 1807 the Rhossili treasure got into the papers, with a second-hand account in the *Cambrian* dated March 7 of recent discoveries. There must have been storms and spring tides to stir up the sands. One of the finds at Rhossili was no more than a wreck that had been there fifty years, from which 'a cask of iron wire' was removed. The other was better. Scattered about were approximately twelve pounds in weight of Spanish dollars and half-dollars dated 1625. It was 'conjectured' (the paper didn't say by whom) that these 'formed part of the cargo of a rich Spanish vessel from South America called the Scandaroon galley, which was wrecked on that part of the coast upwards of a century since.' Persons 'now living' were said to have had relatives, no doubt very old ones, who remembered 'the circumstances' of the wrecking.

Years later, in January 1834, when the *Cambrian* returned to the subject, it gave a more exciting account of what had happened in 1807. Sand had 'drifted very unusually,' and 'part of the wreck, in a very decayed state, became visible, and a great quantity of dollars, with some old iron and pewter, was then dug up from some depth in the sand.' Many local inhabitants were 'much enriched.' But 'the spot where the vessel struck being only open at four hours ebb tide, and the sand having returned to its old quarters, the money-hunters were obliged to desist in their attempts.'

The reason the newspaper went back to what happened in 1807 was that it had happened again – late in 1833, following gales, although the *Cambrian* didn't hear about it till January 1834; the fortune-seekers were trying to keep it quiet. An account appeared thirty-seven years later in an 1870 *Handbook for Travellers in South Wales*, published in London but evidently written with local knowledge.

> In 1833 about 120 ft. of the ship was exposed, and a systematic attempt was made to recover the treasure. About 300 people were at work on this 'Eldorado,' and were well repaid for their exertions. In 1834 she was again visible for a short time, and a large number of Spanish dollars found.

J.D. Davies, two years old at the time, eventually heard the story of 1833 from George Holland. Four men had seen 'an unusual shifting of the sand.' Davies even knew their names, William Taylor, John Taylor, Richard Clark and Thomas Hullin (there is still a Hullin family in Rhossili, but without knowledge of the story). The friends knew the buried-treasure legend, and went to see if the sands were about to oblige again.

> Strange to say, they commenced their search in a spot where a quantity of the dollars lay; but unfortunately for them, the tide was just beginning to come in, and soon overflowed the place where the

> money was; they continued however to dig till the water got too many for them, and they afterwards said, that they lost many pieces, that were washed off their shovels...

They marked the spot with a makeshift buoy, which was gone the next day. But word got out, people flocked to the sands, 'and much quarrelling and fighting took place.' Many dollars were found. 'Some persons from Swansea, named Bell' arrived with circular iron tanks, open at both ends, inside which they dug, with no more success than anyone else.

One or two neighbouring gentry with coins showed them to Davies. He saw Spanish pesos, 'the coins that have been made so familiar to us in the pages of Robinson Crusoe. [All] were much defaced, and the coinage very rough and rude.' The best preserved money had the name King Philip IV and was dated 1625. Davies listed other non-precious objects that were salvaged, including musket balls mixed together with bits of iron, like primitive shrapnel; a marine astrolabe, the beautiful brass instrument for navigating by stars and the sun; and a pair of large cannon, which for years stood outside a house at Llangennith.

Davies even cranked up the story by reporting a tradition that a second Spanish vessel, this one carrying gold, was wrecked in an adjoining cove, Blue Pool, which faces Carmarthen Bay. He said that 'about forty years ago' (meaning the 1840s) coins were found there, in 'crevices of the rocks,' by Thomas Hullin and William Taylor. This was the pair that helped find the silver dollars in 1833.

After their coup at Rhossili they probably saw themselves as professional treasure-seekers. Aware that a fisherman and his wife were said to have found gold coins at Blue Pool a century earlier, they went 'purposely to search this spot,' wrote Davies, 'and strange to say they had not been long at work before they came upon several more of these coins sticking in the crevices of the rocks, and as bright as the day they came out of the mint.' Hullin,

Taylor & Co then began blasting with quarrymen's gunpowder until they were stopped.

Looking for gold, then finding it a few miles round the corner from the silver, sounds a trifle suspicious. Perhaps Davies, who liked legends and ghost stories, was having his leg pulled. But the Spanish Galleon story itself, which is true, has an air of improbability – a rumoured treasure is unseen for centuries, surfaces twice within twenty-six years, and is never heard of again.

It can't all have been found. I once saw a man in the shadow of the headland, quartering the damp sand with a metal-detector. It was a spring tide, ebbing fast. He plodded west, towards the line of breakers far away.

Its situation makes Rhossili the most written-about place in the peninsula – the great bay; the illusion of sea and sky merging into one another; the strange promontory of the Worms Head, jutting out like the prow of the good ship 'Gower.' The village straggles along the main road from Swansea and ends with an inconspicuous hotel, a few houses – once coastguard cottages – and a grass car-park. The miles of north-south beach are below, running parallel to a north-south ridge at the standard height of Gower hills, around six hundred feet; the end of the ridge runs down to the village. Hang-glider pilots step off its slopes and sail above grass, sand and water. From the car-park a headland runs out almost a mile to the south-west. At the end of it is a causeway of rocks, when the tide is out, and the serpentine Worm; this extends for a further mile in an obliging north-west direction, which makes it more visible when seen from the village.

The small church was built late in the 12th century. Its doorway may have come from a lost church a quarter of a mile below, under the hill and close to the beach, where an earlier settlement was overwhelmed by sand in the Middle Ages. Celtic churches hid themselves below the Gower skyline, less visible to sea-raiders. The confident Normans wanted to be seen. Their church at Rhossili came to be used by marine pilots as a marker. Llanelli pilots taking a vessel to sea knew it was safe to hand over to the captain once they cleared the Burry Holms, and the church tower came into view at the other end of the bay.

One or two poets have taken an interest in the place. A great-nephew of the poet Robert Southey (1744-1843), who thought he could be a poet too, is said to have had a table and chair rowed out to the Worms Head so he could write there in a style befitting a man of letters. He is also said to have used a revolver around the village to shoot dogs, hens and donkeys. He definitely paid someone to let him jump into the sea off Port Eynon point, from the scaffolding where a lifeboat station (now a youth hostel) was being built.

Dylan Thomas had known Rhossili since he was a child, and might have gone to live there once. The idea was not his; he fell in with whatever his benefactors were willing to pay for. In 1953, the year of his death, there were problems with the Boat House in Laugharne, where the Thomases had been since 1949, and someone must have thought of the Old Rectory. Writing to a friend he said it was 'an old and ratty rectory owned by a batty farmer.' Nothing came of the idea, which was just as well, given its location, nearly a mile from the nearest shop, in a village with no pub. From the brow of the hill above, you can look north-west across Carmarthen Bay and see the indent in the coast which is the estuary where the Boat House stands, fourteen miles away, but sixty by road.

Two of the ten stories in Thomas's autobiographical *Portrait of the Artist as a Young Dog* are set in Rhossili. 'Who do you wish was with us?' has him and a companion cut off on the Worms Head between tides. In 'Extraordinary Little Cough' Thomas and school friends camp above the five-mile beach – a bit exaggerated – along which 'Little Cough,' a boy named George, who mirrors something of Dylan himself, is goaded into running after dark. He returns exhausted. 'And when I stared round at George again he was lying on his back fast asleep in the deep grass and his hair was touching the flames.'

Dylan Thomas was too urbanised ever to make much of Gower; the two stories in *Portrait* subordinate the locations, legitimately enough, to his endless narrative of himself. Unlike his friend Vernon Watkins, many of whose poems are preoccupied with images of the peninsula, and who lived there, above a sea-cliff at Pennard, Thomas was more of a day tripper, eating his sandwiches, self-absorbed, not taking his clothes off, ever, to go in the sea. When he was young, of course, he would often have walked in Gower. There is a story of him leading a party of amateur actors up Cefn Bryn one night – after they had performed somewhere in the peninsula – and pretending to invoke spirits at Arthurs Stone. A woman who had known him when they were teenagers once told me, 'He'd say, "Let's go roistering and rude bathing", but when we got to Langland Bay he never took his socks off.'

I expect he came to see Gower as a municipal park without park-keepers. When young – before London and America and fame – he may have found it useful as a place to take a girl to. You caught a bus, had a thirty- or forty-minute journey, walked along a beach till you found a quiet sand-dune, and hoped for the best.

There is a photograph of Dylan, aged twenty, with a London girl-friend, Pamela Hansford Johnson, standing awkwardly in a pool on the sands at Caswell and gazing into one another's eyes; her mother took it. He once wrote a letter to the same Pamela, confessing to, or boasting about, a dirty weekend, very likely invented, in a Gower bungalow where he and a young

Dylan Thomas and Pamela Hansford Johnson, Caswell Bay
September 21, 1934

woman with 'a loose red mouth' spent a weekend fornicating and drinking themselves silly.

Vernon Watkins, who was serious about Gower, died in 1967. His widow, Gwen, still lives in the area, near Mumbles Head, and remembers Dylan by the sea. It was 1950, three years before he died. He and his wife Caitlin spent a day at The Garth, the Watkins' house at Pennard, together with the 'Swansea gang,' a few friends from Dylan's youth. They went to bathe at Pobbles, a cove nearby, but 'we had hardly gone to the next headland, when Dylan threw himself down on the grass, panting. "I can't possibly walk any further," he said. "I'll wait here till you come up".' Gwen politely turned back with him, and they sat on the lawn in the shade, Dylan sipping a lager, and talked about the novels of Dickens. Later, everyone eating tea, there were sandwiches of sewin, a Welsh sea-trout, delicately flavoured. Dylan plastered his with Pan Yan pickle.

Because he is by far the most famous person ever produced by the area, his name is enlisted for publicity purposes, and who can blame the publicists? Sometimes they get carried away. The Worms Head, announces a tv website, was 'made famous by Dylan Thomas.' It was on postcards and in guide books before he was born.

CHAPTER 5

ESTUARY

L LANELLI, in Carmarthenshire, has little to do with Gower, except that the town and the peninsula face one another across the Burry Estuary, and the watery sands between seem always to have been a challenge. In the 19th century, Llanmadoc people believed that 'many years ago' it was possible to walk across stepping stones between Whitford Point and Pembrey, a village west of Llanelli. The distance is something over two miles.

Some old person told J.D. Davies that one of the stones was 'the head bones of a horse.' Pembrey inhabitants, Davies was assured, formerly had to bring their corn across and have it milled at Llangennith, obeying 'an old custom.' He wrote it down because he liked old stories, even stories that couldn't be true. Or so I thought, until I was told that a wealthy family called Ashburnham once owned land in both places, Llangennith and Pembrey. An hotel in Pembrey is still named after them. They were the link, centuries ago.

Near Llanelli itself, farther up the estuary, at low water there is not much more than a mile of muddy sand between the two sides, separated by the river Loughor, which marks where anglicised West Glamorgan ends and the Welsher Carmarthenshire begins. Professional cockle-gatherers from Penclawdd, in Gower, move insect-like across the horizon with their trucks, as if floating on water. The estuary is soft-centred, unlike the limestone coast of south Gower. The course of the river shifts. Rough seas with storms behind them have reshaped the sandy Whitford Point and changed the coastline many times. J.D. Davies has an enduring image of an old man remembering an old woman remembering how she milked cows in a 'green meadow' at the foot of Spritsail Tor, near Llanmadoc, before it was sand and sea.

Ships and sailors brought the two coasts together; there were love-affairs and marriages. A two-way trade thrived. A vessel might cross from Llanelli with coal and go back with sand. But the waters were never as safe for shipping as Llanelli liked to pretend. The small vessels that traded with local villages like Llanmadoc, which in maritime terms was a creek in the marshes, could cope with shallow waters. But Llanelli aspired to be a proper port, dealing with France and the Mediterranean.

The town was a thriving God-fearing commercial community, grounded in chapels as well as the monstrous furnaces that poured red light on to the streets after dark. Its steel and tinplate were exported from a couple of modest docks, via channels between sandbanks that shifted week by week. Sea-pilots took frequent soundings to keep track of the sand; sometimes they checked with binoculars from the land, standing on high ground at low water, looking for hidden banks.

Coal was Llanelli's other export. The district was on the western edge of the South Wales coalfield. Some asserted that these coal reserves (most of which are still there), and in fact all the coal in Britain, had been expressly provided by the Almighty as part of a global plan to give the Christian nations the benefit of mineral resources. Britain and America were the most favoured nations. Dr Buckland of the Red Lady believed it to be so, or pretended that he did. He publicly accepted that there was a divine initiative to make Britain 'the most powerful and richest nation on earth.'

Llanelli was doing its bit to advance this master-plan. Like all the South Wales ports, it competed furiously with its neighbours.

> Burry River, at Llanelly, has this peculiar advantage to light colliers bound up the Bristol Channel when caught short with a S.E. wind and blowing hard, and there is no shelter in the Mumbles; they may run for Burry, where they will find smooth water, as soon as they pass the Worms Head, and they may work into Pembrey or Llanelly under close-reefed sails.

In other words, trust us – don't trust that lot in Swansea.

Ships came to grief quite often, though with luck they could be floated off again. At least sand didn't split a hull as quickly as rocks. But a January evening in 1868 proved a spectacular exception, and has become embedded in local history as the sea disaster to end all Gower sea disasters. It was a joint calamity, begun in Llanelli, ended seven miles away at Llanmadoc; an estuary matter.

In Llanmadoc church that evening, Wednesday the 22nd, choir practice was in progress, conducted by Mr Davies. Church music, like church decoration, was to be taken seriously. He had been rector for eight years; a lonely man, in the way of family, enthusiastic about his flock, looked after by his housekeeper, Anne Lewis. For once the choir had no weather to compete with. Exposed to winds from the north and west, the church could be noisy in storms from that direction. As it happened, there had been strong north-westerlies for days. But by Wednesday they had died away, leaving the weather calm and clear.

Someone screamed in the churchyard, 'an indescribable scream of terror,' wrote Davies. He rushed out. On the path he found a parishioner, a young man, his face 'actually distorted with fright.'

> 'What is the matter my lad?' I said.
>
> 'O,' he replied. 'I saw a man without his hat come and look in through the window.'
>
> I brought the poor terrified lad into the church, where he remained some little time before he came to himself.

Respectable people wore headgear. The hatless man was seen later on as an apparition. Davies knew it was what people believed, and may have believed it himself; the figure at the window was the spirit of a drowned sailor. But that version came later. On Wednesday evening the weather was calm, and if anyone saw lights from ships, they took no notice. The man at the window seems to have vanished.

It was not until dawn on Thursday that anyone knew what had happened. A string of sailing ships, perhaps sixteen, perhaps nineteen, had been towed out of Llanelli after dark by a steam tug, each ship strung to the one astern. Or there may have been a pair of tugs, and two groups of vessels. The routine was to leave Llanelli on the ebb tide, be towed down the estuary for three or four miles, and then around the tip of Gower, before being left to make their own way towards open water to the south-west. Some of the ships had a pilot on board, instructed to take them 'to sea,' clear of the Burry Holms.

High water at Llanelli was a few minutes after 5 in the afternoon. The procession moved slowly seawards, in calm conditions, with light breezes, and it was not until ships were rounding the peninsula that they realised the north-westerly gales of previous days had produced violent conditions in the open water. A deep swell kept raising them up and plunging them down again. I was in those waters once, aboard a seventeen-foot cabin cruiser, in a strongish north-westerly wind, and once was enough.

Tug or tugs, having done what they were paid for, let the ships go and turned back to Llanelli. Perhaps they left before the danger became apparent. One account said the sea was so violent, it parted the towing lines. No technical inquiry was ever made into exactly what happened. Coastal waters with sandbanks in them were known to be hazardous, ships were always going to sink, men were always going to drown; it was the natural order of things.

The breeze died away, the tugs had gone, the swell was enormous, and the flood tide began, though not until after midnight. Helpless in the narrow waters, without any wind, ships drifted about, banging into one another or having their hulls broken on sandbanks, the *St Catherine*, the *Amethyst*, the *Mary Fanny*, the *Jeune Celine*; at least sixteen of them. About fifty men drowned.

In 1986, a hundred and eighteen years after it happened, I met a man from Llanelli, Oswin ('Ossie') Roberts, whose great-grandfather was a sea-pilot in the estuary in 1868. Ossie had been a pilot too; the last of the Llanelli pilots before the commercial port died in the 1950s. He knew the story of a ship's boy who became famous, on the night of the disaster, for being afraid. The boy was in the crew of the *Mary Fanny*, a two-masted schooner taking tinplate round the coast to Liverpool. 'Pilot was George Perrott. He took them out to No. 3 buoy. The boy aboard her, he got so frightened, he jumped into the long boat after the pilot, and he was saved. All hands aboard the *Mary Fanny* were lost.'

Most of the ships ended up near Llanmadoc – Broughton Bay was littered with wrecks and bodies – but the *Mary Fanny* came ashore at the Llangennith end of Rhossili Bay. David Morris,

Broughton Bay

Ossie's great-grandfather, purchased the wreck, which had four feet of water in her hold. He and his son, Ossie's grandfather, patched her up using pitch mixed with manure to give it bulk, and a watertight *Mary Fanny* traded around the British coasts for years.

The manure came from a farm at Llangennith, where the younger Morris, Ossie's grandfather, caught the eye of a daughter. They fell in love and were married. Their daughter's memories passed down to Ossie – how, as a girl, she caught rabbits on the Holms, and took them to Swansea market on the big cart they called a gambo.

Nearly a century later another ship was wrecked where the *Mary Fanny* had come to grief. This time it was a warship, a World War 2 destroyer, the former H.M.S. *Cleveland*, on its way to a shipbreaker's yard. 'Where the *Mary Fanny* went ashore,' said Ossie Roberts. 'Right on that spot!' The yard was at Llanelli, no longer a commercial port at all, except that some spirit of the place kept up the pretence. For a few years the Admiralty rented space in the North Dock to keep tank landing craft there, against some future D-Day that never materialised. When they had gone, the breaker's quay was the only sign of life. The occasional vessel was towed in and dismembered. Warships were best, because of the high-value metals. Sometimes ships reached breakers' yards with fittings still in place. A yard in Swansea Bay, at Briton Ferry, once found nine hundred and fifty mattresses and got a pound each for them. There was a grand piano. Neath Corporation bought it.

The *Cleveland*, a Hunt class destroyer built in a hurry, had spent the war escorting convoys. In June 1957, twelve years after the war ended, the Navy was still scrapping ships. This one was being towed round from Cardiff to Llanelli when a summer gale broke the cable outside the Burry Estuary, and drove it into the arms of Rhossili Bay. It got as far as it was possible to go, the line of dunes high up the sand at the Llangennith end, broadside-on to the sea, as if planted there for maximum effect. The *Cleveland* made an attractive seascape, especially at each high-tide, when water lapped against the side and, until the novelty wore off, thousands came to admire, and warm the hearts of ice-cream sellers and the owners of the Kings Head in Llangennith.

Over the next year or so they had several goes at moving her. Excavators dug channels in the sand, a couple of tugs hovered on the other side of the breakers, the cables tautened, the *Cleveland* shivered, and nothing happened. I used the salvage operation in a novel of the sixties based on the incident. All the ship did was shift sideways a few yards, next to a different sand-dune, but never towards the open sea. In the end the insurers' patience ran out, and they blew her up and took the pieces away by lorry.

As for Llanelli, nothing goes there any more by sea, except yachts and motor cruisers, which berth nearby at Burry Port. The estuary still marks a division between territories, but not entirely. The same housing estates stare at one another across the water.

CHAPTER 6

THE PEOPLE

THE FIRST-COMERS, whoever they were, are too distant to seem real. The bones of Paviland's Red Lady catch the imagination for a moment, elements of someone whose world this was. Bacon Hole, a cave in the cliff face at Hunt's Bay, nearer Swansea, hints at human occupation of a date much earlier than Paviland's, but it lacks a skeleton, and the fantasies of a Buckland, to make it famous.

In the long silence between then and the start of recordable history, the only evidence of human beings is in the stone and earth of monuments, most of them associated with the dead of the neolithic and bronze periods, three to six thousand years ago. The lonely pillars of the 'Sweyn Howes,' on the back of Rhossili Hill, are the remains of neolithic tombs. Better preserved, because it has been professionally done-up, and is shut away in a valley instead of exposed on a hillside, is the burial cairn at Parc-le-Breos, near Parkmill. It belongs to the same period as the Sweyn Howes. The bones of forty or more people have been found there, from an infant to a man in his sixties. Animal remains and pieces of pottery suggest that the dead were sent on their way with ritual feasts.

A few miles distant, on the central spine of Cefn Bryn, is Arthurs Stone, the most visible grave in the peninsula, and the most famous. What survives is a capstone weighing perhaps twenty-five tons, with a ten-ton piece broken off. Because the stone is of a kind alien to Gower, there are theories that it came inside a glacier in an ice age, or was transported by fanatics, though it would have been the fanatics' slaves who did the heaving. Even if the ice carried it south, the monstrous object is unlikely to have been neatly deposited on a hilltop. Humans dragged it there.

On a more graspable scale, another Hole of the southern cliffs, Minchin – not far from Bacon – was home (or workplace, or refuge, or all of these) to people in Roman times and afterwards through the Dark Ages. Coins, copper brooches, iron arrowheads, a bronze bracelet, combs and spoons of bone, a missile to be shot from a ballista, a Roman oil bottle, broken pottery galore: all accumulated over millennia. Animal bones from pre-history – lion, rhinoceros, hyena – were there.

Through the peninsula, items turn up at random in fields, beside lanes, under sand. A stone-age hand-axe is picked up in a Mumbles allotment, antlers are dredged from Swansea Bay, Anglo-Saxon coins are found under a stone at Penrice. More than two thousand Roman coins in a bronze pot came to light at Southgate in 1966. Thundery rain at Skewen, on Swansea's east side, in 1919, uncovered a Roman hoard where an oil refinery was being built near the docks; now the refinery is long gone, and its own remains are turning to relics underground.

Walking over the dunes at Broughton Bay in the 1980s I found the brass cartridge case of a 20mm cannon. Aircraft on training missions in World War 2 used to fire at targets there, so it was a forbidden area, with skull-and-crossbone signs. Ejected cartridges fell like hailstones. A farm bailiff was killed. Two schoolboy trespassers were there c. 1943 – the year stamped on the casing – when a pair of Typhoons came out of the sky, firing. We ran.

The texture of the past and its 'ordinary people' is elusive. We have a glimpse of Anglo-Norman Gower in the late 13th century only because William Cragh of Llanrhidian survives in the Vatican archives. Legends – historical gossip – throw a faint light on lives and the way people thought. J.D. Davies wrote some of them down, before folk-memory fell out of fashion.

The tales reached as far back as the Vikings, raiding the British coasts a thousand years earlier:

> There is a tradition in Rhossili, that three Danish vessels came
> to the Burry Holms, and that the crews landed and proceeded to
> Llangennith, where they burned the Church, and slaughtered the
> people; but while they were occupied in this murderous work, the
> inhabitants of Rhossili went to the sands and set fire to the ships.
> This story was communicated to me by Lady Wilkinson.

Caroline, Lady Wilkinson, came from one of the long-established Gower families, the Lucases, and had brought her husband, Sir Gardner Wilkinson (1797-1875), an Egyptologist, to live at Reynoldston, in the house called Brynfield. She heard the Viking legend from 'an old man in Rhossili village.'

Did Davies write down these stories as soon as he heard them, or were they filtered through his memory too? He followed the 'three ships' story with an account of 'a desperate fight which took place between the people on Llanmadoc Hill, and those on [nearby] Harding's Down. I give it verbatim as related by Henry Thomas, of Lagadranta [near Llanmadoc].'

> There was a bloody battle between the people on Llanmadoc Hill
> and them on Arsin Down; they slung stones and pitched *bow arras*
> [bows and arrows] at one another from hill to hill for a long time,
> and then they met and fought hand to hand on Tankey Lake [moor],
> till the blood was up to the tops of their boots: here Tankin, the
> leader on one side, was killed, and the place was called ever after,
> Tankey's Lake. My informant also told me, that the leader on the
> other side was 'one Captain Hardy'; 'Captain Tonkin was,' he said,
> 'a Frenchman, but he had never heard of what nation Captain Hardy
> was.'

J.D. Davies concluded, hopefully, that 'Arsin' was the same as 'Harding' and sounded Danish. There is still a Tankeylake Farm.

Folk-lorists know that the force that drives the legend is the story. People wanted to be entertained, not instructed. They wanted to believe that *of course* an enemy's long-boats burned on the sands at Llangennith, that Vikings in funny helmets rushed about with buckets of sea-water, and all the girls of Rhossili kissed the local heroes when they got back.

On the south coast, at Oxwich, the stone effigy of a Norman knight and his lady can be found inside the church, a small ancient building below the headland, close to the sea. They are in a corner near the altar, well-illuminated, almost a tourist attraction. The bodies, cast in a cement using local sand, are orange-tinted, like the beach. He wears armour, with a close-fitting helmet and a curtain of chain-mail that covers the neck, leaving an oval for his features. She is on his right, the face fully exposed to show a long chin, with a headdress across her forehead. She looks resigned, but you can't tell what mood the sculptor intended for him, if any. Both have their hands pressed together in prayer, and their bodies are close enough to feel one another's warmth, if they were flesh and blood.

These are, or were, the 'Doolamurs,' a corruption of 'de la Mer,' a Norman family once prominent in the area; although they may be somebody else altogether, Normans with another name whose identity was stolen, thanks to folk-memory, by the more famous de la Mers. They have been there since the 14th century. 'From time immemorial,' wrote J.D. Davies, '[their] niche in the chancel had been known among the inhabitants as the "Doolamur's Hole." I have often heard my late father (who was curate of Oxwich in 1830) say, that in his time, it was a common thing for parents to frighten their children when naughty, by threatening to put them into the "Doolamur's Hole".'

Davies finds a story to go with the Normans. A Mrs Wood – another Lucas, who married a Colonel Wood – told him that 'she remembers hearing [...] that the Knight and his lady, who were buried beneath this tomb, were drowned in Oxwich Bay.'

The figures are well-lit now, clean and peaceful. Children have worse things to frighten them. But the church itself, lonely and crouched in Oxwich Wood, can still conjure up a different past in a different Gower. It is outside the village, at the end of a path, stuck in the middle of nowhere. A poem by a contemporary writer, Nigel Jenkins, 'Memorial at Oxwich,' catches the uneasiness of the place. Perhaps I am reading more into it than the poet intended. But I detect old fears, renewed with every generation.

> Man, wife and child,
> a lonely mist of three,
> drifting through a carefully full
> seaside graveyard
> where the flat dead are praised
> by their stone guards.
>
> Her thighs on holiday
> and the infant's child-wide grin
> become the subject of a photograph,

snapped perhaps before a rent
in their vulnerable cocoon,

before the juicy warmth spills out
and the shell becomes winter,
a smiling blue-veined memory
in the folds of a pigskin wallet.

What of the open dead at sea,
what of the pig whose skin,
what of the nipped cocoon,
what of the husband
who could not be in the picture he took?

But all is safe:
they were smiling to him,
he remembers the words that made them laugh.

Imagining the past is easy. Reporting it is more difficult. Plain lives in Gower, plainly described, are the hardest of all to reach. Diaries have survived here and there. An oyster fisherman in Victorian times, John Timothy (1833-1908), kept one for the first four months of 1864. He lived in Pwlldu ('Black Pool'), a small bay and hamlet towards the Mumbles end of the southern coast. Pronouncing the Welsh word was beyond him, often the case in 'English' Gower, and he played safe and said 'Pool-die.'

John worked hard, watched the weather, had an eye for the unusual. 'February 4. Went to sea again, the wind north-west. Went away for day under single reef canvas. Beat to Oxwich Bay. We was 10 of us down there. Caught 2,900. We seen the sun moon and stars in the sky at the same time. Came home at 6.' He didn't fear gales, he liked beer ('Drinked all day,' he wrote on January 2, a Saturday), and he kept on the right side of God:

Sunday February 7. Stayed in Mumbles to dinner, started to go to Bishopston Church at 2.30. The Revd. Jones delivered a sermon on the 16th Chap. [of Numbers], 48 verse. The words 'and he stood

between the dead and the living and the plague stayed.' Came out
of church, snowing very thick. Went out to Murton, drank 1 pint
then went to Kittle. Drank ½ pint there. Went to Poole's house by
Highway. Came back to Murton Chapel and heard a sermon delivered
by John Rosser of Mumbles. The words were as follows, 'As Moses
lifted up the serpent in the wilderness so shall the Son of Man be lifted
up.' Came out at 8. Went a little way and got home at 1.

A family called Gibbs, with a traceable history in Gower going
back to the fifteenth century, has left diaries and letters that are
now in the possession of Michael Gibbs, retired schoolteacher and
archivist. Originally the clan may have come across the Bristol
Channel from north Devon. They were not 'gentry'; some were
farmers, mariners, cattle-dealers, farm bailiffs. A Thomas Gibb
of Oxwich Green (born 1729), a direct ancestor of Michael
(born 1941), was a casual labourer who helped with hedging and
harvesting; his wife and daughters were casual servants at Oxwich
rectory. But when he found himself in dispute with his social
superiors, he challenged them. In October 1787 the Talbots of
Penrice Castle wanted to terminate his lease of a cottage. Thomas
sent them a letter, suggesting they do a deal. The details are
obscure but his resolve is clear.

> Honored Sirs – as you are desireous of this littell place I shall oblige
> you on these terms, which I think is not unreasnabel considderin my
> troubble in moving and other disadvantages which I foresee, so this
> I expect – William Gie's house and John Clark's with a life added to
> the both that is in this and the Lord's rent at ten shillings per year,
> and two lives added to mine in the little house at Oxwich Green,
> with the sum of forty pounds in hand, with all the timber and other
> things except the stone belongging to these houses, for William Gie's
> lofts are very bad, requiring a great deal of repairs. So do the littel
> house at Green. The littel meadow in Penrice parish and half an acre
> of marsh added to William Gie's house, with the leases costing mee
> nothing. So I am your humble sarvant, Thomas Gibb.

The Talbots met all Thomas's demands except one, where a
compromise was reached.

In the 19th century a Harriet Gibbs (1795-1881) wrote letters, kept papers and made private notes, all offering a woman's view of family life, much concerned with health and personal behaviour. She married another Gibbs, a mariner, Samuel, and they had nine children. A daughter, Sarah, suffered from 'indigestion and a sluggish liver,' and was sent to 'drink the waters at Llandrindod' in mid-Wales, a little town that tried in vain to be a spa of the continental kind. She died at Port Eynon aged twenty-four. Another daughter, Mary, born 1817, who had 'attacks' and 'fits' in her forties, was evidently an alcoholic. July 5 1866: 'She have got at the spirits. Oh! What a graceless woman... I have advised her to pray to God to resist this awful drinking.'

February 10, 1867: 'Our dear Mary had dinner and after a while she had an odd feeling about her and poor thing, her mind was wandering and she did not know what she did, as began to take of all her clothes and said she was going to bed.'

Not all Harriet's private memoranda were about domestic affairs. A son, George, born 1827, worked in England as a young man, and was appointed local shipping agent by Lloyd's of London. The proud mother made notes about his work. He was called out on the night of the Burry Estuary disaster.

January 23, 1868: 'at 2 o'clock in the morning, George Gibbs was sent for to Rosilly, a vessel ashore and all perished. It was an awful gale, and sea running mountains. There was a heart-rending scene to look at, 11 vessels all to pieces, having come out of Llanelly in the evening, and the wind died away, the sea mad and they all got ashore on Rosilly sand and Llangenny, Brufton and the banks. The shore was all strewed with the wrecks.'

Harriet's troubles were nearer home. March 14 1868: '[...] on this same day unfortunate Mary came in and drank the raw Gin and went home and could not guide herself, fell and bruised her face, and was upstairs several days. Oh! What a shame and disgrace. How it do wound the feeling's of her aged parents and her poor children.' Mary died a few years later.

Capt. Samuel Gibbs, Harriet's seafaring husband, lived to be seventy-seven. He was an old friend of the Rev. John Davies, senior, the father of the Rev. Davies who wrote the book. When the captain's health was failing, Daniel Davies, the doctor, brought over the senior John Davies, the friend with whom he had explored Paviland cave in their youth, to see him. 'We scarcely know what to give your poor father,' wrote Harriet. 'He takes a little of the calve's jelly [...] we give him often, but he bite the spoon and resist all who try to give him anything, and kick with his feet and through all the close off. He is quite at a loss, does not know anyone and he must be getting very weak [...] he take the sleepy mixture and fall off to sleep.' Samuel was in his eight-second year when he died.

Alcohol was much resorted to. When it turned up unexpectedly, people consumed it on the spot. The Rev. John Collins of Oxwich, another diarist, noted on Thursday March 13, 1794: 'Smuggler chased into the bay at Oxwich by the *Speedwell* cutter and taken. Sixteen men landed and saved some casks [...] several of parishioners got very drunk with gin.' On Saturday: 'Poor Thomas Matthews died owing to drinking a quantity of gin on Thursday.' On Sunday: 'Buried T.M. corpse, Oxwich church, near 200 people at church.'

The sick and injured could send for a doctor, if they were lucky. In April 1864, when Mary Gibbs was having a bad night, Harriet despatched a servant at 11 o'clock on a ten-mile journey to Blackpill, near Swansea, for a Dr Hancorne. The doctor went down to Port Eynon, presumably on a horse, though not till next day. Daniel Davies, the peninsula's first doctor, was in Reynoldston from 1816, less than three miles from Port Eynon. Perhaps he was anticipating the future and didn't respond to calls after 5 p.m.

Medical men cost money; folk-medicine was free. J.D. Davies

quotes at length from the 'commonplace book' of a Mr Leyshon Rogers of Llangennith, which contains entries of the late 18th century.

> For a boyl, take white Bread and butter and chaw it and spread it on a Cloth and put to it.

> For the heart burning is one bean dried very hard, to eat this will stop it soon.

> To keep of any Disorder from any person and to make ye Blood to Surkylate, is to take 1 quart of Decoction of Bark and to mix i Pint of Brandy with it, and then to drink a glass full every night and morning fasting, as long as it do hould.

The active ingredient of aspirin – first synthesised in a stable form in Germany, twelve years after the Rev. Davies copied the entries from Leyshon Rogers' notebook – is salicylic acid. This is found in the bark of trees, notably willow, and is one of the world's most versatile drugs. Gower's poorly could have done worse than brandy and aspirin.

Household furniture and fittings reflect everyday lives. At the death of Mary Bennett, née Lucas, another of the clan, in 1700, her possessions were listed and priced. The most valuable item was 'Her Weareing apparrel,' £5. There was no crockery; her twelve plates were made of pewter, and so were one flagon, three tankards, two dishes, two basins, one cullender, nine spoons and a chamber pott. The full tally included three feather beds, two pairs of blankets, brass candlesticks and kettles, a fryen pan, six stools, one chest and severall old bookes. The total value was twenty-nine pounds 11 shillings and tenpence, the worldly goods of a comfortable life. The poor left few inventories.

A true 'social history' of Gower has yet to be written. Farm labourers, quarrymen and fishermen made their livings unnoticed and generally unreported. Occupations, where they are recorded, show communities enriched with local skills, in a way unimaginable now. Within the extended village of Llanrhidian, in the industrial corner of Gower on the north coast, about thirty trades and occupations could be found in a population of a few thousand, at the middle of the 19th century. Most of the workers were labourers on farms or farmers themselves, or they were colliers or coppermen (there was a copper works) or servants. But dressmaker, carpenter, mariner, sea-pilot, cockle-woman, tailor, miller, laundress, weaver, mason, blacksmith, teacher, gardener, sawyer and ragman were there as well.

From the nineteenth century, 'ordinary lives' begin to build themselves into history. J.D. Davies, writing his four volumes, showed the expected deference to wealth and hierarchy, but uncovered information that told other tales. He noted beds of burnt cockle-shells deep down in the churchyards of Llanmadoc and Llangennith, and concluded that when food was scarce, cockles may have been brought to the church to be cooked and divided fairly. The locals always told him the same: 'There was a great famine in them times.' Davies (born 1831) had seen for himself the 'poorer classes' being unable to afford coal, having to warm their cottage kitchens by burning dried cow dung.

Near the end of the 19th century, a Royal Commission into land ownership in Wales took evidence in Gower, and, for the first time in history, a farm labourer from the peninsula had his words attended to and written down by secretaries. The Gower hearing was on a single day, May 26, 1893, at Reynoldston, inside the King Arthur, which was, and is, the local inn.

Most of the evidence came from tenant farmers and land agents. Aware that the labouring poor preferred to keep out of sight, the commissioners were surprised to discover that one of them was volunteering his services; he was the only one in South Wales who did. So they began by questioning this prodigy to make sure that he was what he claimed to be. His name was David Williams and he lived at Burry Green, a mile or so distant.

He could do most things; he could plough, thatch, make hedges – 'anything on the farm,' except that he couldn't milk a cow. 'It is not a common thing in Gower,' he said, 'for a man to milk.'

Cottages for labourers were not up to much. His previous home, in Cheriton, near Llanmadoc, had been a place where 'farmers [...] would not like to put their animals to lie down in the winter.' Upstairs, three younger children had shared the bedroom with him and his wife. Rain and snow got in through the roof; he had seen snow lying on the beds in winter. Two older daughters were 'in service,' as domestic servants; when they visited their parents, they had to sleep downstairs, where the floor was earth, and a small fire burned in a grate that David had installed. Attached to the cottage was a quarter-acre garden. Now, he said, a daughter, her husband and three children lived there. His present cottage at Burry Green still had only two rooms, but the children were gone and it was sufficient for his needs.

What did they put on the table? A little milk, he said. Butcher's meat at weekends only. 'But we have plenty of potatoes and bacon for dinner, and that is what the labourer in Gower has been brought up on.' Asked about tea, he said, 'I think rather too much tea at the present time. I think if there was something else better than tea, the labourer would feel better, sometimes.'

David Williams may have been lucky and gone regularly to a church or parish school. Not everyone cared about education. Gower children might be kept at home for days at a time to help the family plant potatoes or rake up cockles. A few years later J.D. Davies began evening classes for those who had left school. Writing in his church magazine he was soon regretting the 'utter absence of enthusiasm for self-improvement... The necessary result, that boys and young men will ever be doomed to a life of toil, hardship and privation, will apply here as elsewhere.' He didn't say what girls and young women were doomed to.

A mile from Burry Green and David Williams' cottage lived a boy called Richard Lewis John, born 1890, whose father, a farmer, was keen on education. The farm was Ty'r Coed, near the western edge of Cefn Bryn; it is still on the Ordnance maps. As a small boy Richard walked to school in Llanrhidian, a round trip of three miles. Aged twelve, he progressed to 'Intermediate' school, the Comprehensive of its day, at Gowerton, a village eight miles away that is technically in Gower though it doesn't feel like it. His farmer-father was a governor of the school, and didn't think much of the way people spoke in Gower. A better school would teach his son to speak 'proper English.' But Gowerton meant a more complicated journey.

Every Monday Richard left Ty'r Coed after breakfast, riding bareback on Doll the pony. With him went a bag of food and clothing to last the week, and another bag of books for school. Doll took him to the coast and the old road on the edge of the marshes; at high water on a spring tide, the pony was close to swimming. Part one of the journey ended at Llanmorlais, an estuary village four or five miles away. Doll turned round and found her own way back to Ty'r Coed. Richard got on a train.

The railway had reached north-east Gower by 1866, a single-track line to serve the local coal mines. Passengers came later. A seven-coach train ran on Saturdays to take Penclawdd's cockle-women to Swansea market; the carriages reeked for hours. It was assumed that one day the railway would carry on, west and south, to bring all peninsula Gower into the modern world, but that never happened.

Richard John, catching his train at Llanmorlais, the terminus, travelled eastward past collieries and slag tips, all gone and grassed over now, to Gowerton and the school, four miles away, another small hub of industry, grown out of nothing. During the week he stayed with an aunt who lived a mile from Gowerton. On Fridays, when school finished at 4.30 – already dark in winter – he set off for Ty'r Coed, on foot this time, taking the shortest route, inland across open country, not along the coast. Ancient tracks were still in use, green lanes that have vanished now or are known only to serious walkers. Richard passed close to the village of Three Crosses. Then across commons, alongside a wood, over Welsh Moor (the no-man's-land between north and south Gower, the Welsh and the English), and around the flank of Cefn Bryn, the furnace-glare of Llanelly on his right, across the water. It was an eight-mile walk.

Those who were not ambitious made the best of what they had. North-east Gower, with its new climate of industry, was quicker to shake off memories of a feudal past. In south Gower they poached game at their peril, knowing they could be evicted from their cottages if caught. The Talbots were not rapacious landlords, but everyone kept on the right side of them. A photograph of the reigning Talbot hung in Gower cottages.

People even paid for the privilege. It was another branch of the 19th century Talbots that more or less invented photography, so when the landlord's agent offered the new marvel of a true likeness in a frame, modestly priced, one suspects that even those with earth floors decided they wanted one, or felt it unwise to

C. R. M. Talbot (1803-1890)

say they didn't.

One's class could be recognised at a glance. In 1912 or 1913 someone took a photograph of the geologist W.J. Sollas at Paviland, the Red Lady's cave, which he was re-excavating ninety years after Buckland. Sollas is in his shirt-sleeves, bare-headed, cigarette between fingers; he looks like Orson Welles. Three of the others, standing awkwardly, are local workmen, one of them a Gibbs. They announce their status with cloth caps, collars but no ties, and an uncertainty about what to do with their hands. Sollas, with tie, has a managerial look. The fourth man is younger, wears a jersey with tie visible, and must be Sollas's assistant.

People needed to show respect for their social superiors, though didn't always. The parson at Oxwich, John Collins, complained in his diary, February 1801, 'Painter here from Swansea. Drunk and impudent. Charged me 8 shillings.' A tradesman from Penmaen might have been more polite because the Rev. Collins was a figure in his community. The chap from Swansea lived in a seaport where all sorts rubbed shoulders and broke rules.

Hierarchy in Gower was more tangible. J.D. Davies himself was ever respectful to the Talbots, thanking the current head of the family in Vol. 1, 'C.R. Mansel Talbot, Esq., M.P.', for 'permission to peruse the splendid collection of ancient documents preserved at Penrice Castle [...] probably the finest private collection of old records in the kingdom.' The Talbots had been friendly with his father, so they smiled on the son when he was made Rector of Llanmadoc in the 1860s, bringing his High Church principles with him. Talbot support helped him fend off the evangelical churchmen; as the *Cambrian* put it, he was backed by 'persons of immense influence.'

The clergy had their own hierarchies of respect. Gifts from above were offered and accepted without awkwardness, at least by the Rev. Collins, who wrote it all down in his obliging diary.

21 October 1787 Mr Talbot gave me a handsome bookcase.

30 November 1795 Breakfasted at Penrice Castle. Mr Talbot gave
me a Double Gloucester cheese a cherry tree and a piece of venison.

11 September 1799 Breakfasted at Penrice Castle and went with
them and party to Wormshead. Heavy rain while at dinner in tent.
Cleared up and got home dry.

9 July 1804 Dined at Penrice castle on a remarkably large haunch of
Margam venison.

The curate of Port Eynon, reporting to his bishop in 1799,
apologised for a mistake in the letter 'occasioned by the noise of
my children.' Go back further and the Rector of Nicholaston, a
Rev. D.A. Evans, writes to his patron at Penrice Castle, a Mansel,
the family that preceded the Talbots, about a business matter. It
is 1722. He oils the wheels by declaring that 'I am not able to
express my joy for Mr Mansel's honour's success in ye house of
Comons, wch I heard but late...'

Respect for the Talbots reached a point in the 19th century
where they had a town named after them. This was outside
Gower, on the eastern side of Swansea Bay, where the family
had its stateliest home – Margam Park, originally a Mansel
property – and owned thousands of acres that they were busy
covering with coal mines and iron works. The nearby town was
Aberavon, which had a harbour. The leading Talbot, the C.R.M.
whose picture hung in cottages, had the port developed – he
was a Member of Parliament – and the place was renamed Port
Talbot in his honour, although the parliamentary constituency
stubbornly remains 'Aberavon.' A century and more later there
are locals who resent the theft of their place-name. A woman
who was brought up there in a working-class family of the
1930s, not far from the actor Richard Burton's birthplace, is still
annoyed at the self-importance of the Talbots. 'What a cheek!'
she says.

Everyday life for the underprivileged was not as barren and colourless as it can be made to sound. But it had its wintry side. Rhossili, seventeen miles west of Swansea, and the most admired spot in the peninsula, can still feel desolate in November, with rain sweeping the headland and the car park empty. In the old Gower, any event that broke the monotony was welcome.

In 1854, four hundred children on a Sunday School outing from Bethel chapel at Seaside, Llanelly, arrived in Rhossili without warning, having been taken in boats to the Worms Head by their enterprising teachers, and walking a mile and a half to the village. The church was opened and the bell rung in their honour. When they left, villagers walked them back to their boats and waved them off. It was an event.

The gentry, of whom there were not many, gave people something to look at, a shooting party returning to Penrice, a woman's face at a carriage window. When Florentia Wood, a colonel's daughter from Gower, married William Crawshay, an ironmaster's son from Merthyr, at Reynoldston in 1870, the *Cambrian* described how the bridegroom turned up in 'a chariot' that was 'drawn by six white horses with postilions and outriders,' though presumably not all the way from Merthyr. The bell-ringers, said the newspaper, were so enthusiastic, they broke one of the bells when rehearsing, and the occasion would 'long be remembered and cherished in the hearts of the dwellers in one of the most picturesque and romantic districts in the peninsula of Gower.'

This was not necessarily so; a posh wedding was just a diversion. A Mr Bevan, who had walked over from Horton out of curiosity, left a private account of the proceedings. According to the *Cambrian*, 'the booming of artillery echoed from hill to hill.' According to Mr Bevan, 'Someone found an old cannon and set it off.'

When a Talbot heir was born at Penrice in 1796, an ox was roasted outside the gates of the castle, and bell-ringers at Cowbridge – near the Talbots' principal seat of Margam Park – were still ringing a day later. When recovered, they sent in a bill for two guineas.

Fixed festivals and special days, usually religious, brought distractions. The 'Horse's Head' visited householders at Christmas, in fact the skull of a pony, cleaned with quicklime, held aloft on a pickaxe handle by teenagers, who sang carols for money. The Christmas Play of St George did the rounds, performed by itinerant gangs. St George and a Turkish knight fight with wooden swords, the latter falls down dead, and a Doctor appears:

> I can cure the itch, the palsy, and the gout,
> If the devil's in him, I'll pull him out.

The Knight is given a magic potion and comes back to life. 'One of the party now goes round with a hat,' explained J.D Davies, 'and all retire.'

The height of these sober pleasures was the 'Mabsant,' each parish's annual celebration of its patron saint. Special foods were prepared. A dish called 'whitepot,' made with boiled milk and flour, was popular. In Llanmadoc they had a pie made of chopped mutton and currants. In Llangennith, presumably because their saint, Cennydd, was more famous than the others, the celebrations were louder, and people came from Swansea to join in. The Rev. Davies said there was widespread 'fiddling, dancing, ball playing and various other amusements.' This was too much for strict Christians. A Methodist minister, William Griffiths, who preached to a very small congregation at Llanmadoc in 1819 while their mabsant was going on, denounced the event as 'a meeting of the devil's,' with its 'drinking and dancing.' J.D. Davies had more sense than to go round being shocked.

★

There isn't much in the record about sex. An occasional anecdote hints at romance. The manuscript diary of an anonymous young Englishman records a visit to Swansea in 1821, travelling there from Bath for a brief holiday in August. On the journey his coach was joined by 'six ladies' and 'two maid servants.' One of the latter was 'a very pretty smart girl' who seemed to be having trouble with her clothes. She nearly lost her hat twice, in a high wind, and did lose one of her gloves.

In Swansea he put up at the Mackworth Arms, where he ate a supper of 'real Welsh mutton chops which were stinking,' before going to his bedroom, where he found 'a glove exactly corresponding with the one my pretty young companion had lost.' This was an encouraging development. Had she planted the glove in his luggage? Mr X doesn't speculate. But he found that the family she was travelling with had taken lodgings 'in the Burrows, which are close by the Pier' (Later the site of a dock. Now Swansea's Marina is there, and a stark village of apartment blocks).

Next day was wet. He braved the weather, walked out on the harbour pier with his telescope, and saw her 'at a window at the top of the house looking at the bay.' When he waved to her with his handkerchief, she waved back.

Servants answered doors, not their employers, so when he called, the girl duly appeared, and he was able to return the glove and have 'a pleasant tete-a-tete.' He would have stayed longer ('although very wet'), but a fellow-servant came to say she was wanted by her mistress. Wet or no, he hung about, and they spoke again, this time through a window. It begins to sound like scenes from a low-key tv costume drama, but the diary is (probably) too muted not to be genuine. Mr X managed to fit in some scenery and a visit to Oystermouth Castle. He and the girl had a further conversation, and he had almost decided to stay on in Swansea, before he pulled himself together, afraid of 'gaining too much in her esteem for her future happiness ever to recover,' and 'stole away.'

J.D. Davies stayed clear of such matters. The only carnal touch in the History concerns the episode of St Cennydd, conceived by an incestuous union, and the crucial passage is in Latin, untranslated. Gower, like everywhere, would have had stories to tell, but no one told them. If anything emerges or can be inferred, it is usually from the dark side. A harsh world of sexual need and misdemeanour, a century ago, can be glimpsed through newspaper advertisements and reports in south-west Wales, as recorded in a meticulous paper by Russell Davies. Illegitimacy was common in respectable communities, together with suicides by pregnant girls, backstreet abortions and the murder of unwanted babies. The *Cambrian* in Swansea ran carefully worded ads for substances that were supposed to induce abortion, such as 'Towle's Pennyroyal and Steel Tablets, Woman's Unfailing friend. Guaranteed to correct all irregularities, remove all obstructions, and relieve the distressing symptoms so prevalent with the sex.'

Between 1901 and 1907 a Professor Deaking, 'Herbalist,' of Alexandra Road in Swansea, not far from Gibbet Hill, used the *Cambrian* to advertise 'French Novelties,' which meant condoms. These cost sixpence each, £2 now. Or you could have a dozen for three shillings and sixpence, postage extra.

Many didn't bother. In 1907 a young coal-miner from Trimsaran, near Llanelly, intent on seducing Catherine Rees, took her for a weekend to the Metropole Hotel in Swansea, having bought a ring so that when the manager looked at her hand he would think she was married. They had what sounds like a good weekend, costing £20, say £1500 today. Unfortunately he had not been to see Professor Deaking first, and found himself in court, being ordered to contribute to the baby's upkeep.

Every Thursday the Professor went ten miles to Llanelly, town of chapels, to sell his 'rubber goods,' in the phrase of the times, at the Saddler's shop, round the back of the market. My paternal grandfather, an immigrant English labourer in a Llanelly steelworks, was busy adding children to his family: at least eight between 1882 and 1904, of whom four lived to be adults. Would he even have known that Prof. Deaking existed? I doubt it.

'Progress' by the end of the 19th century had brought steam-driven machinery to thresh corn and move heavy loads. J.D. Davies wrote admiringly in his Vol. 4, 1894, 'the traction engine and steam-saw traverse the roads; truly we may exclaim: "Old things have passed away, behold all things have become new".'

A few years later, in 1901, he was telling readers of the *Gower Church Magazine* about the wonders of the modern world: X-rays, chloroform, photography, typewriters, electric power and wireless telegraphy. He guessed that the 'air car' was coming, although he got the name wrong. The phonograph, the primitive recording machine of the time, had already come. The idea intrigued him, no doubt because so many Gower voices had told him things that vanished into thin air. A speech or a sermon, he thought, could be 'reported and stored up in a small box for an indefinite time.' He saw other implications. 'As such things are in existence, it should make people careful of what they say. There may be a silent witness hidden away under the sofa, in the piano, or in a corner of the room, registering every word...'

Meanwhile, in early 20th century Gower, labourers went on labouring. Any rumbles of change came from Swansea, where the streets were paved and lit by gas, and the town even had the telephone.

The singer Adelina Patti, an international figure in her day (she had no local associations), bought a remote mansion at Craig-y-Nos, twenty miles away at the top of the Swansea Valley, just short of the mountains, where she could enjoy privacy. In 1893 a Mr Legg of Swansea was 'commissioned to fit up a long telephone line to Craig-y-Nos, thus enabling Madam Patti to speak to London or Paris.'

Local industrialists built villas and mock castles close to Swansea, preferably up-wind of the fumes that could wither trees. The place had outgrown its past as a market town, as well as an experiment with gentility early in the 19th century, when it aspired to be a resort, a Welsh Brighton. Prosperity followed. In 1848, when the British Association for the Advancement of Science was meeting in the town, Sunday worshippers at the parish church of St Mary put £81.6s.8d in the collection plates, £6000 or £7000 now.

Metal works and the port became the principal employers of labour. A strike at the end of April 1892 annoyed the authorities, with marching men, a broken window or two, and a threat to throw a policeman in the dock. Incoming ships were diverted, and the port lost 30,000 tons of trade. For middle-class Swansea, these were dangerous signs in the sky. The *Cambrian*, voice of progressive ratepayers who didn't want to be too progressive, shuddered at the 'tyranny of the mob.' On May Day a rally brought out five thousand demonstrators for a procession, which included floats with men at work, sail-makers stitching, boiler-makers hammering, massed cyclists and comedians bringing up the rear.

A 'Souvenir' prepared for the occasion was a book of two hundred pages, which hinted at a Utopian future when 'the wage system' might give way to a 'partnership' between capital and labour. Designed to impress delegates with the importance of the venue, it had the calm air of an era when it was taken for granted that the town and its surroundings would prosper for ever, advancing towards a tomorrow that was not defined but was sure to be satisfactory.

His Worship the Mayor, a patriarch in his robes of office, shown gazing confidently at new horizons, gave the book his blessing. A

photograph in it of 'Swansea Sands' at holiday time, with its straw hats and full skirts, makes the scene look achingly sombre, as if the seaside, too, was meant to be taken seriously.

A longish poem, an 'Ode of Welcome' to the T.U.C., was included.

> Welcome to these our busy toil-worn vales [...]
> Welcome great Congress to our toiling Wales!

The toilers the poet had in mind were in coal mines and iron works, not fields and cow sheds. The best the *Souvenir* could do for Gower was trot out 'legends' – one about fairies at Scurlage, another featuring the tormented spirits of two murderers on the shore, trying to make a wreath out of sand. J.D. Davies has a more original version.

Gower's fresh air received a mention. 'The Copper Works may throw off much more sulphur than an ordinary pair of lungs can inhale with comfort, but the bracing breezes of Clyne or Fairwood Common provide an easily secured antidote.'

A century later, Swansea's copper works, docks and the rest had gone. The bracing breezes of Gower were still there, together with walking, swimming, surfing, angling, horse-riding, rock-climbing, bird-watching, sun-bathing, archery, hang-gliding and doing absolutely nothing. Tourism thrived, and with it came prosperity, better late than never.

CHAPTER 7

RACE RELATIONS

GOWER PEOPLE once fell into two groups that were separated, not socially, by class and means, but geographically, by racial origin. How deep this ran in recent centuries is hard to tell, and there was intermarriage even in medieval times. But the distinction was always there.

The racial divide is part of a wider Welsh history. The existence of a country called Wales speaking a language called Welsh had been recognised, by outsiders as well as by the Welsh themselves, long before the Norman conquest. After it, medieval Wales retained a character of its own, at least in the north and west, ruled by princes, most of them related to one another. But it never became a sovereign nation, a political entity. Although the original inhabitants of Wales, 'the people,' the Cymry, retained their language and dreams of independence, they were joined by English-speaking invaders and migrants who came, over time, to assert that they too were Welsh. In later centuries, and especially when South Wales was industrialised in the 19th and 20th centuries, these 'Anglo Welsh' ended up outnumbering the 'Welsh Welsh,' as they still do. Much of modern political discourse in Wales implies that the nation is Cymric, burning for independence and the universal use of the Welsh language. It is not. Some of the nation is; some of it isn't.

The cultural fracture has been there a long time. English-speakers in Wales have sometimes accused the Cymric Welsh of maltreating them. In Tudor times an Englishman, Robert Craven, took a farm in Llanelly, and was hounded out by Welshmen, or so he claimed at the fast-track tribunal in London, the Star Chamber. 'Assault upon complainant and his wife' was alleged, 'because they, being English folk, took a farm at Llanelly; illegal imprisonment in the stocks at Llanelly by the constable.' More than four hundred years later, in 2008, an Anglo-Welshman was writing to Wales' only national newspaper to complain about 'vitriolic letters in these columns ostensibly about tourist provision but clearly anti-English in terms of linguistics and people.' One could, he pointed out, speak no Welsh but still *be* Welsh. It is an obvious truth, not always acknowledged.

The late Professor Rees Davies has suggested that by the 13th century the distinction between Welsh and English people within Wales was already 'deeply entrenched and institutionalised... Wales was to remain a land of two peoples. This meant that the word "Welsh" was henceforward contentious. In a fashion it has remained so ever since.'

The Welsh-English border country, the 'Marches,' was disputed territory which for centuries produced racial bitterness and conflict. Gower was far to the west, but because it was a small, attractive region that the Normans settled intensively, it became a miniature March, a compact local stage where the two cultures could hack at one another. Its smallness was part of its appeal to fighting men: there could be a clear-cut result, a peninsula that belonged either to one side or the other. The Normans built numerous castles, of which half a dozen remain, packed into a small space, hinting at fear. Most were in the south of the peninsula, where the good arable land could be parcelled out to their adherents. Gower's Welsh-Welsh were dispossessed, 'ethnically cleansed,' left with thinner soil and colder winds in the north-east corner, along the estuary. The only northern castle still standing is on a stretch of cliff above the marshes, at Weobley. Directly beneath it, a thin track of hardcore and broken concrete runs out for more than a mile across the marsh to a hut on stilts, left over from World War 2 and a gunnery range.

The marshes from Weobley Castle

Weobley was not an early castle. It was designed for domestic as well as military use, and is sometimes called a 'fortified manor house.' But its great walls and commanding situation feel fortress-like. When local labourers built it, overseen by armed men, it was the start of the fourteenth century, only a decade or two after the 'hanged man' episode of 1290 (Chapter 2). Llanrhidian, where William Cragh lived, is not far away. There ought to be a story about the Welsh patriot/terrorist saved by a miracle, whose village became a focus for unrest, who caused the nervous occupiers to build an extra castle at Weobley, a couple of miles down the road. *(Cragh, the man they couldn't hang, tells villagers they have nothing to fear but fear! Normans respond with new fortress.)*

When guerrillas from wilder parts of Wales came raiding, they were as violent as the Normans. A hyperactive West Wales princeling, Rhys Gryg, attacked the area in about 1212, 'destroyed... all the castles of Gower and their fortifications, and expelled all the English population that was in that land without hope of their ever coming back again, taking as much as he pleased of their chattels and placing Welshmen to dwell in their lands.'

None of this made for a happy history. The last time Welsh warriors made themselves felt in Gower was at the start of the 15th century, when Owain Glyndwr (b. 1359), an enduring Welsh hero, was busy terrorising the English throughout Wales. His rebellion appealed to the French, who sent an army to Milford Haven in 1405 to support him. In the House of Lords a nervous peer suggested that were Glyndwr to succeed, 'there would be an end to English speech and to England.'

Swansea and Gower got ready. Clerks at Swansea castle recorded extra expenses. Firewood had to be purchased to warm the bedrooms of visitors in connection with 'the rising of Oweyn Glendourdy.' Three extra men-at-arms were hired for twenty-eight days at a shilling a day, and eighteen archers at a modest daily rate of sixpence. Total cost of a month of reinforcements was sixteen pounds and sixteen shillings, but special measures failed to save the castle from damage, though the records are vague about what happened and when. The Welsh certainly swept through the peninsula, and local patriots, stirred by this prince from the north, joined them in butchering the English; it never happened again. Glyndwr himself kept away, warned off by a prophecy that he would be captured if he went there.

The man was a serious threat. It is tempting to think that his enemies tried to make him seem less menacing by poking fun at him. 'Glyndourdy,' alternatively 'Glyndourdo,' sound belittling, and might have done so in the 15th century. This attractive theory is rather spoiled by the fact that, as Professor Prys Morgan points out, one of the family's variant spellings was 'Glendowerdy.' But I still see the trace of a joke; English is good at belittlement. Four hundred years later Mr Talbot's 'Sea Fencibles,' a maritime Home Guard, were at Port Eynon, waiting, like the rest of southern Britain, for Bonaparte's army to invade; they are recorded as preparing to deal with 'Old Boney.' The British responded to Hitler by saying his real name was 'Shicklegruber' and circulating a song about the genital shortcomings of the Nazi leaders.

Shakespeare, two centuries after Glyndwr's insurrection had come and gone, saw comic potential in a voluble Welshman, as the English still do, when he wrote part one of *Henry IV*, and made the rebel (anglicised into 'Glendower') boast that 'I can call spirits from the vasty deep,' prompting Hotspur's 'Why, so can I, or so can any man. But will they come when you do call for them?'

When the real Glendower had finished with Gower, the official assessment was gloomy: 'The two parts of the lordship are worth a hundred pounds and no more because the lordship in great part is destroyed by Welsh rebels.'

In the end, of course, there was compromise. English-Welsh fighting in peninsula Gower seems to have created no legend, unless J.D. Davies's 'bloody battle' on Tankey Lake Moor is a scrambled version of a skirmish between Anglo-Saxons and Celts. Davies also cites a dubious report – it is connected with the 19th century forger, Iolo Morganwg – of an English-Welsh encounter on the slopes of Cefn Bryn.

The violence receded long ago. R.S. Thomas's poem 'Welsh Border' gives it a glance:

> People have died here,
> Good men for bad reasons,
> Better forgotten.

What did survive in the peninsula until the last century was a trace of social hostility between the two Gowers. Historically the accents were different, Welsh in one, a soft drawling Englishness in the other. Port Eynon, Nicholaston, Oxwich, Ilston, belonged to one culture; Penclawdd, Llanmorlais, Llanrhidian to another, although the division was never as sharp as that makes it sound.

The name 'Rhossili' has Welsh roots but the village is anglicised and is in south Gower. 'Crofty' sounds English but is in Welsh Gower.

Literary travellers and travel books liked to emphasise the difference, and overdid the hostility. An 1823 Swansea guide said flatly that 'The English people of Gower' rarely intermarried with the Welsh. *Black's Picturesque Guide through North and South Wales* (1860) assumed that anywhere in the peninsula that was outside English Gower was not Gower at all: 'Even at this lapse of time the Gowerians have kept themselves tolerably aloof from their Welsh neighbours, neither "marrying nor giving in marriage," and preserving their distinctiveness in customs, dress and language.' A.G. Bradley, *In the March and Borderland of Wales* (1905), wrote: 'It used to be said that when an English Gowerian was asked for the house of a Welsh neighbour just over the line, he generally replied, "I donna know; a lives somewhere in the Welsherie".'

What Welsh Gowerians said was not reported. In any matter affecting Anglo-Welsh relations – not just in Gower – it is easier to know what the English thought about the Welsh than vice-versa. Welsh opinions in their own language are less accessible, and in any case the conquerors write the history; they even write the guide-books. *A Handbook for Travellers in South Wales* (published by John Murray, London, 1870, author unknown) dealt briefly with Gower but included a four-page essay, a 'Social View' of South Wales, which attributed 'a sad want of truth and straightforwardness, and a love of prevarication' to the Welsh. As for their harp-playing and poetry, the author was not impressed. He conceded that the music at their *eisteddfods* wasn't bad, but it was 'mixed with much buffoonery.'

Perhaps the person to blame for all this is Giraldus Cambrensis, Gerald of Wales, the 12th century son of a Norman knight and an aristocratic half-Welsh mother. A churchman and author, he wrote seventeen books, two of them about Wales: the first an account of a journey on ecclesiastical business, the second a description of its people. So we have at least half an Englishmen saying what he thought about the Welsh, as well as half a Welshman assessing the English. His journey didn't take him into Gower. After a night at Swansea castle, in March 1188, he and his party made their way across the inland edge of the peninsula, forded the river Loughor and went on into west Wales.

English Gerald found the Welsh bold, agile, frugal and modest. There was no begging; everyone's home was open to strangers, and new arrivals (presumably at homes like his mother's) were entertained by girl harpists until nightfall. Verbal wit and a hot-tempered disposition went together. So, unfortunately, did a general cunning and craftiness, a Welshman's readiness to perjure himself. The Welsh were greedy too, and prone to sexual misdemeanour. They married their cousins. They also had a habit of slaughtering near-relatives in disputes over land.

Gerald's English conscience was bothered by the violence used against the Welsh. But at one point he thought, or pretended to think, that the problem of Wales could be solved by ejecting the entire population. 'Further, I would not know how to hold a land so wild and impenetrable, and inhabitants so untameable. There are some who think that it would be far safer and more advised for a prudent prince to leave it altogether as a desert to the wild beasts and to make a forest of it.' He had second thoughts about this final solution, and deleted the passage from later editions. In his Welsh hat, Gerald had some terse advice for his half-brothers: unite under a single prince and train the entire population to bear arms. Like most of his successors, Gerald failed to rake through English shortcomings as thoroughly as he raked through the Welsh. His genes were rather less than half Welsh. But he was conscientious enough to make a moral distinction between the two causes. The English want power, he said. The Welsh want freedom.

It is a long way from Gerald's Wales to racial unease in Gower. Social mobility has put an end to that unease; to most of it, anyway. A trace of it can still be seen, in the obligatory Welsh place-names that now appear on signposts, alongside the existing English ones, if they exist. This happens throughout Wales, but is more noticeable in a place like south Gower where English has such a long history. The policy has had curious results. The village of Bishopston, known as such for the best part of a thousand years, has had its pre-Norman name of 'Llandeilo Ferwallt' revived, though its chances of displacing 'Bishopston' are not good. It is a gesture, satisfying or irritating in relation to one's Welshness, depending on whether it's Cymric or Anglo.

Such differences aren't new. When the Ordnance Survey was planning its first map of Gower in the 1820s, the Swansea industrialist L.W. Dillwyn, whose origins were English, was one of the local gentry the surveyors consulted over their draft maps. The place-name 'Cilfrwch' on the south-west edge of Fairwood Common, where Dillwyn expected to see 'Kilvrough,' caught his eye, and he queried it with the map-makers. The Welsh spelling, he said, 'may possibly be more correct,' but it would puzzle the Swansea postmaster. It was, he added, 'a handsome Gentleman's seat [which] is always spelt Kilvrough especially as it is in Gower Anglica where no Welsh is spoken.' The house is no longer a Gentleman's seat, but the O.S. Explorer 10 map, 1995 revision, remains loyal to Kilvrough Manor and Kilvrough Farm. For the moment Reynoldston stays Reynoldston; there was no pre-Norman settlement. Ilston stays Ilston.

Gowerton, on the other hand, does not stay Gowerton, or not entirely. The village is an anomaly of its own. Before the industrial revolution, it was a small settlement to the north-east of the peninsula, a damp nowhere on the edge of a moor, conceivably the one where five hundred and sixteen dead Englishmen were counted on January 1, 1136. The name of the village was Ffosfelin,

Yellow or possibly Mill Ditch. In the 1850s the main-line railway arrived, swinging to the north-west from Swansea, on its way into Carmarthenshire. Ffosfelin, with ample coal and water in the area, became an industrial village. Passenger trains stopped there, and the railway company, not fancying 'Yellow Ditch,' named it 'Gower Road,' since the road into north Gower runs through the village. That confused the postal service, and at a meeting of local elders in 1885, a colliery manager called Thomas Jones proposed they add the English suffix 'ton' to 'Gower' to make 'Gowerton,' the 'town of Gower.' Jones was a figure in the community (His son, Ernest, would be a pioneer of psychoanalysis, colleague of Freud and his biographer.) English was the language of progress. 'Gowerton' was adopted.

This wouldn't happen now. In recent years the English name that was proudly invented in 1885 has required a Welsh alternative. The original Ffosfelin was not much fancied. So 'Gowerton' has had to be translated back into Welsh, and lives on as Tre Gwyr, Gower's town. Bilingual signs greet the visitor. The Explorer 10 map says 'Gowerton' prominently, '(Tre-Gwyr)' less so. The two Gowers remain.

CHAPTER 8

FAMILY AFFAIRS

FROM THE 18ᵀᴴ CENTURY, the 'big house' in Gower, where social authority and wealth could be found, was Penrice Castle. Hidden from the road, amid parkland, it overlooks Oxwich Bay discreetly, and is more or less invisible from the sands. Until the 1950s the estate owned most of the land in peninsula Gower. Today holiday cottages and car parking provide much of its income.

There is a mild confusion about the name, which appears twice on the O.S. maps, first as Penrice Castle and then (in black type to indicate an antiquity) a quarter of an inch away, as **Penrice Castle**. The antiquity is a 13th century ruin, and has a keep, high walls and little towers. The other castle is the house, a Georgian mansion built by a Talbot in the late 18th century. The two are close together. The real castle is on higher ground, the base of its romantic walls level with the top of the domestic chimneys. People called Methuen-Campbell, descended in a complicated way from the Mansels via the Talbots, occupy the house now; this branch of the family has lived there since the end of the 19th century. Both buildings are in private parkland, although a public footpath runs between house and castle.

The house makes the most of the setting. Tall windows take in sea and landscape, the grass falling away to a man-made lake and a south-easterly view of headland, bay and Bristol Channel. Once it was a place apart, self-contained, manned by servants. Now it is a large old house in a world of small ones, kept going by diligence, pride and a sense of its own history. Unseen and unheard below, on every summer day hundreds of vehicles roll in to the car park, on Penrice-owned land by the sea, where the ticket man waits.

The original masters of Gower were the Mansels. The only acknowledgement they get now is in the given names of male descendants; the Methuen-Campbells routinely have a 'Mansel' slipped in somewhere. A John Mansel was the first to appear, in 1201, when he witnessed a legal document. Unsurprisingly, no one is sure when or how the family arrived in Gower. Some websites allege that Mansels (or Maunsells or Munsels) were alongside William the Conqueror when he crossed the channel in 1066. Professional genealogists say wearily that no more than about twenty guaranteed Norman warriors who came with him can be named. There was a Robert de Beaumont, a William de Warenne, a Hugh de Montfort. There was no Mansel.

The Rev. J.D. Davies, who took these matters seriously, included a vast mistaken pedigree of the Mansels in his Vol. 4 that traced them back to the Conqueror. He worked from an original version that he had seen at Penrice Castle, which 'measures 8ft. 6in long by 3ft. 6in. wide,' and sounded sorry that it was too large to reproduce full-size in his *History*. As it is, the abbreviated pedigree runs to four folded sections, which open out to a total length of two and a half metres. It says that 'Phillipe Mansell Esquire came into England with William Conqueror,' and shows him marrying 'Daughter of Montsorell.' The story is untrue, but there must have been lesser gentleman-soldiers and officials who came in the wake of the Conquest. Imagine a Phillipe Mansel with a unit probing into the west that found Gower, deciding to stay or being persuaded to. Invaders become settlers.

By the Middle Ages the Mansels were significant land-owners in Gower. They used daughters to marry their way into money, as they did in the 14th century with a family called de Penrice (or de Penrhys), who built the stone castle in the 13th century and lived in it. When the Penrice family died out, around 1400, their land passed to the Mansels.

At first there is no sign of them, in their second-hand castle. In 1464 a Philip Mansell forfeited his lands for some political misdemeanour, but a couple of decades later the family returned to favour when Philip's son, Jenkin, gave his support to Henry Tudor, fought with him at Bosworth Field in 1485, and so was on the victorious side when the Wars of the Roses ended. There was a family talent for advancement. At some point the Mansels left Penrice Castle – perhaps had left it before Bosworth – and moved closer to Oxwich village, to another old castle on a ridge above the sea. A son was born there in 1487 and named Rice or Rhys. He was to be the significant Mansel, a soldier and administrator with powerful connections.

Rice Mansel had three wives – death in childbirth was unexceptional – and the last, Cicely Daubridgecourt, had friends in high places. Mansel and his private army fought in Ireland and he was given a knighthood. In Gower he spent money restoring Oxwich Castle. What he produced was more of a manor house, made to resemble a castle for decorative purposes; warfare had moved on, and sieges, bowmen and boiling oil were already in the past. This mock-fortified house is the present-day Oxwich Castle, the most visited ancient monument in Gower, a well-kept place. It is also a useful site for enacting mock battles at weekends. Mansel received a further reward from the Crown for services rendered. Around 1540 he was invited to buy an estate centred on Margam Abbey, twenty miles from Penrice, near the present Port Talbot. Henry VIII's 'dissolution of the monasteries' was in progress, enabling the Crown to raise money by closing religious houses and selling them off. Sir Rice Mansel was offered Margam and its lands for around £2,500, a fortune at the time; it took him years to pay it all. The Abbey had been owned by Cistercians, the 'white monks,' who believed in piety through hard work, and the purchase brought Rice Mansel land and wealth on a scale impossible to achieve in Gower. From the remains of the Abbey buildings he made a large and comfortable gentry house. But he held on to Oxwich Castle, the old headquarters.

In the middle of the 16th century, not long after the Mansels acquired Margam Abbey, they were involved in a violent episode, along with a cast of characters who included a rival knight, a concerned aunt, armed men and French sailors, together with sundry villagers and men from Swansea, eleven or twelve miles distant. These minor players had such English names as Purcell, Dunne, Curteis and Gybbe, along with Welshmen – Owen, Morgan, Gitto and, a minor player with a major part, someone called Watkyn John ap Watkyn. As in the case of the hanged man from Llanrhidian, events left a written record.

The affair began simply enough, with a wreck on the coast in December 1557. A storm blew a French merchant ship into the bay and on to the rocks at Oxwich Point. This happened at some time before midday on the 26th, St Stephen's Day, our Boxing Day. Perhaps villagers saw it happen, but the first to know about it officially was the local clergyman, Richard Cosin, and his guests, who had been invited for a midday meal. While they were eating, some half-drowned sailors arrived. At the time the rectory was directly below the church, between it and the sea: into which, a couple of centuries later, it fell, and had to be rebuilt elsewhere. Church and rector were close to the scene of the wreck. There is a hint, a feeling that Richard Cosin was not indifferent to the benefits of what came up on the rocks.

England being at war with France, as it was for most of the 16th century, the Frenchmen were locked up, and the village got on with the business of looting the ship. The cargo included raisins, figs, almonds and wool; the ship's timbers and fittings were also worth having. Among Cosin's guests was the head of Rice Mansel's household, the steward, Gruffydd ap Owen, who probably left at once to supervise proceedings, if only to ensure that his employer was the chief beneficiary. Rice Mansel himself was not at home; he could have been spending Christmas at Margam Abbey, his principal residence for years. His eldest son Edward, still a young man, was in Gower, though not at Oxwich on St Stephens Day. Married to an earl's daughter, Member of Parliament for Glamorgan since 1854, he remained a lesser character than his father.

A second family now became involved, the Herberts. They were at least as powerful as the Mansels in South Wales; they also had a reputation for violence. Sir George Herbert of Swansea claimed rights over the coast, and when he heard about the wreck the following day, December 27, he sent two men to guard it. They were either too late or too few, and seem not to have brought the paperwork necessary to establish their authority. As soon as they reported back to Swansea in the small hours of the 28th, Herbert put together a force of seventeen men, one of whom was Watkyn John ap Watkyn. Another was Sir George's bastard son, William Herbert. They left for Oxwich in the dark. A clergyman, a Mr Price, went with them for moral support. Price would have known that December 28 was Childermass, Holy Innocents day, when the Biblical Herod is supposed to have slaughtered male infants for political purposes. Childermass was an unlucky day, when nothing important should be undertaken. But he probably kept his mouth shut.

At Nicholaston, a few miles short of their destination, the unit met, as in a farce, four men riding the other way with a quantity of figs, which they claimed to have found 'hidden in a bush.' The figs were seized. Herbert and party pressed on. In Oxwich they went straight to the rectory and banged on the door, or possibly broke it down. It was 'about the breke of the day,' around 8 o'clock. Herbert appeared in Cosin's bedroom (there were hints that relations between Cosin and his housekeeper were not what they should be), demanding he hand over property from the ship, if there was any. The rector said, 'I trust, Mr Herbert, that you will not take from us our own goods.' Meanwhile some of Herbert's men broke into an outhouse and found figs – more figs – and gunpowder.

From the rectory Herbert went up the hill to the Mansel residence, officially 'the Mansion Place of Oxwich,' although people still called it 'the Castle.' Herbert was admitted, but was told that none of the Mansels were at home. Edward, they said, might be at the house of his steward, Gruffydd ap Owen, at Slade, a mile or so down the lanes. Or he could be at the home of Mrs Anne Mansel, his aunt, at Llandewi, in the middle of the peninsula. She was an aunt by marriage, the widow of Rice Mansel's brother, Philip, and was another Daubridgecourt.

Before he left, Herbert had three French prisoners removed from the house, but he took no property. He then rode to Slade and had words with ap Owen. The steward knew what was coming. He had already sent word to Llandewi, where he knew Edward Mansel to be.

> Ap Owen: How now, my lord, I had not thought to see you venture abroad in such foul weather.
>
> Herbert: Hadst thou but done thy duty as a true steward, then had I no need to come.
>
> Ap Owen: Frenchman's goods it is, and our own, for such as took it ought to have it.

Attempts to placate Herbert by suggesting that the matter wasn't serious angered him, and he made the unfortunate remark that he would send Edward to his father 'trussed like a bantam cock.' While Herbert was at Slade, his unit searched the premises and seized a barrel of raisins, a sack of wool and the inevitable figs, in this case three baskets of them.

The raiding party went from house to house, removing goods, then doing the same at Oxwich Green, nearer the village, while Herbert sat on his horse and waited for Edward Mansel to return from Aunt Anne's. Perhaps her house 'at Llandewi' was the Mansel property called Henllys (Old Palace), on the track that runs due west from Llandewi, where the road bends sharply, leading to the back of Rhossili Hill. It is still there (2008), a whitewashed building on a green lane that could be a small farmhouse, slate-roofed at one end, a cat at a window peering through net curtains; now known as Old Henllys, which is Old Old Palace. It was a larger property then. The road, or track, to Oxwich, running south-east from Llandewi, is now a public footpath. It passes through open country, skirting the Penrice woods. Oxwich Green is no more than three miles, with a further half-mile to the castle, or Mansion Place.

Once he was up and dressed, Edward could have ridden to the Green in a quarter of an hour. But he was told that Sir George Herbert was waiting for him there, and so he took a different route, perhaps through the Penrice estate and down to the foreshore, then back up to the castle, half a mile to the east of the enemy. Caution seems a good idea, though it might have looked like hesitation to others, and even to Edward, once he was safe inside the gates. One imagines his father, Sir Rice, galloping up to the Green, telling Sir George to bugger off. Having behaved properly, the son may have felt a pressing need to demonstrate that he could behave badly as well.

Matters were not helped by the arrival of Aunt Anne. She seems to have followed her nephew almost at once, because it was still barely light when she encountered Sir George at Oxwich Green, unaware that Edward had bypassed him. She said there was no need for so much trouble over so few goods. Herbert was unmoved. It was not for the goods, he said – shifting his ground – but because her nephew had 'abused his officers and servaunts, as good gentlemen as the said Ed., whom he wolde teach to know the worst s'vante in his house.' Anne Mansel carried on to the castle and they opened the gate for her to ride in. Having a female relative arrive to support him may have made Edward even more anxious to prove his manhood.

Behind the bluster, Herbert was willing to compromise. He sent a friend to the castle, William Griffith, who had been staying with him in Swansea, and had come along on the Oxwich expedition. Edward apparently agreed that an inventory could be taken of the salvaged goods. But when Herbert and his troop arrived, they found him outside the gate, sword in hand, backed by four or five men in suits of armour and carrying weapons. A back-up force with staves – thick sticks – was behind him, inside the gateway. Aunt Anne was also inside the gate, about eight feet behind her nephew. In the confusion, perhaps, a 'ring brooch' of gold set with rubies was dropped inside the castle, and lost for four hundred years – or so it was decided in the 20th century, when it was found again.

According to the written record, Edward Mansel shouted, 'How now, are ye come hither to rob and invade me?' They

Oxwich Castle: the gateway

then proceeded to have a skirmish. Swords were waved. Edward caught sight of Sir George's son, William, and cried, 'Villain, whither comest thou?' Young Herbert then seems to have given young Mansel a slight wound in his arm. No other casualties were reported.

However deep and long-standing the quarrels between Mansels and Herberts, perhaps both sides were beginning to sense the absurdity of men in armour fighting over figs. But Watkyn John ap Watkyn, in the Herbert camp, made an unfortunate move. He had a sword in his hand, and a buckler, a small shield, on the other arm. At his feet was a stone, not very large. Presumably out of frustration or boredom, he thought to liven things up. He moved the sword to the other hand, picked up the stone and threw it hard at the Mansels in the gateway. It went over their heads and hit Anne Mansel on her forehead. She collapsed, amid cries of 'Murder,' though she was still alive. The wound was 'the breadth of two thumbs, and the depth even to the brain.'

Attacking a woman was against the rules. Everyone sobered up. The affray was over. The Herberts withdrew hurriedly and returned to Swansea. Anne lived another four days, until New Year's Day, 1558. The inquest comprehensively indicted the Herberts and their men for aiding and abetting Watkyn John ap Watkyn.

It was bad news for the Herberts. The Mansels took the case to the Star Chamber, the all-purpose tribunal, at a time when open enmity between two prominent families sent the wrong message about the state of Wales. The Acts of Union, which brought Wales under the English jurisdiction, and looked forward to a more peaceful Principality, were still recent; warring gentry were out of fashion. The case went against the Herberts, who had to pay fines and compensation to the Mansels. Sir George seems to have been briefly imprisoned. A common-law trial for the killing was envisaged, but the outcome, if any, is unknown.

If a woman hadn't died, there would have been no inquest and no Star Chamber proceedings. The events at Oxwich would have been a minor affair, unrecorded. Even the affray and the killing were forgotten over the years. According to J.D. Davies, it was not until a visitor examined the Penrice manuscripts in 1840, and unearthed the story of the incident, that the truth re-emerged. In Davies's lifetime, fifty years later, it was still not common knowledge.

> A local tradition is current, that during the building of the castle by Sir Rice, a stone fell from the wall and killed Lady Mansel, Sir Rice's wife, whereupon he determined not to finish the building, considering it a bad omen, and went to live at Margam.

In this version there was still a stone and a dead woman, but it was all an accident. The truth was better forgotten.

For a couple of centuries after Rice Mansel's time, the family prospered without achieving any particular fame or notoriety. Another Edward Mansel, who lived at Henllys (d. 1723), was an unpopular character known as 'the Captain,' who features in the tale of a 'ghost carriage' or 'spectre chariot,' in which he is driving desperately across Rhossili sands, possibly with silver stolen from the Spanish galleon. The Captain had financial problems, and the fable hints at them.

J.D. Davies wrote (not in his Gower book) that Ed. Mansel had 'large estates and great influence' in West Gower, and terrorised the inhabitants. He kept bloodhounds to deter trespassers, and trained a large boar to attack anyone who happened to use a footpath near Old Henllys. Davies goes on to paraphrase 'J.W., an old man (a mason) now dead,' telling a story that had been handed down in J.W.'s family for generations.

> My great-great-grandfather [also a mason] was early one morning going to a job of work at Paviland [the farm, not the cave], and to shorten his journey, took the footpath by Henllys. Crossing the stile

which leads into the road close to the house, he was immediately attacked by the boar. Luckily he had his heavy spawling hammer in his hand, and he struck the beast a tremendous blow on his head, killing it on the spot.

It is said that the people, driven to desperation by a number of tyrannical acts, rose up in arms and surrounded the house, with a determination of executing lynch-law upon him. But Mr Mansel, having received some intimation of the visit, had made preparations by keeping a horse ready saddled and bridled in some part of his house. Concluding that no mercy would be shown him, he mounted the horse, and ordering the door to be suddenly opened, leaped out among the people, and riding through them galloped off, and as some say, was never heard of any more.

This, wrote Davies, must be a mistake, because it is 'well-known that he passed over to Ireland, where he was seen, and afterwards died. Be this as it may, he never came back in the flesh to Henllys.'

Another Mansel, another legend.

The long reign of the family in Gower came to a close in the 18th century, when they ran out of male heirs. They had acquired a peerage in 1711, but the title was short-lived. Thomas, the first Lord Mansel, died in 1723. His eldest son Robert died before him, so his grandson Thomas succeeded, but in 1744 Thomas died of syphilis, caught when he was having his mind broadened by the Grand Tour of Europe. Thomas's uncle Christopher (Lord Mansel No. 3) died next, followed swiftly by his other uncle, Bussy, fourth and last of the line.

In the meantime, a strategy had been devised to make the best of a bad job. The first Lord Mansel's daughter, Mary, now the family heiress, had married someone called John Ivory Talbot. His father was a Sir John Ivory of Ireland, who had married an Ann Talbot of Wiltshire. Their son, the one who married Mary Mansel, added his mother's surname to his own, to become John

Ivory Talbot. The genealogy of wealthy families is complicated by the demands of land, money and succession. The Wiltshire Talbots had estates and a stately home. Ann Talbot was said to be descended from the earls of Shrewsbury. Eventually the Ivory Talbots would drop the Ivory altogether and be just Talbot.

John Ivory and Mary had a son, Thomas, born at Margam in 1719, who became an Anglican clergyman. An indistinct figure, he spent his adult life as rector of Colingbourne Dulcis, near Salisbury, in Wiltshire. When the last male Mansel died, this son, the Rev. Thomas Talbot, inherited the estates of Penrice and Margam. What was Mansels' was now Talbots'. It took another generation to produce a Talbot able and willing to exploit the old Mansel properties. The Rev. Thomas and his wife Jane had a son, christened Thomas Mansel. T.M. Talbot (1747-1813), grandson of Mary Mansel, was to be the agent of change. In his early twenties Thomas was sent off on a Grand Tour. Italy was his prime destination. One travelled to see classical works of art, and bring back as many of them as possible. Thomas shipped twenty-three cases of 'Marbles, Pictures, Etc' from Leghorn to the Mumbles.

The larger part of his estate was the land at Margam and its decaying mansion, which was knocked down before the end of the 18th century. Margam was left without a family headquarters until a strange new house was built there by his son in the next century. Thomas was more interested in having a foothold in Gower, and commissioned a house at Penrice beside the old Mansel castle, calling it his 'villa' or 'shooting box.' That was in the 1770s. The villa is now Penrice Castle. The marble fireplaces (shipped from Italy) and mahogany doors are his; so is the parkland, with its landscaped slopes and trees and lake. He was unmarried for years after he built it, until a friend, the Earl of Ilchester, stayed there with his teenage daughter, Mary Strangways. He fell in love with her and they married in 1794; she was seventeen, he was forty-six, the same age as her father.

Travellers used to wonder why Talbot took such trouble over a rural backwater. C.F. Cliffe (*The Book of South Wales*, 1848), sniffed at the house as 'a tasteless structure.' Henry Skrine, who wrote *Two Successive Tours Throughout the Whole of Wales* (1798), called it 'a highly ornamented villa' with 'luxurious appendages' but wondered how its owner could 'desert the noble seat of Margam, in the midst of a populous and plentiful country, to form a fairy palace [which it is not] in a dreary and desolate wild, far from the usual haunts of man, and near the extremity of a bleak peninsula [which is incorrect].' Sydney Smith, the sardonic clergyman-author, who was there at about the same time, praised the flower garden but complained that 'for any communication with the human species, a man might as well live in Lundy Island.'

T.M. Talbot was before his time in seeing the merit of lonely places. Perhaps he wanted to be different, to unload some of his Grand Tour acquisitions in a location that no one had ever heard of, and enjoy them in rooms with romantic views. Most educated persons saw the peninsula as a blank sheet of paper. Thomas fancied leaving his signature. He wasn't much interested in the local gentry but he liked people with ideas. It was from Penrice Castle in 1823 that William Buckland set off for Goats Hole and returned with the red skeleton of Paviland. Talbot would have enjoyed the excitement, but by then he had been dead ten years. His daughter, Mary Theresa, was the one who busied herself with natural history, who liked to poke about in caves.

Ultimately the Talbots became one of the richest families in Britain, thanks to the coal under their land in south Glamorgan, and the enterprise of the next generation. They caught the wave of industrial development, leasing mineral rights, profiting from iron and copper works. If it moved and made money, the Talbots wanted some of it. Gower was part of their empire, but after the time of Thomas Talbot, they were never a 'Gower' family in the way the Mansels had been.

CHAPTER 9

DYNASTY

THE TALBOTS, like the Mansels before them, had problems with male heirs. Thomas and Mary Talbot produced five daughters who survived childhood, but only one son, Christopher Rice Mansel, C.R.M. Talbot, known to the family as 'Kit'. His career as Victorian landowner and industrialist was enlightened for his day. He was also a mathematician, a chess-player and a pianist, and Glamorgan's Member of Parliament for most of his adult life. Talbot did whatever he thought necessary to advance his interests. By living through the greater part of the 19th century – born 1803, died 1890 – he saw his world change, and became part of the process of changing it. In the Mansel-Talbot dynasty, he casts the longest shadow.

Unlike his father, who loved Penrice, he was comparatively indifferent to Gower. Margam was the centre of operations. He built a new mansion there, with turrets and battlements, scenic chimneys, and an extravagant interior filled with paintings and antiques. As with Penrice, it came to be called a castle. I went there once – it still exists, a day-out museum-piece now, publicly owned and open to all – with a Methuen-Campbell, Lucinda, a great-great granddaughter of C.R.M. Talbot. She lives in Gower. She shook her head at its faded splendour and said that she used to dream of winning the lottery and buying it back for the family. We didn't stay long. In the distance, towards Swansea, a steel works breathes smoke and lies low, distant descendant of the works and collieries that Kit Talbot licensed to use his land and make his fortune. He owned 44,000 acres, most of them in south Glamorgan, the rest in Gower. He was said to be 'the richest commoner in England,' and it may even have been true.

His High Church leanings endeared him to the Rev. J.D. Davies, and Talbot supported him against evangelical critics. Davies's *History* says little or nothing about contemporary figures. But he writes warmly of Talbot. They were both keen sailors, which must have helped, even though the Rev. Davies's craft was home-made, and the waters it cruised in were Carmarthen Bay, not the Mediterranean. Davies wrote:

> [He] was the owner of several fast-sailing yachts; the first was the 'Guilia,' in 1822; the next was the 'Galatea,' in 1825, a topsail schooner, in which it is said he met with some curious adventures. On one occasion, while in foreign waters, he was nearly boarded by a pirate, which ran very close to the yacht, but not liking her looks and her stalwart and numerous crew, and the sight of some polished brass guns which she carried, she sheered off.

Davies added a footnote to explain about the crew. 'They were all picked men, none of them standing under 5 ft. 9 in., and were nearly all Gower men, of whose seafaring qualities he had a high opinion.'

Another of Davies's admiring anecdotes has Talbot riding on the outside of a mail coach as it passed south of Margam Park, as the house was then called, when a fellow passenger ('a Scotchman') noticed the oak woods there, and – not knowing who Talbot was – said he wondered why the proprietor didn't cut them down and turn them into cash. The proprietor replied that from the point of view of profit, no doubt the Scotchman was right, but 'perhaps the owner of the woods would rather have the trees than the money.' The Rev. Davies doesn't mention pit-heads, smoking chimneys and dismal cottages that were blighting other parts of the proprietor's land, but could hardly have been expected to. By the standard of the times, Talbot was the countryside's friend.

On behalf of progress, he was keen to get railways into South Wales as soon as possible, and in 1849 he paid vast amounts when the South Wales Railway Co., of which he was chairman, needed more capital to extend the line from Gloucester to Swansea. It crossed his land; he made sure his gamekeepers had the right to pursue poachers along the track. When he was getting old, Talbot was briefly involved with another railway proposal, to extend the line a few miles into a rural area where farmers, tradesmen, shopkeepers and people in general were being deprived of the benefits of modern transport. It was a local matter of small consequence. But the rural area was the Gower peninsula, and it would have mattered later on.

The Great Western Railway was the company involved. The South Wales Railway, where Talbot was once chairman, had been taken over by the Great Western in 1863, and Talbot was now on the board of the GWR. He and a party of GWR directors were visiting the peninsula when the idea of a line into Gower came up. Wouldn't a branch as far as Reynoldston, say, be a grand thing? 'A grand thing for a railway,' said Talbot, 'but a devil of a thing for Gower. No, no! No rail here. We can come here and enjoy the country. The rail would destroy it all.' Thanks to his outburst, the GWR changed its mind, or so the legend says; another legend.

The anecdote was in the vast obituary they gave him in the *Cambrian*. He knew the editor, so perhaps it was true. Or, perhaps for the same reason, it wasn't. The obituary also said he was 'worshipped by his tenants,' which seems improbable. He was quoted as telling a Gower Farmers' dinner how much better off they were than their predecessors.

As for a Gower railway, other proposals came and went in the next century. A syndicate with a Swansea solicitor called Wilson as its mouthpiece once planned a line, with stations at Three Crosses, Cilibion and Frog Moor – near Reynoldston

– and its terminus at Port Eynon. The scheme was approved by Parliament, but the company failed to raise the money. Perhaps C.R.M. Talbot's earlier opposition had blighted the whole idea. No doubt the GWR's railway would have brought light industry, more houses and bigger villages. It would also have changed Gower long before its status as an Area of Outstanding Natural Beauty came to save it (to an extent) from bricks and concrete.

Talbot's reason for being anti-railway may not have been entirely to serve the public good. He may have feared train-loads of noisy visitors who would frighten cows, pheasants, and the sheep that grazed salty grass on Worms Head; their meat went up to his London house in Cavendish Square for dinner parties. And who was the 'We' in 'We can come here and enjoy the country'? But whatever his motive at some forgotten outing of men with beards and watchchains, Kit Talbot was Gower's first conservationist. He has an attractive air. He told a story about travelling from Paddington on a Great Western train in the company of his friend Isambard Brunel, who built the line. Near Reading there was a complicated system of points where other railways met and crossed. Talbot, expecting to be reassured, remarked to Brunel that he was always glad when they got past Reading without an accident. Brunel said, 'So am I.' Previously no one in the Mansel/Talbot family had left behind much detail of their life. Now letters were being kept and stories remembered for long enough to be written down in disrespectful times, including the splendid story that the first Lord Mansel (1688-1723) fathered many illegitimate children, possibly seventeen, by his housekeeper, Catherine Thomas.

C.R.M. Talbot's career prospered; in private he had problems, although the matter of succession seemed to be solved when the first child of his marriage – to an earl's daughter, Lady Charlotte Butler – was a boy, born 1839. They named him Theodore Mansel. Girls followed: Emily (1840), Bertha (1841), Olivia

(1842). In four years his wife bore four children. In spring 1845 she became ill with 'consumption,' our 'tuberculosis,' and they went abroad to find milder weather. By the following January her condition was worse. They were in Malta, and she was coughing up blood. Talbot wrote, distracted, to an aunt. Charlotte was worse, their English cook had died, their English doctor had gone mad.

> I cannot really say I have had a single comfortable moment for months and months. The lines of Byron continually haunt me.
>
> > My days are in the yellow leaf,
> > The thorn, the canker and the grief,
> > Are mine alone!
>
> I fear I have done wrong in coming out here...

Charlotte died a few months later, aged thirty-seven, and the yacht 'Galatea' brought her back.

At least Talbot had his son and heir. When Theodore came of age in 1860, the 1st Glamorgan Rifles paraded at Margam Park, a Grand Dinner was held in the Orangery, and his father made a speech in which he spoke of his son ('yet but a young man') as an heir who would surely appeal to Welshmen because 'he thought Wales the best part of England,' which was how they looked at things then.

Talbot was then in his late fifties. In his early seventies he was still thriving. So was Theodore. The son was said to be deeply religious, even 'saint-like.' Ancient gossip says that before he was converted to High Church Anglicanism he was a 'philanderer.' He was unmarried. A family story hints that he was gay. Balding and bearded, he liked sports and recreation, and could be seen on the sands playing a game with the locals, a sort of violent hockey called Bando in which participants get whacked with sticks. Having the heir to Margam in the game meant they were able to whack him as well.

Theodore's passion was fox-hunting. A reckless rider, he had many falls, and in autumn 1875 had one too many, landing heavily on his head and chest, and breaking his collar-bone. He received other injuries, probably spinal, from which he never recovered, and died at the Cavendish Square house in June 1876. His father wrote of 'the desolate vacant blank' that was left.

Lawyers were kept busy. The estate had been 'entailed' to the next male in line after Theodore, which would have meant a boy born to one of his sisters. C.R.M. Talbot broke the entail, and when he died in 1890, everything went to the eldest daughter, Emily. Unmarried, fifty years old, she inherited lands and a fortune worth nearly £6 million, perhaps £500 million at today's values. She was the richest heiress in Britain.

If it ever occurred to her that a woman might be incapable of managing a great estate, she kept the thought to herself. 'Miss Talbot' ran Margam Park and its gardens as a business, with a staff of painters, masons, carpenters, gamekeepers, gardeners, housemaids, footmen, butler and the rest. Good causes, especially if they were religious, received large sums. So did the docks and railways she invested in. She stalked the house with an eye for detail, and is described as doing what house proud women used to be known for, using fingers or a handkerchief to check for dust on polished surfaces.

Deciding that arrangements for indoor activities were not satisfactory, she commissioned a billiards room with carved panelling to keep the gentlemen happy. You feel that she played there herself when she was in the mood. She enjoyed connecting with a man's world, whether it was opening a new dock, going off on holiday to the south of France or entertaining the king. Apparently there was no shortage of male suitors, which is not surprising, given her wealth. A local industrialist and land owner, Arthur Vivian, would have been happy to join his empire to hers, but made no progress. There was a 'devoted companion,'

a Miss Houlton, succeeded by a devoted Miss Boyce; no doubt Emily had tendencies in that direction. A painting shows not unattractive features, with the prominent Talbot nose and a suspicion of contempt about the mouth.

Miss Talbot took an interest in Gower, and sometimes lived at Penrice. The staff would shift trunk-loads of possessions from one house to the other, including the family silver, which had to be in place at Penrice to grace the dining table. The peninsula saw her as a figure to be wary of, kindly to the poor, but a landlord, or landlady, who would stand no nonsense from tenants. She did good works and made improvements. Turf on the top of Cefn Bryn is said to have been laid at her direction for the benefit of horse-riders; Penrice Castle is near the foot of the hill. The tenants were not always as friendly as polite histories suggest. An elderly Nicholaston farmer, David Harry, appeared at Penmaen petty sessions in June 1893, charged with shooting at Miss Talbot's land agent, Richard Essery, with intent to murder. He had a revolver, described as 'old and rusty,' and missed. He was sent for trial at Glamorgan Assizes, but the jury, perhaps with a prejudice against landlords at the back of their minds, failed to convict.

She had strong views on alcohol, and when Rhossili residents, smitten by Methodism in the early 20th century, decided that their pub, the Ship, was the work of the devil, they petitioned Miss Talbot and the Ship was closed. Rhossili still has no pub as such, a rare situation in Gower. It has an hotel with a licence instead.

J.D. Davies had dealings with Miss Talbot when he was at work on his History, and needed to consult the Penrice manuscripts. She loaned him material to copy, one item at a time in case it went astray in his study, which she didn't trust. When her young niece, Evelyn, was staying at Penrice Castle, the child would ride over to Llanmadoc on her pony, taking a single manuscript, then wait to take it back again. After Emily's time, Evelyn would be the owner of Penrice. The name 'Talbot,' like 'Mansel' before it, would disappear. Emily did what she could to leave her estate in good hands. Her brother Theodore was dead. Only one of her sisters was married: Bertha, who married a Scotsman, John Fletcher, of a wealthy and long-established family (they claim to be descended from Robert the Bruce). Evelyn was one of their children.

But Evelyn was not made sole heir. Aunt Emily divided her properties, separating the estates that had come together c. 1540 when the Mansels of Penrice acquired Margam. Penrice was to go to Evelyn Fletcher (b. 1870), Margam to her brother, Andrew (b. 1880). Perhaps anticipating this happy event, he had been given fore-names to enhance his Welsh side, making him Andrew Mansel Talbot Fletcher. He had been in the army and was known as 'Captain' Fletcher. The plan for Penrice worked. Evelyn went on to marry another Scotsman of a reliable family, Brigade-Major Sir Archibald Campbell, who later inherited the family title to become the fourth Baron Blythswood. He died in 1929, leaving Evelyn as the popular widow and eccentric of Penrice Castle, Lady Blythswood, until her death in 1958.

On the Margam side, Captain Fletcher was not a success. Emily had had her doubts. He used to run up gambling debts and apply to her to bail him out. He liked fast cars and was once arrested for 'furious motoring' in Piccadilly, 20 m.p.h.; it was 1902. He was not a safe pair of hands. So Emily gave ultimate control to a trust run by cautious men, who lacked the imagination to see Margam through the difficult years ahead, as taxes rose and sympathy for landowners diminished. Penrice would survive; Margam would not.

Miss Talbot died in 1918, and the new owner of Margam, Captain Fletcher, whose family estates were at Saltoun, East Lothian, made Margam his second home. Sometimes a party came down from Scotland and they spent the summer there. During World War 2, the estate fell apart. To Fletcher's dismay, the trustees decided to sell the Margam land, retaining the house but disposing of its contents: the pictures, the books, the silver plate and candlesticks, a harp, a grand piano, the Regency writing desks, a Persian carpet, some old armour. It was a household clearance on an imperial scale. They even sold the hand-painted wallpaper in the 'Chinese Bedroom,' which was purchased for 28 guineas on condition that the buyer peeled it off at his own risk. The sale took four days. It was October 1941. The war was not going well, and it may have seemed reasonable to turn art into cash, in case Germany won and Goering sent his treasure-seekers to loot the stately homes of Britain.

The sale realised £29,213, more than a million now, but a fraction of present fine-art value. Margam Park was stripped bare, and the house went into decline. British and American soldiers were billeted there, rank and file in outbuildings, officers inside the house. General Eisenhower paid a visit before D-Day.

The land was sold to a syndicate of business men. The house

was in the hands of a South Wales brewer, Sir David Evans-Bevan, who did little or nothing with it, except let the fabric decay. He tried to give it away, but no one was interested. By the 1950s, ceilings were collapsing, windows were smashed and lead had been stripped from the roof by thieves, which let the rain in. Evans-Bevan seems to have been reluctant to install a caretaker. Perhaps too many Mansel and Talbot ghosts were abroad for a lone watchman; in recent years 'paranormal investigators' have spent the night there, though with modest results. 'Cobweb-like sensations' have been reported.

When Margam Castle was well on the way to ruin, the local authority came to the rescue, buying house and gardens, and began the long process of restoring them. 'Margam Country Park' has become a well-managed attraction, though it feels detached from its history.

Like a mocking commentary on the decline and fall of Margam Castle, in 1993 a man came on the scene with claims that he was the rightful heir to Miss Talbot's millions. A Mr Ken Matthews of Port Talbot, when consulting a doctor, was asked if there was diabetes in his family. All he knew of his ancestry was that in 1937 he was born to an unmarried mother in a poor-law institution at Pontardawe, in the Swansea valley - 'the workhouse,' one of the gaunt refuges for the destitute that lasted well into the 20th century.

He learned more. The child was taken from the mother, whose identity Ken Matthews didn't know, and adopted by a local family. His interest in diabetes was soon overtaken by an interest in inheritance. He believed that he was the child of Ivy Pinn, a housemaid in her mid-twenties at Margam Castle, where her father was a woodman. She was undoubtedly pregnant, was dismissed, and left the castle in disgrace. Much of the information was hearsay from local people with long memories. Written statements were collected, video recordings made. It was not the servant-girl who mattered, it was the man who seduced her. That became Ken Matthews' obsession.

Ivy's lover, said the gossip, was the young heir to Margam, John ('Jock') Theodore Talbot Fletcher, son of Captain Fletcher. The son's relationship with Ivy lasted for years, renewed each time he stayed at Margam. Off they'd go into the countryside in his car. The love-affair evidently became one of those tit-bits that make people grin and wink at past naughtiness and say, 'We all knew.'

The tale of Ivy Pinn, which Ken came to believe, changed everything. If he was the son of a Fletcher, even a wrong-side-of-the-blanket son, he was, or he might be, entitled to make a claim – perhaps – in principle – depending on the law and lawyers (whose shadow is all over the story) – as a result of which he might, other things being equal, which they never are, be entitled to undreamt-of wealth, at present wrapped up in some impenetrable trust, which no one outside legal circles seems to have got to the bottom of, that was created by the will of the hard-boiled Miss Talbot.

It is a long chain of uncertainty. Ken Matthews found many documents, never decisive but now and then suggestive. He pointed to anomaly and coincidence in the story, and devoted years to the quest. With his wife Penny he dredged up information as if they were a television research team preparing a series about hanky-panky among the rich.

Jock Fletcher had a wife, whom he married in December 1933, eight or so years after he seduced Ivy, assuming he did. The wedding, to Norah Gabbett-Mullenhan, was in London (in the chapel of a military barracks), but apparently it didn't stop him carrying on with Ivy. The marriage was a disaster, as he mentions more than once, in passing, in his barely comprehensible memoirs, published 1991.

18 March 1936. The trouble between Norah and myself is reaching a climax. I had a letter from Mum today; she thinks an annulment of our marriage is the best solution. More trouble and worry for Mum, I'm afraid.

After three years Norah sought a divorce on the grounds that the union had not been consummated. To prove this, Jock and Norah had to present themselves (not at the same time) for medical examination. Two London doctors were appointed as Inspectors, as though in some medieval inquisition, to examine his 'parts and organs of generation' and 'report in writing whether he is capable of performing the act of generation.' The unfortunate Norah was examined to make sure she was still a virgin. The result was that Jock's parts were found wanting (one wonders how, exactly); he was declared to be incapable of having sex, and Norah was granted her divorce. The decree nisi was dated June 21 1937, eight days after Ken Matthews was born in the workhouse. Norah's price for going quietly was a settlement of £25,000, a million today.

It is not clear how the episode proves anything, except the fallibility of doctors and the ingenuity of lawyers. The theory is that John Theodore Talbot Fletcher was pushed into marrying Norah by his domineering father; there is some evidence that the Captain did bully him. So Ivy had a lover who was potent and Norah had a lover who was not. They just might have been the same man. Genetic evidence would be needed to prove it.

At one stage, in 1998, the *Scotsman* newspaper reported that Ken Matthews was keen to examine the mummified heart of Robert the Bruce, the Fletchers' supposed ancestor, who died in 1329, and is said to be buried in a lead-lined casket at Melrose Abbey. There is certainly a casket and it has something in it. If it is King Robert's body-tissue it might in theory be made to yield a usable specimen of DNA. This is not going to happen. The only realistic way to establish the coding of Fletcher (or Mansel or Talbot) DNA, to see if it was transmitted to Ken Matthews, is by obtaining a contemporary sample. Nobody is rushing to provide one. The Matthews camp is still hoping, and has plans to send any DNA that becomes available to America for analysis. It is a forlorn venture.

Early in his investigation, in 1994, Ken Matthews went in search of John Fletcher, who was still alive. He found Fletcher's address by knocking on the door of Penrice Castle and asking for it. Christopher Methuen-Campbell, then the head of that branch of the family, seems to have been entertained by this visitation. He told him that Jock Fletcher lived at Epping, in Essex, and the claimant hurried there. Jock was ninety. His carers were on holiday, and he answered the door himself, wearing pyjamas and dressing gown. When they were inside, Penny Matthews, who was with her husband, came to the point at once. 'You might remember Ivy Pinn,' she said. 'This is Ivy's son.' The website describes him closing his eyes and refusing to say a word. Mrs Matthews says, 'The look on his face will be with me to my dying day.'

That was it. Fletcher died the following year and was cremated. It is difficult to follow all the attendant hints and allusions because they are based on an obsession. More than a decade has been spent picking at these old bones. Ken Matthews died in 2008. I never met him. His widow says, 'The fight goes on.'

CHAPTER 10

THE ESTATE

MOST OF THE LAND that Evelyn Fletcher inherited has gone, sold back to Gower tenants in the 1950s. But her direct descendants own what's left, and they still live in the 'Castle,' which remains a private property. Evelyn made a better job of her inheritance than her brother the Captain made of his. Perhaps she was luckier.

After her husband, Lord Blythswood, died in 1929, she grew more attached to Penrice, and became part of the Gower scene, 'her ladyship,' a small vivacious woman, fond of fast cars in the Fletcher way, and notorious for whizzing along the lanes, eyes just visible above the steering wheel. She owned 30,000 acres, and to begin with employed dozens of people, on the principle

that servants had always been there and always would be – cooks, housemaids, footmen, gardeners. After World War 2, all that had gone or was going. The house itself was in bad shape. Evelyn Blythswood wouldn't spend money on repairs. She economised on cleaning materials. If the housekeeper asked for two large tins of polish, she was told to make do with a small one.

The estate was benign and old-fashioned. No one was very efficient, but no one was very greedy either. Rents were not raised as they might have been. Penrice ran at a loss, subsidised by the Blythswood estate in Scotland. There was one Blythswood child, a daughter, to keep the family line going. This was Olive, born 1896, known as the Hon. Olive Douglas Campbell. As a young woman Olive attracted the attention of the social columnists. In 1923 the Prince of Wales (the one who later went off with Mrs Simpson, and abdicated after being King for less than a year) was said to be involved with her. *Time* magazine reported: 'The anxiety felt in the Empire over the protracted bachelor days of the Prince of Wales was considerably aggravated by the denial of another marriage rumor. Lady Blythswood said there was no truth in the report that her daughter Olive was to marry the Prince. In the meantime court circles are growing desperate.'

Eventually, in 1927, Olive married a Methuen, son of a Scottish field-marshal. From a haze of ancestries – the Methuens, the Douglases, the Campbells – emerged Olive's son, who would later own the Penrice house and land. His full name was Christopher Paul Mansel Campbell Methuen-Campbell, born 1928. Before the estate reached him, it was supposed to go to Olive, his mother. Taxation being what it was, Lady Blythswood was advised to make her daughter a gift of the estate, and so avoid some of the inheritance tax. But seven years had to elapse for the gift to become tax-exempt, and Olive fell ill and died in 1949, before the seven years were up. More tax had to be paid, not less. Olive's son, Christopher Methuen-Campbell, was left to save Penrice, which he did, just in time.

Lady Blythswood was there until she died in 1958, a relic or a family treasure. Christopher's first wife, Oona, who now lives in Suffolk, where she moved after they divorced in 1973, saw house and inhabitants as they were in the late 1940s, and will not be again. Christopher himself died in 1998. He had remarried and had a son, Thomas Rice Mansel Methuen-Campbell, by his second wife, formerly Judith Ann Crowther of Swansea. Thomas, born 1977, now runs the estate.

Oona is a slight, quick-witted woman without apparent resentment at where she finds herself. She met Christopher in London after World War 2, at the last gasp of debutantes and their social scene, that strange marriage-market where the privileged young sought likely wives or husbands. Groups of suitable candidates were put together for the purpose, and events organised where they could mingle.

> It was at Lancaster House, rather a posh dance, terrifying, it was, the King and Queen were there – you hardly dared move because if you bumped into someone, you didn't know whether to curtsey or hide. It didn't exactly make for a relaxed evening. Anyway, I was in the same party as Christopher, and that's where I met him. Some of them were all right. Some of them were Brigade types, all terribly suitable. Now, when I read the Court Circular, there are quite a lot of names that I didn't realise at the time were anybody in particular. When some of them became quite important I realised I'd missed my chance, in a sort of way. It was such a different world, that London. Like a different planet.

Later, when she was introduced to the family, she was nervous of Lady Blythswood, who was said not to like women. They got on well enough ('I was only nineteen, so perhaps I didn't count as a *woman*, as a rival'), but life at Penrice Castle took some getting used to. The fabric of the house was deteriorating. It was cold and damp.

In the drawing room she used to sit on the sofa with one bar of the electric fire on, the window open, and the door open as well so she could hear the telephone. I don't know how she didn't die of hypothermia. She was very thin. But she was very kind and very nice. Above her head – all the downstairs ceilings are high – there was a sort of hammock of cobwebs which the dust had landed on over the years, which gently wafted in the breeze. She reminded me of Miss Havisham in *Great Expectations*, in the wedding dress turned yellow, except it certainly wasn't Lady Blythswood's wedding dress. If I left something behind, cardigan in a drawer or something, you'd find her wearing it. She never went shopping.

None of Oona's predecessors at Penrice Castle chatted to the world at large about how awkward a house it was to live in, although it was obviously less awkward in earlier days, when it was full of servants. As long ago as 1969 she was being admirably direct to a reporter from the *South Wales Evening Post*, saying that the place still had no central heating, so 'we perish in winter. I wage a constant war against draughts, going round with damp absorbent kitchen paper which I poke into the gaps with a meat skewer and seal up with Sellotape. It is surprisingly effective.' She added, no doubt with irony, that the walls of the drawing room were covered in gold silk and portraits of the Mansel family.

She was saying much the same in Suffolk in 2007. 'The grand dining room had one of those hot cupboards, mahogany lined with zinc. We used to heat up bricks in the kitchen range and put them in the bottom to keep the plates warm.' Kitchen and dining room were a long way apart. 'I got an awful lot of exercise there, and if you were looking after babies and trying to cook, it wasn't exactly convenient.' Things improved, said Oona, when they hired a former butler and his wife. 'She cooked when she was well enough, and he – poor man, having been a butler all his life – if things had been as they were he would have had a couple of footmen under him – instead of which, poor man, he was bringing up buckets of coal himself. He did occasionally sigh a bit.' Repairs and improvements were made. The house was saved.

Christopher and Oona had four children. Joanna (born 1951), is a writer and genealogist, Dr Joanna Martin, and lives in Suffolk. James (1952), a writer and musicologist, lives at Corsham Court in Wiltshire, where Methuens have been for generations. Lucinda (1959), a teacher, lives in Gower. Catherine was born 1965.

Lucinda was the Methuen-Campbell I visited Margam Castle with, the great-great granddaughter of C.R.M. Talbot. Aged about eight, she went there with two of her siblings and her father, Christopher, who broke into the house so his children could see what they had missed. That was before the local authority took it over. Inside it was derelict, a haunted place. By the main staircase was a tableau of stuffed animals; an ostrich and a tiger were rotting away. The Chinese bedroom still had the hand-painted wallpaper that someone paid for but never took, and her father tore off pieces so they could all have some. Lucinda has mislaid hers. She is melancholy about the lost mansion of Margam. She feels much the same about the lost mansion, as she sees it, of Penrice Castle, where she is free to visit but never does. Her childhood, she says, came to a sudden end when her parents' marriage was breaking up, and she had the option of going with her mother to Suffolk, or staying at Penrice. She stayed. Her father married again. At the next Gower show, a local event every August, held in the Penrice Castle grounds, Lucinda, aged nineteen, staged a protest against life in general. Her father was show president as usual, this time with his new wife, Judy. Lucinda, a good-looking woman, got herself drunk, took off her clothes and ran around the show-ring naked. The local Press picked up the story ('... a tall blonde woman... she was there long enough for the beer tent to empty') but didn't know, or didn't say, that it was the lord of the manor's daughter.

Lucinda talks about the attics at Penrice, and the treasures she found there as a child. Another lost land opens up. The top of the house was where the servants had their quarters, the maids and footmen: old cupboards, forgotten treasures. She keeps returning to the subject. 'We used to explore up there. It's all stone floors and arched rooms, nothing had changed. You never knew what you were going to find, a dead bat, or stuffed birds, or lots of uniforms from ancestors, amazing uniforms. Or African spears. You might find a shrunken head. You never knew.' Her mother, Oona, remembers David Attenborough visiting Penrice when he was in Gower as a guest of the Glamorgan Naturalists, and being taken by Lucinda, then a small child, to see the attic's treasures. Lucinda remembers it too. Attenborough was staying at Penrice. During a lunchtime reception he vanished and couldn't be found. Lucinda had invited him to see the wonderland under the roof. Perhaps he heard the legend of the bees. Generations of them once lived up there. When they were expelled, long ago, prodigious amounts of honey in blackened honeycombs were found. Some say it weighed a ton. Others say it was two tons. A lorry took it away.

Her father, Christopher, was often up there, searching for things he could sell. Once, says Lucinda, it was a rare work called *The Pencil of Nature*, containing photographs taken in the 1840s by W.H. Fox Talbot. Only a handful of copies ever existed, each with the photographs placed in by hand. Christopher, who belonged to another branch of the Talbots, believed that Penrice had a copy, if only he could put his hand on it. He searched for days. Lucinda doesn't know if it ever came to light. She remembers a painting by the 18th century Allan Ramsay, of the second Lord Mansel with his siblings. As a child she thought of the pictures as friends, danced in front of them, even talked to them. One day the Ramsay wasn't there. The Tate Gallery bought it in 1989.

In Lucinda's eyes, her father had a desperate air. She remembers him visiting her boarding school in Kent on sports day, looking a bit tramp-like, avoiding men he had known at Eton; perhaps making some undefined protest at the class of minor gentry he belonged to, or at its twilight. He had no illusions about the place of a private estate like Penrice. At times he saw it as a burden, and his own existence – far down the line from the early Mansels – as 'completely archaic.' Yet he was determined to preserve it for his family. He enjoyed the farming (he had a degree in agriculture) but he began to look for alternative income.

Car-parks by the sea became a business in his time. Oona saw it happen. 'Do you remember old Mrs Slocombe at the Oxwich car park, who used to take the money? If there was anyone local, anybody she recognised, they got in free. There was great excitement one week, we made forty pounds, great money in those days. That would have been in the early nineteen-fifties. In those days the estate owned Oxwich and Port Eynon [car parks], and I suppose Rhossili too. I know there were at least three because Christopher spent his whole time rushing from car park to car park, checking up, shooing away the people he didn't approve of.'

Methuen-Campbell died in January 1998, leaving three and a quarter million, most of it represented by the estate itself, which Thomas, his son by his second wife, has carried on preserving. He and his mother live in Penrice Castle. Fifty years after the death of his great-grandmother, Lady Blythswood, he says that the estate still feels the effect of her years of frugality. 'She would not spend money on the house. That is how she was. In one way it was brilliant, things were preserved. In another way...'

Farming continues, but land is no longer the principal engine. Thomas makes the most of the new Gower, the holiday peninsula. If the estate and its house-called-a-castle is to endure, he has no option. The grounds have 'traditional self-catering cottages,' with tennis court, lake for fishing and parkland thrown in; T.M. Talbot's 18th century landscaping comes in handy. Down the hill at Oxwich is the estate's surviving car park. Half a century after Mrs Slocombe used to wink at people she knew and let them in for nothing, it makes serious money. On Google Earth the tiny roofs are like red and black symbols on a military sand-table, fleets of armoured vehicles drawn up by the beach, ready for action. There were around five hundred the day I counted. Parking (2008) cost £2.50 per vehicle.

The Mansel repertoire of family tales includes one from the 20th century about a Mansel descendant, a Methuen-Campbell who, when young, looked remarkably like the Prince of Wales, the one who abdicated. The descendant was (and is) David, the younger brother, by a year, of the late Christopher. The latter was born to Olive in March 1928, David in August 1929. A painter by profession, he lives in London but keeps a cottage in Gower. He remains deeply attached to Penrice Castle; to the *idea* of Penrice. 'One felt very secure as a child. I liked all the people around there.'

'Evidence' for a royal connection is slim. The Prince of Wales was known to have an appetite for married women. Years before Mrs Simpson, he stayed at Penrice Castle, where a tennis court was created for his benefit, which of course he never used, though no one suggests that hanky-panky, if there was any, took place in Gower. 'David' happens to be the last of the prince's seven given names, and is the one he was known by among friends and family. It seems rare if non-existent in the Mansel/Talbot/Methuen-Campbell families before it was given to Olive's second son.

None of that amounts to much. The social-gossip item of 1923, when Lady Blythswood denied publicly that her daughter was going to marry the prince, does suggest that Olive and the prince had a relationship of some sort. Or it could all have been in the gossip-writer's imagination. The face is, or was, the nearest thing to evidence as far as most people were concerned – certainly in Gower, where the story of a royal parent was widely told, accompanied by the usual winks and assurances that 'We all knew.' Even as a new-born baby – it was said – the resemblance was uncanny. As it happens I met David Methuen-Campbell in the 1950s. Primed by the gossip, I suppose I imagined a similarity, but thought no more of it.

The story is a family joke. David knows snippets about the prince-at-Penrice episode – how the royal visitor walked his dog on the Oxwich shore, how he failed to play tennis on the virgin court. Personally he never saw a resemblance.

> I don't know when it was that people started telling me. People have told me it all over the place, even when I went to America. I'm quite certain it's actually untrue. It's just a coincidence, you know? It's a strange rumour. I know when I was at the Royal College of Art, in the life-painting class, there was a Chinaman posing, and he said exactly the same thing to me. He was standing there, supposed to be leaning against the wall, but being a Chinaman he leant about two inches off the wall, and he suddenly said, 'You look just like the Prince of Wales.'

David prefers to talk about his childhood at Penrice, growing up as a country boy. The gamekeeper was called Woodward, a Gloucestershire man. 'He used to take us out when we were learning to shoot, my brother and I. He was quite prepared to put down the gun and talk about birds.' Woodward took him to the salt marsh below the house; to the woods on Oxwich Point. He knew where the ancient lanes were. Then there was Jack Jenkins, the estate carpenter. 'He was a great pony man. We used to go for miles across the Bryn, over Hardings Down, then up to Rhossili Down, visiting people he knew on the way.'

If he hadn't been a painter, David says, he would have been a farmer, like his brother. In World War 2 he was at boarding schools in Scotland and England, and eventually at Eton. 'I always dreamed of Gower,' he says.

His nature seems different to his late brother Christopher's: less aggressive, more thoughtful. That hardly counts as evidence of anything, does it. Does it?

CHAPTER 11

CRIMES AND PUNISHMENTS

For EIGHT HUNDRED YEARS, from the coming of the Normans to the end of the old Penrice estates in the 1950s, the crime of crimes in Gower was poaching. Stealing a landowner's rabbit, let alone anything larger, was an offence. Most poachers got away with it most of the time. In 1984 a writer interviewed a woman who, as a child, had lived at Walterston, a forgotten settlement below the north-eastern slopes of Cefn Bryn, during the 1930s. She told him about the poaching that flourished in the 'forbidden woods' of Parc-le-Breos a mile or two away, and how poor cottagers at Walterston were looked after by the poachers. Parc-le-Breos, originally property of the wicked Normans, is now a holiday centre. Poaching is forgotten, though pheasants have been bagged by greedy lads with air-guns, and unattended lobster pots off the southern coast are preyed on by the occasional diver.

Rural crime and urban crime seem far apart, but the countryside can be less law-abiding than it looks; there are mean lanes as well as mean streets. Sheep-stealing has a long history. The last Gower practitioner to be hanged for it was a 'desperate character' called John Hugh, from the Llandewi area, known as Johnny Hatchet, executed at Cardiff in 1795. Deliberate wrecking, using false lights to lure ships on to rocks, might have been a crime, if it ever happened. But anything brought in by the tide was seen as fair game, and still is if nobody's looking. The Penrice estate has certain manorial rights over Oxwich beach. If a waterproof bag containing fivers was found by a hard-up day tripper, would it be handed over instantly? On the other side of the Burry Estuary, the village of Pembrey had a reputation for behaving badly over wrecks. When a French vessel, *La Jeune Emma*, was wrecked on the Cefn Sidan sands nearby in 1828, the corpse of a French girl, aged twelve, had its fingers chopped off and gold rings taken.

In modern times there was discreet looting in Port Eynon Bay after a pleasure cruiser, the *Prince Ivanhoe*, with four hundred passengers, struck a submerged object off the coast on a fine August afternoon in 1981. It opened up the hull and she had to be beached. Everyone was saved (two passengers had heart attacks) and the *Ivanhoe* was there for a long time, with no one much interested in salvaging her. Persons unknown swam or waded to the ship and rescued crockery bearing the company crest. Some of it was seen in Gower kitchens.

Family violence never goes away. The diary of George Holland of Llanmadoc has an entry for Sunday November 21, 1841: 'Elizabeth Thomas stabbed her brother John Thomas in the belly with a knife. Died on Monday.' At around the same time a Morgan Davies of Neath was convicted of attacking his wife with a poker and leaving a wound six inches long, after shouting 'Damn you, you whore. I will make thee say what I ask thee.' It was not clear what he had asked her, but they were in the bedroom at the time. Financial crime was savagely punished. At the same court, in Swansea, a man who obtained money from the Aberystwyth savings bank with a forged cheque was sent to spend the rest of his life in a colony, working in chains. A man who had stolen a pound's worth of halfpennies, which would be four hundred and eighty, together with two hats, presumably to put the halfpennies in, was sentenced to death.

Toll gates in the 19th century made tempers rise; the keeper of a gate at Cartersford, on the north road across Fairwood Common, was killed when someone threw a stone at him. Records survive of court proceedings. A Williams hits a Lewis with a stick and draws blood, fined 20 shillings (Oystermouth, 1677). Five men fight in public, each fined six shillings and eightpence, one third of a pound (Oystermouth again, 1680). A sea-captain dumps ballast on a beach; fined ten shillings. Mary David, a widow, fails to repair her hedges (Weobley, 1716). George Gwyn keeps a mangy horse on a common (Weobley, 1725); outcome of both cases unknown.

Theft thrived, regardless of penalty. Another diarist, J.G. Hancorne, born 1794, went from his home at Kittle, near Pennard, to consult a lawyer in Swansea one Friday in May 1840. He drove in an open carriage, a phaeton, accompanied by a girl servant. She did the shopping, purchasing an 18-pound joint of beef to be used when feeding the neighbourhood sheep-shearers. They returned with it on the back of the vehicle. The servant would have sat facing the rear, but when she got out to lead the horse along a difficult stretch, there was no one to keep an eye on the meat. It vanished. Hancorne guessed that 'some damned thief' had been following them, biding his time. He should have applied to the Gower United Association for the Prosecution of Felons, set up in 1810. Rewards were paid for work in the community, ranging from a few shillings in a case involving turnips to five guineas for catching robbers. Their first case concerned a Mr Holland, who had his pocket-book pinched. He was a founder-member.

A police force was taking shape in the 19th century. The South Wales Police have sportingly published the 1859 notebook of a young constable with a large moustache (P.C. 207 Lewis Jones), whose Swansea beat included Gowerton and parts of north-east Gower. Days and weeks go by, devoid of excitement. He moves gypsies from a common, stops a fight outside a pub, hits a blind man over the head at Gorseinon Fair; policemen were expected to be handy with their fists. P.C. Jones's career had a setback when he recovered a strayed horse and made the owner give him the ten-shilling reward. He also overslept and was found in bed at 9.30 a.m. Jones had to resign. He joined the Neath police instead.

Smuggling was always a popular crime, aided or tactfully ignored by most of the population, especially in remote, badly-off areas like Gower. Old-fashioned smuggling went with lonely coasts and shallow sands, and the peninsula had its share of business in the eighteenth and early nineteenth centuries, when successive governments in London imposed punitive taxation on 'luxury goods' (brandy, wine, tobacco, tea) to finance wars. Much of the contraband came into Britain from or via France, a nice irony, since France was the principal enemy. The Bristol Channel was less convenient than south-east England. Its coasts, though, were not so rigorously guarded.

J.D. Davies knew the stories and might have spoken to old men who had lent a hand when they were young. He said that the last contraband to come into Gower was landed on the north coast at Whitford Point. Previously two strangers had been in the neighbourhood, telling people they were miners looking for lead ore. A lantern and a bag were found hidden in a cave. It sounds a hopeless enterprise, and when a boat eventually came in with brandy, it was seized by Customs. Davies gives no date. Rhossili Bay, which caters for all tastes, has a smuggling history. One episode, in 1805, was reported by the *Cambrian*, when a hundred kegs of smuggled liquor were seized on the sands by Customs officers, backed by the local marine militia, the Sea Fencibles. In them was eight hundred gallons (3600 litres) of brandy, gin, rum and wine. It was February 16, a waning moon, spring tides, high water in mid-evening. Trafalgar was eight months away.

Smuggling was in the mind of Dr Buckland or his Welsh friends when he found the red bones at Goats Hole, a few miles round the corner from Rhossili, in 1823, and thought at first that they might have belonged to an exciseman killed by smugglers. J.D. Davies mentions a cave called Hounds Hole, 'many a time filled with kegs of brandy.' Hounds Hole is close to Goats Hole.

Highway, the name of a farm and a wood near Pennard, is said to have been a, or the, centre of the trade, a strange choice: it is closer to Swansea and the forces, such as they were, of law and order. Kilvrough, one of Gower's gentry houses, is nearby; perhaps it extended a discreet patronage to the men in masks. In April 1804 excise officers seized hundreds of casks of brandy at Highway. In the process of guarding them, they and the mob that gathered made seventeen casks disappear. Official accounts of such behaviour sound pained, but as Michael Gibbs of the Port Eynon family says, the records 'do not convey the grinding poverty and sheer drabness of the lives of [...] labourers in Gower.' He quotes the 18th century Oxwich diarist, Rev. John Collins: 'To Molly Stephens for brandy 1 shilling.' Gibbs comments: 'Molly was the wife of one of the labourers living in Oxwich at that time and she did not keep a shop. Perhaps I am being unjust to her memory when I suppose that the bottle of brandy which she sold to the parson was not one which she had picked up on the sands after a benevolent high tide.'

Smuggling was a raw edge between Them in London and Us in Gower. Another was press-ganging, when 'eligible men of seafaring habits' were seized, and – if they couldn't be persuaded to enlist – taken for the navy. The random conscription was much hated, and there was violence on both sides. Nottle Tor cave near Llanmadoc (it no longer exists) was used as a hiding place. J.D. Davies explained:

A good look-out was kept from the top of Llanmadoc Hill, and as soon as the man-of-war's boat was seen coming from Llanelly, the intelligence was conveyed to the inhabitants, and all the young men, whether seafaring or otherwise, retired for safety to this cave [...] My informant (George Evans) told me that during this time a brig called the Weasel, commanded by a Captain Grey, was stationed in the Mumbles Roads for the reception of the pressed crews, and that having got together a complement of somewhere about one hundred men, she left, and was lost [near] the entrance to Appledore Bay, Devonshire, and all hands perished except one man, who made his escape from the vessel the day before she sailed.

Unless Davies's informant was muddling up the stories, something similar happened on the south Gower coast in 1760, when an Admiralty vessel, the *Caesar*, was raking in men for the Seven Years' War with France and others. On the morning of November 28 she was anchored off the Mumbles with eighty pressed men locked below decks. The weather was bad, and when she sailed, bound for Plymouth, the lieutenant in charge chose to leave on an ebb tide, to help her down the Bristol Channel. High water was 10 a.m. Four hours later, in worsening weather, the *Caesar* was still off the Gower coast. The ebb was slackening; soon after 4 p.m., when it was getting dark, the flood tide would begin. The *Caesar* turned to go back to Swansea Bay, but mistook Pwlldu Head for the Mumbles, and ran on to a reef. She ended up jammed in a cleft between rocks. Those on deck escaped; the captives below did not, and as the tide rose they drowned. The place became known as 'Caesar's Hole'; the O.S. maps say 'Graves End.' A poem by Vernon Watkins, 'Ballad of the Equinox,' though not explicitly about the incident, is in its shadow:

Pwlldu – an eternal place!
The black stream under the stones
Carries the bones of the dead,
The starved, the talkative bones [...]

On the northern side of the peninsula, the shallows of the Burry Estuary were equally attractive to the smuggling trade. Cargoes might be dropped off at Weobley, below the castle, and stored nearby. In November 1730 excise officers seized brandy and secured it temporarily inside the castle itself; some of it was promptly stolen. J.D. Davies has a paragraph about 'The Brandy House, the name given to a cottage that stands on the edge of the marsh at Llandimor, and was built about 100 years ago for smuggling purposes. The floor was excavated to a considerable depth and then arched over, forming a capacious cellar. As far as I have been able to learn it was never used more than once as a smuggling place, and was then filled with tobacco and silk. It was afterwards converted into a dwelling-house.' The place is no longer a cottage, and the 'capacious cellar' has been concreted over, but it is still lived in. They make jewellery there, looking out on the marshes. It remains 'The Brandy House.'

Alcohol featured in most smuggling stories. Thomas Prance was a famous sailor, originally from Devon, who became a Customs officer in north Gower, in charge of the Burry station. Having distinguished himself in a last-ditch action against the French in 1793, he was awarded a thousand guineas by the government. He lost both his hands in the action, but had himself fitted up with a mechanical apparatus; then married a Penclawdd woman and went in for law-enforcement in the estuary.

Drink nearly did for Prance, indirectly, in December 1815, when men under his command, with others from Llanelly, boarded a dismasted French vessel in the river. He left them to keep an eye on her and went off for his dinner. The ship's cargo consisted of brandy and wine, so while he was away, naturally everyone got drunk; then one of the Llanelly officers fell overboard and drowned, and the ship caught fire. Prance, one of a thousand footnotes to Gower, is buried at Penclawdd, in an unmarked grave.

J.D. Davies has little to say about crime, but he made an exception for a murder, on account of the gravestone. An elderly widow was attacked with a poker, probably by a thief she disturbed in her cottage at Penmaen; it happened in 1829, two years before Davies was born. His short account is in manuscript, and may have been intended for Volume 5 of the History that he meant to write but never did.

> On the 5th October 1829, the peninsula of Gower was startled by the report of the commission of a terrible crime in the village of Penmaen, which was soon ascertained to be only too true. In a cottage (still standing) quite close to the left hand side of the high road, leading to Swansea, lived a widow named Mary Cavanagh, who supported herself in tolerable comfort by letting lodgings. On the morning of the day above mentioned, she was found dead in her house, with her skull fractured with a blow of the kitchen poker. It was supposed that the murderer had been disturbed, as nothing was found missing. Several persons were arrested on suspicion, but the evidence was not sufficient to convict them, and consequently this outrage must be added to the list of undiscovered crimes registered in the criminal annals of this country. It is however a very remarkable fact, that one of the persons arrested, afterwards died, as I have been informed in a most singularly dreadful manner. He became afflicted with that rare disease called Phtheriasis, the lousy disease, and was literally devoured alive by vermin. Washing and cleansing were useless, for no sooner were the parasites removed from his body, than they reappeared in swarms.

Phtheriasis affects the eyelids, and is caused by pubic lice. They get into beards too. It is hardly a fatal condition. But Divine judgement evidenced by bizarre infestation was always popular. (Gerald of Wales recalls a young man visited by 'God's judgement' in the shape of a plague of toads, who ate him.)

The victim's gravestone, in Penrice village churchyard, is a 'murder stone,' with a space left for the murderer's name, when discovered. Mrs Kavanagh's sister commissioned it.

> TO THE MEMORY
> of
> MARY
> Wife of James Kavanagh of
> Penmaen who
> was Murdered by
>
>
> the 3rd of October 1829
> Aged 73 Years

The blank space is still there.

A variant style of stone is at Cadoxton, near Neath: Margaret Williams, aged 26, found dead in a ditch, 1822. Another is at Nebo chapel, Felindre, in upland Gower: Elenor Williams, aged 29, found dead in a well, 1832. The wording in both cases is similar. Like 'victim statements' of the 21st century, the stones provided a public platform for private outrage.

> ALTHOUGH
> THE SAVAGE MURDERER
> ESCAPE FOR A SEASON THE DETECTION OF MAN
> YET
> GOD HATH SET HIS MARK UPON HIM
> EITHER FOR TIME OR ETERNITY
> AND
> THE CRY OF BLOOD
> WILL ASSUREDLY PURSUE HIM
> TO CERTAIN AND TERRIBLE BUT RIGHTEOUS
> JUDGEMENT

Mamie and Georgie

> *Frankie and Johnny were lovers.*
> *Oh Lordy, how they could love*

Mr George Shotton, marine surveyor, and Miss Mamie Stuart, dancer, were born and reared far from Gower, in north-east England. One day they came to Caswell, a mile or two into the peninsula from the Mumbles; an unsettling story.

They met in Sunderland in July 1917, in the middle of World War 1. George spent his time visiting ports across the country, a self-employed man, thirty-seven years old, slightly built, smartly dressed. Sometimes he had a moustache; he reminded people of Charlie Chaplin.

His home was in Penarth, a port with its own dock not far from Cardiff. He had a wife, born May Leader, a sea-captain's daughter whom he married at Newport, Monmouthshire, in 1905; there was a son aged three. But George was away most of the time, superintending ship repairs, keeping tonnage afloat to stop the nation starving. He was fond of women too, and well-placed to enjoy them. He had money, he was often alone in cities, and half the fit men in the country were in the trenches or dead already.

In July 1917 George was in Sunderland to oversee work on a Norwegian ship. He and the captain spent the evening of July 3 together, and around 10 o'clock they picked up two girls (not 'young women,' not in 1918). What the captain did is not reported, but George and his girl went for a walk and had sex, presumably in a park or a back-lane.

This casual encounter became a love-affair. Mamie, twenty-four years old, was a 'fast' woman, in times when fast women were viewed as an unfortunate consequence of the war. Social inhibitions were beginning to dissolve. George must have seen

Mamie as a gift, a sexy woman who was bright and attractive, not one of the faceless seaport pick-ups.

Perhaps he wanted someone amusing and passionate to come home to. Divorce wasn't much of an option. In the year he met Mamie there were only seven hundred divorces in Britain. His wife may have been one of the unhappy thousands whose upbringing had vilified sex. A popular booklet of the time, *Marriage Before and After,* suggested that nothing could do more harm to a happy marriage than 'an insistence in either party on too frequent indulgence in sexual intercourse.' Mamie liked a bit of fun. She smoked, she played the piano, she even saw herself as a professional dancer. Her given name was 'Amy' but she had turned this into the more glamorous 'Mamie.' There had been a 'Mamie Stuart' (real name Annie Danks) on the stage a decade earlier.

George's Mamie was appearing in northern music-halls before the war as one of The Five Verona Dancing Girls. By 1914 these had shrunk to The Three Dancing Glens. Then they vanished altogether, and when George found her in 1917 she was at home, living with her respectable parents. Her father was another sea-captain, now employed on a local tug-boat. She had a sister, Edith, who had similarly improved herself by a change of spelling and become Edythe. Edythe was Mrs Brass, married to a man in the furniture business.

Mamie was a half-hearted rebel. She wanted what her family wanted for her, social upgrading, a husband who wore a trilby hat and had a well-paid job that didn't get his hands dirty. For a while she was content to lead a compromised love-life, with a George who came and went. He rented rooms in London – at Bayswater, at Notting Hill – where they could make love in a proper bed. But Mamie fancied marriage. So did the nation: after the nightmare of the war, family life was more important than ever. Local newspapers carried long reports of presents received by happy couples. In 1925 a Swansea bride's list ranged from fur coat and riding crop to glass bon-bon dishes and ostrich-feather fan. The groom's list was just as long, silver cigarette box, brass chestnut roaster...

Edythe had doubts about George. Then, in spring 1918, after they had been lovers for eight months, he did the decent thing. On March 25 they went to the register office in another north-eastern port, South Shields – George's movements dictated by his ship-surveying timetable – and got married. His abode was given as a local hotel, Mamie's as the Notting Hill address in London, in Elgin Crescent. The witnesses were the Registrar and his deputy.

Happy couple

You wonder what went on in his head. Was George so much in love that fear of otherwise losing her was enough to unbalance him? Men were known to marry in order to get into bed with someone, but he and Mamie had been sleeping together for eight months. She may have threatened him with an attack of chastity, or more likely she both wept and threatened. If he was a violent man, uneasy at his own nature, he could have taken his mad decision in order to make himself feel a better person. Bigamy was not all that uncommon: divorce would remain difficult for decades, and spouses who wanted to begin a new life occasionally took a chance, abandoned the other, went to live far away and married someone else. George didn't take this route. Having married Mamie, he used his work schedule to stop her finding out about May, as he used it to stop May finding out about Mamie.

It was complicated, having two wives, but for a while he managed it. The better person inside George could make both of them happy. Mamie went with him on his travels. When he was at the London docks they stayed in Notting Hill; they were in Bristol, they were in Liverpool.

On visits to the north they stayed with her family, where Edythe, despite her scrutiny of the marriage certificate, was still dubious about this smooth little man who didn't seem to have a home.

Keeping wife No. 2 happy when he was working in Welsh seaports and having to spend time with wife No. 1 can't have been easy. Perhaps Mamie, who had friends in London, didn't mind being left behind at Elgin Crescent. He spent money on her. She dressed well. She may have had another lover on the side. But early in 1919 George and Mamie were together in Swansea, living in rooms on what has become the Mumbles Road, near the gasworks (now a Tesco) and the prison, looking out across the great circle of the bay. May Shotton was less than forty miles away in Penarth.

Their landlady, Mrs Hearne, took an interest in this sober professional man and his flighty young wife with bobbed hair and shining eyes. She liked cigarettes and thumping out tunes on the piano. In the street, people turned to look at her, but at night she and George quarrelled. Mamie confided in Mrs Hearne. She pined for the stage, she regretted her marriage. In July their lives began to unravel. Something happened outside the George Hotel, on the front at Mumbles. Mamie and Mrs Hearne saw George with a woman and child. In what seems an act of self-destruction, he had positioned his wives four miles apart at either end of the Mumbles Road. He told Mamie he was going on a business trip. Instead he went down the road to see May.

George said the woman and child belonged to the hotel; it was an innocent misunderstanding. Although Mamie left him next day and returned to her family, he bombarded her with letters ('my own little darling'), and in September he was at Sunderland in person, promising a new start in Swansea, where he had bought a motor car. Edythe tried to stop her. She knew that George was violent. Letters from Mamie told the folks at home how he bruised her arms and face. 'He just went on laughing,' she said. Edythe had even seen a bottle marked 'Poison,' labelled 'J. Blake Benjamin, Chemist, Penarth.' There was also a revolver. Mamie had found one in George's luggage. It was loaded.

None of this deterred her. By November she was back in Swansea, arriving at the station dressed to kill, in black sealskin coat with fox-fur collar, black silk hat, port-wine jumper with three biscuit stripes, white cotton underskirt, other underclothes of white lace, black suede shoes and, somehow inevitably, black stockings. George had taken a six-month lease on a property in Newton, part of the Mumbles. It was called Ty Llonydd, House of Peace, a gloomy Victorian dwelling with trees in the garden. Soon Mamie was writing to her family to say that George was ill-treating her again. He was in touch with them too, complaining that Mamie meant to leave him and go to London. He sent a telegram to her father in Sunderland, asking for his advice. This was November 1919; George was preparing for Mamie's disappearance. Captain Stuart replied to say that if she went to London, he would have nothing more to do with her. Then a letter he sent to his daughter at Ty Llonydd was returned by the Post Office marked 'House Closed.'

Devious George was renting a second property. It was three-quarters of a mile away, at Caswell, a small scenic bay, beyond Mumbles, where the peninsula begins to stretch out to the west. The road from Swansea descends almost to sea-level, and a narrow valley opens to the beach; then the road rises again to cliff-height, before turning inland to Bishopston. The house, Grey Holm, was on that west-side ascent.

Three unmarried sisters developed Caswell in a genteel manner during the late 19th century and went to live there. They created cliff gardens, planted pines and exotic trees, and had a few houses ('villas' sounded better) built there to rent. Grey Holm (originally Craig Eithin, 'Gorse Rock') was the first, designed by an architect in 1891. This was where George took Mamie, in late 1919 or early 1920. The house remains, under yet another name to distance itself from its past.

Grey Holm was still comparatively isolated, although by this time Caswell was known as a bathing beach. (A century earlier a literary traveller said it was 'frequently visited by the neighbouring nymphs.') The bay was much photographed. A landowner in the valley declined to repair a chapel, built there on the site of a holy well, for fear it would induce 'Swansea people' to 'enter the land and leave behind them broken hedges, broken gates, broken bottles, bits of paper & worse refuse.'

Exactly when George took Mamie there is unknown. Dates have vanished from the record between November 1919, when Mamie wrote to her family, and March 1920, when the police were told about a curious find at a Swansea hotel, the Grosvenor, of a large suitcase and a small bag, containing, among other things, four pairs of women's shoes cut into pieces; a silver wrist-watch inscribed 'From George October 31st 1917 with love'; a lady's handbag, a visiting card and case, a cigarette case, a toothbrush, a pair of wire cutters and a novel called *Molly Make Believe*. There was also a Bible, which obligingly contained the family address in Sunderland, including Edythe's. A person unknown had left this collection at the hotel.

The Swansea police wrote to the Sunderland police – it was what they did then – and the Stuarts were informed. They said they were anxious about their daughter because of her husband's 'eccentric ways.' As a result, inquiries were made in Swansea, and on March 23 the chief constable was able to tell the Sunderland police that all was well. Bag and contents had been traced as Shotton's property and returned to him. Shotton had been interviewed by a detective-superintendent (who was 'well acquainted with Mr and Mrs Shotton and their child,') and all were in good health, and living at Caswell Bay. On March 29 Sunderland sent a puzzled reply. There is no child, they said. So there had to be two Mrs Shottons.

George had left enough clues to incriminate a saint. If he wanted to be caught, if self-destruction was his aim, it was a brilliant success. But at the same time he denied everything. Mamie, he said, had run off and left him. He continued to live in Caswell with wife and child while his shadow-world collapsed. Charged on May 25 with bigamy, and tried in the summer at Swansea, he mounted a ludicrous defence of impersonation by somebody else at the register office.

It took the jury five minutes to find him guilty, and he was sent to prison for eighteen months' hard labour.

Mamie Stuart had her moment of fame. People all over the world said they had seen her. She was working in a London hotel. A miner's wife from Sunderland saw her in London in a blue linen costume, accompanied by a fair-headed man. She had sailed from Swansea to Canada in the five-masted sailing vessel *Cumberland Queen*. She was with a troupe of dancing girls in Karachi. She was in Ireland and Aberdeen. In Hastings she was seen getting into a taxi. In Brighton a spiritualist found her in the world beyond: her mortal remains, still wearing clothes, were buried a yard deep, under a red-brick floor.

Detectives had roughly the same idea. No public accusation could be made. There was no evidence of murder, although the newspapers were full of hints. Police dug up gardens at all George's houses, in Penarth, in Newton and in Caswell, where they also took the fireplace apart. They searched the Gower cliffs. When 'the dissected body of a female' was washed up in one of the bays, Edythe Brass hurried down from Sunderland. It wasn't her sister. The newspapers were as disappointed as the police. It was only ten years since Dr Crippen had been satisfactorily convicted of murdering his wife and burying her under the coal cellar of their house in north London. He hanged, of course. Perhaps George saw Crippen in his dreams.

When he came out of prison, his old life was over. May divorced him. He became an itinerant mechanic. Once, he threatened his sister with a gun and went to prison again. In World War 2 he was in Bristol, working at an aircraft factory, his history a secret. He still managed to attract young women.

In November 1961 three men from Bishopston went caving on a Sunday, on the cliffs between Caswell and the next bay to the west, Brandy Cove. More exactly, they went down a narrow air or rescue shaft, at an angle of about 30 degrees. It had been constructed for one of the small lead-and-silver mines developed there in the mid-19th century. Twenty feet down they reached a narrow tunnel, blocked off by a slab of stone. Behind it was a human skull and other bones.

Forty years late, the police arrived. The remains of Mamie

were there, still with scraps of clothing, a piece of black silk, hair clips, a gold wedding ring; the skeleton sawn in three by someone in a hurry, who left hesitant saw-cuts in the bones, who had put the pieces in a sack, bits of which were still there. The spirits in Brighton had had the right idea.

It was a few hundred yards from the house at Caswell. George was fond of walking in Gower, and the shaft must have caught his eye. Farmers used it to dispose of dead animals, so a smell of decomposition was only to be expected. Who would crawl into such a place with a bag of body parts? In 1961, the first officers who arrived were too large to get through the tunnel, and the cavers had to go back inside and bring them some sample bones. The search for George began. Police traced him to Bristol, to a woman who had invited him to lodge with her because he was kind to her mentally handicapped brother, when both were in an old people's home. He lived in her house for years, a 'superior' kind of person, she said, a little grey-haired man who smoked a pipe and accompanied her to church. (An earlier landlady recalled that he 'used to creep about the house and appear behind you'). He had been alive until three years earlier, dying at the age of seventy-seven.

Mamie's bones disappeared after the inquest, where they were displayed in court. It is said that the family didn't want them back. There is nothing left, not even a ghost-legend of the cliffs, a tormented figure with a sack who dissolves into the air behind a gorse bush. A retired postman came forward at the inquest and said he saw George carrying the sack out of the house on a winter afternoon. George is supposed to have said, 'Oh my God, I thought you were a policeman.' The postman omitted to tell anyone at the time.

The extraordinary thing is that George got away with it. The other extraordinary thing is that at one point he may have wanted to be caught. Perhaps at first he intended to drop the incriminating suitcase into the sea but couldn't bear to let it go, inscribed wrist-watch, *Molly Make Believe* and all, and left it at the Grosvenor Hotel in despair at himself. As events moved on towards retribution and the hangman, his courage failed, and he reverted to the villain who sawed up his lover but didn't want to die for it.

When the police stopped searching, and he had the rest of his life to cope with, did he dream of Caswell and the cliffs, and walking there with Mamie? The bay was busier every year. It was the first in Gower to have busloads of day-trippers from Swansea. 'The sight on a summer's day,' says an old guide-book, 'is one to be remembered, the hundreds of bathers with various coloured caps bobbing up and down in the water.'

George met people in England later on who recognised his name and knew his history, but he shrugged his shoulders and said he had been wronged. Few people come to terms with everything they've done. George had another thirty-eight years to create fictions that he could live with while he aged.

Oh Lordy, how they could love.

CHAPTER 12

HISTORY MAN

J.D. DAVIES, collector of local history and legend, is now part of the process himself. His habit of writing down stuff that no one else bothered with has kept him alive. 'It is hard for us to see ourselves in our antecedents,' wrote E.W. Nield in the journal *Gower*, 'and harder yet, in transport- and tourist-tamed country, to see, for what they were, the very places which they knew and were part of.' Davies helps.

In his world, legends were treated with respect. He didn't ridicule them. He devoted fifteen pages to the Latin and English versions of Capgrave's account of St Cennydd, sent down the river in a basket and reared by seagulls in Rhossili Bay. He smiled at the monk's tale but made no comment.

He had read John Leland, the sixteenth-century traveller and writer, on the subject of Worms Head.

> Leland [...] speaks of a wonderful 'Hole at the Poynt of Worme heade, but few dare enter it, and Men fable there that a Dore within the spatius Hole hathe [been] seen with great Nayles on it [...]'

Davies wrote that a Llanelly sea-pilot, William Lewis, had told him how he once rowed a boat into an opening at the base of the Worm, and found himself in 'a very spacious cavern, which he described to be as large as a Church.' The pilot saw no door with 'Nayles.' No one else seems to have found a cavern there, though it would be nice if someone did.

West Gower blurs fact and fiction. It speculates about the Helwick sands, the shoal south of the Worms Head, and Davies wonders if 'Helwick' might be the Anglo-Saxon 'Helewick,' which, he believed, meant 'hidden town.' If so, it agreed with 'a very ancient tradition [...] that there was once a road along these sands, and that pieces of iron horse's shoes had been dredged up there.'

Inundations, which were actual enough along the South Wales coast, intrigued Davies. At low water the remains of trees, fossilised into unappetising clumps of what looks like softened rock, can be seen in Swansea Bay, and here and there along the peninsula.

> There is a very old building in Llanmadoc village, called the 'Mansion house,' the beams of which are said to have been cut on Whitford Sker. There is no reason whatever to doubt it. Henry Thomas, a labourer in my employ, since deceased, informed me that when a boy, he remembered seeing trunks of trees 40 feet long, in Broughton bay, in places where the force of the sea had exposed the native soil, which underlies the sand at no great depth in this bay [...] I should say, that it was quite possible that some few trees might have been *in situ*, and flourishing within the area of Broughton bay two hundred years ago [i.e. towards the end of the 17th century].

Davies worked out that the forest of Whitford might have suffered from an event, a storm of some kind, as early as the start of the 16th century. He may have been right about the event though wrong about the date. A century later, in January 1607, an extreme storm caused floods and deaths throughout the Bristol Channel, as water was driven into a narrowing space. There is a recent theory that a tsunami was involved, a tidal wave produced by an earthquake under the Irish Sea. Monmouthshire was the worst affected part of Wales. Pamphlets with such titles as *Lamentable newes out of Monmouthshire* and *God's warning to his people of England* circulated. But Monmouthshire (and the English coast on the other side) were more significant regions, nearer to Bristol and London, than a backwater like Gower. If it was the same event that drowned the forest of Whitford and changed the shape of the estuary, it went unreported.

The supernatural is another Davies favourite, hovering between fact and speculation. His four volumes are almost silent about his own life, but he devotes a couple of pages to the 'singular story' of an incident at Oxwich, where his father was rector. His 'elder brother, now deceased,' then aged thirteen or fourteen, had been out with their father fishing in the bay. By the time they moored the boat it was almost midnight.

> They had just gained the top of the beach, which here abuts the narrow path leading to the church, when my brother happening to look behind him, saw what he described to me, to be a white horse walking on his hind legs, and proceeding leisurely along the path towards the church gate; having called my father's attention to this strange spectacle, he turned round, and they both stood for about a minute and watched the creature, or whatever it was, until it reached the gate, or rather the stone stile by its side, which the animal crossed, apparently without the slightest difficulty, still going on its hind legs. The uncanny thing then disappeared. The only remark my father made was, 'come along.' They were soon inside the rectory, which was only a few yards off. This strange adventure was never afterwards spoken of by my father, nor alluded to in any way. I have often been on the point of questioning him about it, but some vague feeling of undefined alarm always prevented me. Both eye-witnesses have since passed away, so nothing further can be learnt on the subject.

Oxwich Churchyard

John D. Davies was born in Oxwich in 1831. Three years later his father moved to a new living in Reynoldston. John had a brother, Herbert, two years younger, as well as his older sibling; in any case, it sounds like a story that was elaborated for, or by, a small child. A horse had reared up; for a moment in the dark it seemed to be walking on two legs. But Davies preferred the unexplained. A feeling of 'undefined alarm' suited his nature.

There were other supernatural events. The drowned sailor looking into the church (Chapter 5) appealed to Davies. So did the tale of a predecessor at Llanmadoc and Cheriton, a Rev. John Williams, resident a century earlier at the 'Great House,' which was haunted by the spirit of a woman farmer who had cheated locals with short measures of milk and butter. Her ghost roamed the house, moaning 'Weight and measure, weight and measure,' accompanied by 'dreadful noises' and an invisible presence rushing to and fro. The Rev. Williams exorcised it by cracking his whip and talking Latin, condemning the spirit to remain on Llanmadoc Burrows till it succeeded in making ropes of sand. 'It is perhaps not generally known,' says Davies, with clerical humour, 'that evil spirits are particularly afraid of Latin.'

He did see one ghost for himself, and wrote about it in the *Gower Church Magazine*. On June 25, 1894, he was on his way to Penrice Church to meet the diocesan architect at noon. It was a warm, sunny day.

> I drove over from Llanmadoc, and having left my conveyance at Penny Hitch, I walked down the old lane which leads to Penrice village. Those who are acquainted with the locality will know that when you come to the bottom of this lane, you arrive at the iron gates leading into Penrice park [the grounds of Penrice Castle]. A few yards further on there is a bridge, under which flows the small rivulet which feeds the ponds in the park. Crossing this, the road bends to the right, towards Penrice mill, where it forms an angle, and from that point it turns to the left, up a very steep incline for a hundred yards or so, until it reaches a kind of plateau.

People on foot never follow the course of this winding road, as there is a short cut straight up by a footpath, which shortens the distance considerably. I had gone rather more than half way up this pathway, and casually looked up, when I distinctly saw a very tall man, dressed like a clergyman, with a long frock coat, wide awake hat, and dark trousers; he was standing quite still on this plateau, looking straight down at me, as if he had been expecting me, and yet at the same time with a sort of hesitation, as if he did not exactly know whether or not he should come down and meet me.

I was at the time perhaps about forty yards distant from him. I then cast my eyes downwards, and walked on a little further, and upon again looking up I perceived him walking slowly down the main road leading to the mill, thus conveying to my mind the idea that he wished to avoid me. I also observed that he did not take the middle of the road, but walked on the bare edge of it nearest to me; his side was then turned towards me, and I had a distinct view of his figure from head to foot. His whole appearance now seemed to have assumed quite a grey colour, and his hat, which appeared to have the brim turned up, the same.

I could not have been at this time more than ten yards from him, and in less than half a minute I stood on the exact spot where he had been standing just before. I then turned round and looked in the direction in which I had observed him going: but not a vestige of him was to be seen; he had completely vanished; and as I could see down this road for at least a hundred yards from where I was standing, it seemed absolutely impossible that he could have hid himself anywhere.

It did not strike me as anything supernatural at the time, I only thought it was something singular, and that was all. It was not until some days after, when I began to reflect upon the matter, that the strangeness of it occurred to me. If the person I saw was really a human being in the flesh, and not a phantom, I only hope that, if this story comes to his ears, he will communicate with me [...]

Much of Davies's *History* is taken up with ancient lawsuits, inventories and other documents, quoted at length, not always in English, and of largely antiquarian interest; except that now and then a phrase stands out. Leuky, a local heiress, leases ten acres at

Landimor to Sir Robert de Penres in November 1314. The rent will be 'a chaplet of roses at midsummer.'

Although Davies never published a fifth volume, he collected material for it. Writing to a correspondent on June 8 1901 he said, 'No. 4 is the last vol of my history that I have published; I have lost so much money by this book that I can't afford to go on with it; I have plenty of matter, but the means are lacking.' Davies added that 'my health is not as good as it was,' though he lived another ten years. At his death he left £6,047. He may have received a legacy between 1901 and 1911, but on the face of it, poverty doesn't explain the non-appearance of Volume 5. Like most writers, he was aware of rivals, real or imagined. In Volume 4 he began his account of Penrice Castle by saying that 'it is difficult to say very much without treading in the footsteps of others, to which I have a very decided objection.' Perhaps he felt that Gower was coming to be too well-known, and that he would be seen as just another scribbler.

Had he gone on to write that further volume, Davies might have incorporated exciting new stories about Gower pirates and other goings-on that appeared around 1908, in a work that came from nowhere, *Lucas Annotation No. 1*. This rambled on for six thousand words about the pedigree and the past of the important Lucas family, which had been in Gower for centuries. It was prepared by a Rev. Dr. J.H. Spry, a theologian with Gower connections. Someone send Davies a copy from Birmingham. He was keen to make use of it, in the Vol. 5 that he never got round to.

Two sections must have caught his eye. First there was a fight in Cheriton churchyard in 1770 between rival branches of the Lucas family, convincingly described, with John Lucas telling a relative, 'Uncle is in church, Anne, don't cry' – her father, a clergyman, having been locked inside because it was 'offensive to shed blood in sight of clergy.' Second was the story of an earlier

John Lucas, a man 'of fierce and ungovernable violence,' who went to live at 'ye Salte House' on Port Eynon Point, 'washed by ye salte water at flow of ye waves,' where he 'succoured ye pirates and ye French smugglers, and rifled ye wrecked ships and forced mariners to serve him' Again, there is entertaining detail.

Two years after Davies received his copy of the *Annotation*, the same material appeared in a circular from an unidentified publisher, referring to a planned work in ten volumes, *County Families of England and Wales*. This was never published, but the *Annotation* took on a life of its own. When the Cambrian Archaeological Association met at Swansea in 1920, members went on a trip to Port Eynon, and readings were given from this mysterious work on a wet afternoon by the sea.

Few seem to have questioned its authenticity. Davies the scholar might have had doubts about using the *Annotation* in his Vol. 5, but Davies the raconteur would probably have won. Swansea central reference library had a copy in the 1950s. I made notes from it then, relishing the drama and the detail. People went on wanting to be convinced by it. Then Robert Lucas (1916-2006), a solicitor by profession, returned from England to Gower in the 1970s, and began to research the family history.

At first, he took the *Annotation* seriously. In a 1972 article he quoted the passage about the fight in the churchyard. By 1980 he had realised that the genealogy didn't fit. He also had doubts about the pirates of Salthouse, which was no more than a building where sea-water was evaporated for its salt. Michael Gibbs found evidence that at a time when Lucas the pirate was supposed to have been resident there, it was occupied by a Mrs Gribble. (Mrs Gribble, Pirate of Port Eynon, has possibilities.) Lucas let the pirates go the way of Cheriton churchyard. '... the Salthouse story is a work of fiction,' he wrote in *Gower*, 'and while John may have consorted with pirates it is much more probable that he was, like the other Lucases of those times, no more than a busy farmer.'

Lucas's reappraisal dismissed the *Annotation* as a hoax, and found a candidate for the hoaxer, a Gower clergyman, the Rev. William Lucas Collins (1815-1887), related to the Rev. Collins of Oxwich who kept the diary. Obscure motives of one-upmanship within branches of the Lucas family were proposed as an explanation. In any case, the false legends were finished. Except that they weren't.

The pirates and the churchyard affray had already infiltrated Gower folk-lore. Excavation at Port Eynon has since found evidence that the Salthouse was 'fortified with musket loops for all-round defence.' The very musket balls were discovered. It all helped with the mythology. 'SECRETS OF PIRATE'S LAIR UNEARTHED' said the London *Independent* (January 22 1988), its story adding that 'The ruins of Lucas's lair are only 30 miles from the island of Lundy, once notorious as a major pirate stronghold.'

The legend is lodged in books and websites, and will last for ever. As with the '18 straight whiskies' that Dylan Thomas is supposed to have died of, but didn't, nothing beats a satisfactory myth.

J.D. Davies was a practical man. He built boats and carved wood, which can still be seen in Llanmadoc church, among others. The building dismayed him when he arrived. The roof wasn't safe and the floor was bare earth, wet in winter. He raised nearly £600 for restoration, over £50,000 now, sufficient to more or less rebuild the place. A hundred pounds of the fund came from C.R.M. Talbot; rather more than that from Davies himself. His practical side was the one that people knew. The careful observer, accumulating detail for the History, was less obvious.

Once, a literary-minded visitor did the observing, when he was taken to visit Davies in April 1872. Davies was then in his early forties and had been rector for twelve years. The visitor was the diarist Francis Kilvert, also an Anglican minister, though still only a curate hoping for better things. He was in Gower briefly, staying at Ilston with Westhorp, the vicar, who was a friend.

Kilvert's parish was seventy miles away at Clyro, near the English border. A compulsive diarist, he was unknown until long after his death in 1879. It was the Westhorps who took him to visit Davies, who emerged from the rectory looking 'like a Roman priest, close shaven and shorn, dressed in seedy black, a long coat and broad shovel hat.' Shovel hats sat low on the head and had wide brims; clergymen liked them. Davies asked the visitors to stay for lunch, and they contributed their picnic basket. 'We were waited on by a tall clean old woman with a severe and full cap border who waits on Mr Davies and is so clean that she washes the kitchen four times a day. She used to wash her master's bedroom floor as often till he caught a cold which frightened her and she desisted.'

The rectory ('thoroughly untidy and bachelorlike') had the rigging of a boat in the hall, together with cabinets and bookcases, made by the rector to raise money for church restoration. 'He is very clever and can turn his hand to anything,' wrote Kilvert. 'Besides which he seemed to me an uncommonly kind good fellow, a truly simple-minded, single-hearted man.'

This is not quite the diarist at his best. Kilvert, aged thirty-one and waiting for preferment, probably felt deferential towards the older man, established in his own parish. Kilvert's nature was inquisitive and romantic. He also had a discreet interest in young girls and their unclothed limbs, on which he commented from time to time. During a later visit to Gower (but not to Davies) he picnicked at Langland with the Westhorps, their daughters and someone called Annie Mitchell. They drank wine from sea shells, and the girls helped him gather seaweed. 'A very happy day,' wrote Kilvert, 'made happier by sweet Annie Mitchell and her lovely innocent trustful blue eyes.'

This wasn't J.D. Davies's style. He would have kept his gaze on the sea from under the brim of his shovel hat. But he was popular in his parish. He gave instructions that he was to be buried at Reynoldston, alongside his younger brother (the one who may have been involved in the horse-on-two-legs affair).

His parishioners weren't having that. He is in the churchyard at Cheriton.

CHAPTER 13

HILL COUNTRY

THE OLD ROAD from Swansea to Brecon goes out to the north-east, along the floor of a valley that has almost forgotten it was ever industrialised. The River Tawe, which runs down the middle, marks the ancient boundary of Gower in the east. Despite a new bypass, much of this Swansea Valley route keeps to the western side of the river, and so remains within the 'lordship,' as it once was.

Travelling north up the valley, higher ground is away to the left, half a mile distant. Viewed from river level it has no features, no presence, for most of its length, except for a sense of crags at the northern end. But up there is the wilderness, the true 'Upland Gower.' Driving in it once, I lost my way. An approaching 4x4 swerved off the narrow tarmac to make room, and I stopped to ask the route down to Clydach, a post-industrial village in the valley, perhaps six miles from where we were. The driver, a young woman, shook her head. She was from the far side of the moorland. 'Never heard of it,' she said. 'Sorry, mate.'

On a clear day there are sudden views, from the highest moor, of what at first looks like a lake far away to the south-west. This turns out to be the Burry Estuary, about twelve miles distant, with the northern edge of the peninsula on its left, the Llanelli coast opposite on its right. Trackways, some ancient, cross the yellow-grassed moors. Journeys between mid-Wales and the coast would have been safer up there than in the valleys. Into the 19th century, coach-and-horse traffic came across the moors, and there were milestones indicating distances between Carmarthenshire and Swansea.

The area was once used by Welsh nobility from south and west Wales as a hunting ground. Most of it was forested then, and formed part of Ystrad Tywi, roughly modern Carmarthenshire. The Normans and their successors found the same use for it. In medieval times there was a hunting lodge at its northern edge, where the moors give way to lowland. Traces of the manorial mill can still be found there, at Neuadd – it means 'Hall' – by the Amman, which runs east to west, and is where Gower ends; more of a stream than a river, with smooth stones you might find on a beach, and trees at its edge no thicker than a wrist.

When I was there in 2007, a woman in a smallish house insisted that it had been the actual hunting-lodge of Welsh princes, so don't argue. I knocked on another door and found a retired headmaster, Ifan Davies, who greeted me as if I had been expected, and told me about the Welshness of the area.

In sentiment and outlook, the inhabitants here had little to do, historically, with either peninsula Gower or Swansea, those riskier places down south. Rural Carmarthenshire – where people spoke Welsh, reared fat cattle and didn't go in for novelty – was on the other side of the Amman. The Black Mountain (not to be confused with the plural Black Mountains of eastern Breconshire) rises like a fortress to 1500 feet just north of the Amman; another country. The top end of Gower has a further anomaly, a strip of coal-mining land, where pits were sunk in the 19th century, bringing with them the clutter of mining valleys, except that the Amman's is not the shut-in cleft of the Rhondda and other former coal districts in eastern Wales. But it has the mining-valley atmosphere. Rows of small decent dark-brown houses crouch beside barnlike chapels, the Bethels and Beulahs. Cemeteries, rugby pitches and working-men's clubs are all in business. Coal is still dug nearby, in quarry-like opencast mines.

The district has an air of proud under-privilege, unlike the self-assurance of peninsula Gower. Cwmtwrch, one of its villages, means 'Valley of the Twrch,' a tributary of the Amman, and 'twrch' means wild boar. A legend has King Arthur hurling the stone that slayed the rampant boar that was terrorising the community. There are traditional South Wales jokes about the place, as if 'Cwmtwrch' was a byword for somewhere remote and obscure, like a Welsh Timbuktu. The village decided long ago that it came in two parts, an Upper and a Lower. This is no laughing matter in Upper Cwmtwrch. A sign in 2007 said 'Gourmet Restaurant.'

But it is the high moors that define Upland Gower. In the middle of the wilderness, just off the road, is Penll'er Castell, a minor mystery of fallen stones, a bank and a ditch, overlooking the sweep of moorland to the north. The name means 'the head of the place where the castle is.' Morgan's *East Gower* (1899) says simply, 'Absolutely nothing is known about this Castle, when or by whom erected, or what it was called.' An indeterminate place of grass and stones, bearing no resemblance to a proper castle, it has the reticent air of all these unreported hills.

The site has a commanding position, 1220 feet above sea-level, 370 metres, and is the highest point anywhere in Gower. Its height and visibility may have given it a role as a relay-station for smoke-and-fire signals between beacons. There is a line-of-sight from Penlle'r Castell to the hills above Swansea; to Rhossili Hill at the far end of the peninsula, and to the watch tower of Carreg Cennen Castle in Carmarthenshire, eight miles to the north. Later research identifies it as a makeshift fortification, built in a hurry in mid-13th century by a de Breos – very likely the one who failed to hang William Cragh in 1290 – to protect a vulnerable frontier. The Welsh were contesting his control of the uplands, and the area between the high moors and the river Amman to the north became known as the place of strife, 'Stryveland.' A quick castle was run up to keep the rebels back. At some stage the Amman river boundary had to be redrawn farther south, near Penlle'r Castell. The Normans were not quite the masters that they were in less demanding places. The geography was against them. In peninsula Gower, Englishness has flourished for centuries. In the uplands there was no political victory, and Welsh is widely spoken.

The area has, or had, other curiosities, chiefly an entrepreneur known as Death Ray Matthews. In the nineteen-thirties the doings of this mischievous engineer made him a celebrity, of a sort. Now he crops up on the net, an English inventor or magician who eventually brought his 'laboratory' to Upland Gower, where he hid himself behind fences and barbed wire near Penlle'r Castell, trying to perfect the secret weapon to end all secret weapons. At least, that was his story.

His house and laboratory are still there, and, strangely, so is a high fence and padlocked gate, though the occupier is not working on a death ray. It is two and a half miles south of Penlle'r Castell. The area is called Tor Clawdd, which means a bulging bank of earth, or something of the sort. Newspaper reports of the Death Ray man in the 1930s, when he flourished up there, usually assumed it meant 'Cloud Mountain.' Hardly anything in the Matthews story is what it seems.

Harry Grindell Matthews was a farmer's son from the village of Winterbourne, Gloucestershire, born 1880, an inventive electrical engineer who first came into the news in 1911 when he set up a radio-telephone link between man in aeroplane and man on ground. Radio-telephony was being developed by others. Matthews' contribution was to use it in a novel way that got into the newspapers. The man in the aircraft was a 'pioneer aviator' of the day, Benny Hucks. This association with celebrity magnified the event. Matthews had a company called the Grindell-Matthews Wireless Telephone Syndicate, which went bankrupt and was wound up in 1914. Most of his business ventures went the same way. Yet he flourished.

During World War 1 he offered his services to King and country. This was long before he went to Tor Clawdd, when he was still based in south-east England. A clever man, ahead of his time, he proposed the use of light-controlled vessels and aircraft

Death Ray Matthews

as observation platforms. The war was not going well, and his ideas found a receptive audience in circles where no one knew much about science and technology. Grindell Matthews had a reassuringly English look. His suits were well-cut, his face was square and trustworthy, big-browed under heavy dark hair.

Among the people he impressed was Admiral 'Jacky' Fisher. Before the war the admiral brought new thinking to naval policy ('Scrap-the-lot' Fisher), and he remained a senior adviser, heading the Board of Invention and Research. Then in his mid-seventies, he advised everyone to back this go-ahead young chap.

The surviving Government documents are in an Air Ministry file. The inventor's proposal is first referred to in a *Secret* document of October 8 1915. Fisher writes that the Matthews invention is 'so fraught with immense possibilities that it will certainly if successful produce incalculable results as regards the termination of the War.' Yet, wrote Fisher, the idea was 'so simple and obvious that an Admiralty charwoman would detect its secret instantly and consequently the most stringent secrecy is imperative.' The admiral summed up the invention in a phrase: '*A mechanical man with mechanical vision (far more than twice human vision) who can be placed in any sufficiently stable vessel in air or water and directed to take that vessel anywhere that the observer wishes without possibility of interference by the Enemy.*'

No details were supplied. Matthews' price for a convincing demonstration was (perhaps) £25,000, a modern million or two. A trial was arranged using a launch called *Dawn* on one of the Pen Ponds, artificial lakes inside Richmond Park in south-west London. Late in the afternoon, when the sun was low behind the trees, a handful of senior officers and members of the Government saw a searchlight beam used to control light-sensitive selenium cells and steer the launch. The file has no report of the demonstration, and any accounts of it come from Matthews.

The trial was in October. A *Secret* note from Fisher on

November 15 said, 'The inventor has fulfilled his bargain and ought to get his money.' Presumably Matthews was paid. Years later, when the inventor was again seeking Government finance, Whitehall officials couldn't work out which department, if any, had written the cheque. In 1915 they had played pass-the-parcel. Should the Admiralty pay? Why not the Treasury? Perhaps it was a matter for the Secret Service. A civil servant had to point out that Secret Service payments were supposed to be secret. The file doesn't say what happened. As in most things concerned with Grindell Matthews, a fog descends.

Remote control of craft was a far-sighted endeavour. But Matthews was not the first to experiment. Four years earlier, in the summer of 1911, an American engineer, John Hays Hammond Jr., demonstrated 'a wireless apparatus' that could control a boat from the shore. He spent the summer doing it with an old 40-foot house-boat in the harbour at Gloucester, Mass. Distinguished visitors came to see, and he had patents pending for his 'telautomatic' device. The American work sounds more practicable than beams of light; perhaps Matthews knew what was going on in Massachusetts, and saw his selenium cells as a way of getting in on the act. Whatever his strategy, it succeeded. He smiled and took the money.

The file mentions another piece of kit altogether. A note from Fisher to a senior civil servant, December 22 1915, said that 'a mission leaves tomorrow for France with a splendid letter from War Office to Sir Douglas Haig with 3 sets of apparatus for blowing up mines or any other service it is desired to carry out.' What was this device? Was it ever used? Did it get further than a warehouse at a dockside? Rays or beams came to be the signature of a Matthews story. Soon after the war, newspapers were reporting that he had a ray which exploded a bowl of gunpowder, and could do the same with an ammunition dump.

Lethal rays were becoming popular. The H.G. Wells novel,

The War of the Worlds (1898), had given its Martian invaders an unstoppable heat ray. Real warfare itself was now coming to depend on technology, and in the 1920s death rays were being invented in many countries, if you believed the newspapers. A ray to which there was no defence would make war unthinkable, an early version of the nuclear stalemate in the 1950s, the MAD doctrine of 'mutual assured destruction.'

Grindell Matthews seized the opportunity. By the early 1920s he claimed to have a 'ray' or 'beam' that could stop an engine by de-activating the magneto. Or destroy living creatures. Or both. Newspapers tended to report more than Matthews claimed in public, and between his deviousness and their enthusiasm, the death-ray arrived on the scene. His fame spread. 'A switch is turned,' reported *Time* magazine (August 25, 1924). 'Terrible energy flows along the beam. The mouse jumps into the air, quivers, is dead.' The *Star* in London sent a reporter to see an experiment at the 'laboratory' in Matthews' West End apartment. He made gunpowder explode from a distance of 18 feet. At the far end of the room was a petrol engine driving a wheel. Matthews pointed his ray at it and pulled a lever. The engine stopped.

The Air Ministry in London was cautious but interested. In 1922 the military wanted to know if any work was being done on 'electrical interference with aeroplanes in the air or explosives.' The Germans were said to be experimenting. The file notes that a Count in Switzerland claimed to have a ray that stopped aircraft engines; that a Frenchman had an engine-stopping ray which also killed rabbits.

On March 6 1924, Matthews was interviewed at the Air Ministry by a wing-commander, a major and a senior civil servant. He told them that his 'present invention' was an apparatus that produced 'a beam of rays' of very short wavelength.

> He stated that he had with these rays set fire to paper, wood, cloth etc at distances up to 200 yards. He used 1 K.W. of energy in his

apparatus. Recently he supported a piece of metal the size of a florin [a smallish coin] between two pieces of glass. Such rays would be exceedingly injurious to human beings. He hoped eventually to be able to set fire to aircraft material etc up to a distance of four or five miles.

This was not a journalist distorting a hint, this was the inventor claiming that he had a death ray. At the same time, Matthews was trying to raise private money for his magic rays, presenting them as a way of transmitting electricity via beams of light.

The Air Ministry seems to have been as fascinated as Fleet Street by these marvels. A small group headed by a major went to Matthews' laboratory (presumably in London) to see a demonstration. Nothing much happened. An assistant held a lamp, not connected to anything, that was made to glow. A small motor-bike engine was stopped, allegedly by 'the Ray.' The visitors were not impressed, and wanted to repeat the engine experiment under stricter conditions. Matthews refused, but he told the Ministry that he was planning to 'erect a large experimental station away in the country,' and that he would give a demonstration there. It was another ten years before he moved his operations to the bungalow laboratory in Upland Gower, although he may have gone somewhere else in between.

After the 1924 demonstrations, the Ministry began to lose interest in him. A young Government scientist, H.T. Tizard, had become involved. Twenty years later he was Sir Henry Tizard, a powerful figure in World War 2, the person delegated to take Britain's atom-bomb secrets to share with America. On March 25 1924 he wrote, 'Personally I should say that the man is trying to bamboozle you.'

In the 1920s Matthews went on making news and attracting support. Other countries were reported to be after his secrets, one day France, next day America. Private investors came and went. He is said to have experimented successfully with adding a sound-track to film, but if so, it was at the wrong time and place. To keep the public's interest, he used searchlights to project images of angels on clouds over London (1930) and did the same trick with the American flag in New York. Newspapers and radio remained susceptible to his ingenuity.

The Air Ministry had written off Matthews as a fraud, but the idea of magical weaponry still appealed to them. In 1935, with Nazi Germany rearming, a radio research establishment was asked to advise on whether weapons 'of the type colloquially called "death rays" ' were feasible. The answer was no. But while they were thinking about such matters, someone recalled that radio waves were known to be affected by aircraft. This perception led to radar, just in time to have it ready when World War 2 started. Matthews could claim that indirectly his 'death rays' had helped.

In 1934, he had gone to Wales and set himself up behind barbed wire at Tor Clawdd. From now on, this was his headquarters. He let it be known that he was concentrating on the air defence of Britain. A backer may have emerged. The wealthy Lady Houston has been suggested. A former chorus girl known as Poppy, she became rich via husbands and lovers, and gave money to causes that benefitted the country, among them aviation. Her feverish patriotism, it was said, caused her to stop eating during the Abdication crisis of 1936. It also led her to believe, correctly, that Britain was not spending enough to defend itself properly. Grindell Matthews would have appealed to her.

Although air warfare was Tor Clawdd's priority, the submarine threat was not forgotten. All the work was supposed to be secret. At the same time, journalists were told about plans for aerial torpedoes and aprons of steel suspended above London. It is conceivable, if unlikely, that Matthews was given covert official encouragement for his fantasies, in the hope of convincing foreigners, especially Germans, that Britain was developing an armoury of secret weapons. Everyone seemed to know about his secluded hide-out. Upland Gower, though a lonely place, is not all that far from the haunts of men. In the Swansea Valley, below the moors, was Clydach, where the Mond Nickel works employed hundreds. Had Matthews seriously wanted seclusion, mid-Wales or the Scottish Highlands would have been better. The medical officer at Mond, Dr John Gwynne Morgan, invited him down to dinner at his home. Mrs Morgan was disconcerted when he arrived in full evening dress.

A Colonel Etherton, traveller and author, was at Tor Clawdd to write an article for the *Sunday Express*.

> I have just visited, on a mountain-top in South Wales, a lonely English inventor who is working to conquer the air, war and death [...] [H]e is living in a bungalow and laboratory, guarded by barbed-wire fences and secret-ray burglar alarms. He found his retreat by flying over the mountains. He has his own aerodrome, large enough to receive bombing aeroplanes [*It was a landing-strip for light aircraft*].
>
> [...] Some of his work is nearing completion. Here are his objects:
>
> To perfect a device for detecting the presence of submarines thirty miles away.
>
> To discover a ray to kill disease germs.
>
> To set up a new aerial defence for London, or any other city, by rockets and steel-wire aprons which will hang in the sky.
>
> To devise rocket aeroplanes to travel at the incredible speed of six miles a second, with which man might be able to reach the moon.
>
> They are objects so fantastic as to rival the imaginings of Jules Verne and H.G. Wells. But when you hear this quiet, confident scientist talk about them you have to remember that in his bungalow he already has machinery that will transmit rays strong enough to kill a rat sixty feet away or stop a motor-car.

The story that car engines were mysteriously failing, though minutes later they could be restarted, circulated in the neighbourhood.

Children were not encouraged to go near the fence. There were unspecified goings-on. Mysterious visitors came and went. Someone knew someone who had seen a man, on a ridge above the road, point a box or a cylinder at a car passing below, which came to a stop, causing the driver to jump out and fiddle with the engine, which restarted at once. The tales circulated in Swansea. In the late 1930s a charge-engineer at Tir John, the town's new power-station, drove around the moors in his Riley 9, hoping to encounter the ray. He must have been reading the *Sunday Express*. The trip was uneventful, which disappointed him, and disappointed me as well. He was my father, and I was in the car.

It is not clear who, if anyone lived with Matthews at Tor Clawdd. An earlier Mrs Matthews had long disappeared. In 1937 he married again, this time to someone whose career, like his, was built on fantasy. This was Madam Ganna Walska, a Polish or Russian opera singer (born Hanna Puacz, of humble parents), whose several husbands before she encountered Grindell Matthews had made her wealthy. She was fond of jewellery; a 95-carat diamond called 'The Walska' is known to exist. So do elaborate gardens that she founded in California, 'Lotusland.'

Walska's fantasy was that she could sing, which she could not. When her concerts flopped in America she raged at the critics and moved to Paris, where she did no better. A beautiful and forceful woman, she had a particular problem with top notes; what came out was more of a squeak. Audiences laughed, but her husbands, or some of them in turn, encouraged and funded her. She is said to have bought a theatre in Paris complete with orchestra.

On August 23 1937 the London *Times* in its 'Forthcoming Marriages' slot said, 'A marriage has been arranged, and will take place shortly, between Harry Grindell-Matthews, of Tor Cloud, Clydach, and Ganna Walska, of Chateau Galloise, Paris.' Madam Walska was seen at the bungalow. They made a fine pair of fantasists. Matthews may genuinely have believed it was his destiny to save the nation. In that case his stories were not lies: they merely anticipated a future that he convinced himself he was capable of reaching. Or that may be a romantic view, and he was really no more than a self-serving villain.

His biographer, a reporter on the Swansea *Evening Post*, was E.H.G. Barwell, an undemanding observer, whose book *The Death Ray Man* (1941) was sub-titled 'The Biography of GRINDELL MATTHEWS Inventor and Pioneer.' Barwell quoted a letter he received from Walska, who said that Matthews 'carried in him the vision of his Ideal, but never expected it to materialise. When his dream came true he feared to burn his wings, and hesitated, almost preferring illusion to reality. But, God's favourite, he was allowed his dream to come true, and met his twin soul [her, presumably], who, like himself, had given her life to her work.'

The bit about illusion and reality sounds true enough. The marriage didn't last. Death Ray Matthews died not long after, in 1941, two years into World War 2. The internet keeps his story going. His reputation lingers in Upland Gower and the Swansea Valley, but not in the peninsula.

CHAPTER 14

WAR AND MEMORY

THANKS TO TELEVISION, forever recycling World War 2, we know more about the Normandy beaches and Stalingrad than events in British backyards. The latter may not have amounted to much, but they mattered to people at the time. Provincial life was changed in ways barely remembered. Famous air-raids, as in Coventry or Swansea (Swansea's not very famous outside Wales), give a dramatised picture. In the Gower peninsula there wasn't much to dramatise. Whatever happened in Port Eynon or Penclawdd went unreported.

The mood is hard to capture. The Gower doctor before and during the war was W.E. ('Will') Moreton, of Reynoldston, a country GP of a kind no longer found. First-aid equipment and stretchers were stored in the cellar of his house, Brynfield, together with rations for the wounded, in case the enemy came, surging over the beaches or whizzing out of the sky in gliders. Moreton was not a man of nervous disposition, but his elder daughter swears that he kept half a dozen phials of morphine in the medicine cabinet, to make an end of his family if the Germans overran Gower.

Local invasion would have been hampered on the beaches, it was hoped, by stout posts driven into the sand. They were planted at Port Eynon and Rhossili. It sounds like desperation.

The sea soon did for them, tore them out and turned them into driftwood. At Rhossili they were replaced by steel girders. These in turn were bent and abandoned. Here and there along the coast were landmines, in wired-off areas marked with skull-and-crossbone signs. On the dunes near Broughton, wind eroded sand and exposed the mines, like little saucepans. We thought, a pair of us, of lobbing stones from the other side of the dunes, but didn't have the nerve. Swansea had anti-tank blocks of concrete, boy-high if not man-high, lining the edge of the bay, with landmines sown between them. A boy who did have the nerve blew himself up.

The sky, not the sea, was the direction that trouble came from. Since the mid-1930s the Home Office had been begging local authorities to consider air raid precautions, 'A.R.P.' Poison gas was the principal fear, and Swansea sent police and firemen on training courses. But not much happened in the town (and less in Gower, at the time separately administered) until 1938, when Parliament made A.R.P. compulsory, and the initials passed into the language.

The first air-raid warning siren was on top of Cefn Coed, the town's mental hospital, which gave rise to jokes. Trenches for people to jump into during attacks were proposed, and there was trial digging in Singleton Park, but the holes filled with water, and the authorities decided to build public shelters. This programme was still unfinished in 1941 when aircraft from bases in northern France bombed Swansea on three successive nights, 'the Blitz,' culminating on Friday February 21. An early German war directive had Swansea on a short-list of ten ports to be attacked. Whoever wrote it was aware that in the Bristol Channel, with its wide tidal-range, a port could be closed if the sea-locks were destroyed. In the three-night attack, more than 300 people died, hundreds were injured and the town centre ceased to exist. The sea-locks continued to function.

Bombs fell intermittently on Gower. Some residents believed

that fake lights were displayed on hillsides to confuse the enemy. Ilston was showered with incendiaries. Along the north coast bombs exploded in estuary mud and frightened the sheep. A Dornier that had just bombed Swansea was shot down off Port Eynon.

Earlier in the war, nervous citizens panicked and escaped to the peninsula. Bombing had begun in a small way in July 1940. The first serious attack was on the night of September 1-2, and even this was a modest affair, making it possible to count how many high-explosive bombs were dropped: one hundred and six, according to the historian of Swansea air-raids, J. R. Alban. About a thousand incendiary bombs also fell, thin canisters the length of a forearm. The raid killed thirty-three people and injured more than a hundred. Dylan Thomas, in England at the time, wrote to Vernon Watkins in Swansea to say that his mother reported people 'sleeping on the Gower beaches, in barns and hedges.' This may have been exaggerated, knowing Mrs Thomas. But in February 1941, the days of 'the Blitz,' my own mother insisted, to my dismay, that she and I evacuate ourselves after the Thursday-night attack, when a bomb hit the bungalow next door but one. (My father was at Tir John power station on the far side of the town, beyond the docks.) On Friday evening we walked two miles to a suburban rail station, making a detour down a lane to avoid an unexploded bomb, and travelled another ten miles in an unlit train to Llanelly, where we had relatives, arriving in time to see the first German parachute flares floating over Swansea and the fires start to burn.

This kind of flight had happened before, but in reverse. J.D. Davies wrote about 'stirring times' in the early 19th century, when the wicked French seemed likely to invade or at least attack the coasts. 'Gower being particularly exposed in this respect, the inhabitants were continually on the alert day and night; occasionally there were false alarms which caused a stampede to

Swansea, the fugitives leaving everything behind, except what they could carry away on horseback...'

After 1939 there was a general nervousness. A man sailing a dinghy at Oxwich was swept round to Horton, a couple of bays to the west. Police were on the beach waiting to question him. Vernon Watkins, always subject to minor mishaps, went out in a canoe with a friend. When they came ashore at Rhossili after dark, a Home Guard unit decided they were survivors from a crashed German aircraft and arrested them.

Damaged ships, mined or torpedoed in the Bristol Channel, staggered ashore where they could. Swansea smelt of crude oil for weeks at the start of the war when a leaking tanker, the *Seminole*, was beached at Southend, which became a favourite site for emergencies. Over the years, tankers, freighters, landing craft came to rest there, were patched up and towed away. Oxwich Point had an unrepairable wreck that had to be dismantled on the spot.

Much of Fairwood Common, the first open country to the west of Swansea, became R.A.F. Fairwood Common. Before work started in the summer of 1940 there was just time for two Bronze Age burial mounds to be excavated. To secure foundations in the marshy ground, waste material from the vast slagheaps of the lower Swansea Valley was dumped on the common. While the airfield took shape, the Battle of Britain was being fought above southern England. Just down the road in the other direction, at Penrice Castle, Lady Blythswood and guests were able to fit in some sport. In the 1940-41 season, shooters there bagged one thousand one hundred and fourteen pheasants; a meagre haul by past standards.

It took a year to construct the airfield, which opened in June 1941 as a fighter station.

Runway at Fairwood Common, 2008

Fairwood was a bleak place with minimal facilities. Women ground staff, the WAAFs, suffered more than the men, which was not surprising because officially a WAAF was rated as being worth two-thirds of her male equivalent. Telling her story after the war, a two-thirds recruit said that in winter 1941 she and her unit reached Killay rail station at 3.30 a.m., then marched in full kit to the airfield, two miles away. 'We were given a bucket and two blankets, no pillows ... and were told, "Don't use the bucket in the night, it's for getting water to wash with in the morning." We were called out at 5.30 for breakfast.'

Beaufighters, Hurricanes, Spitfires, Typhoons and other varieties were based at Fairwood over the years, and saw action. Later in the war it became an 'armament practice camp' for crews who spent their time, before and after the Normandy invasion, attacking targets in the dunes at Broughton. James Farrar, a pilot (aged twenty) in a fighter squadron, who was there for two months early in 1944, wrote about Fairwood in a story, later published. Officers were billeted in one of two country mansions near the airfield. Farrar may have been at Kilvrough, with 'A view of brown woods, dales, distant hills and headland. [..] There is a farm near the house, run by two Land Girls and a small boy [...] We run a good line in evening excursions here – a small gang of us go out in cars to neighbouring Hot Spots and proceed to liquor up and get to know the inhabitants.' Farrar was posted elsewhere and killed over the English Channel a few months later, the last summer of the war.

Some of Fairwood's buildings and runways survive in a modest way as Swansea's airfield. There is no trace now of a small radar station, associated with Fairwood, that appeared on Rhossili Hill, near the top of the ridge, high above the Old Rectory. Personnel lived in damp brick huts, a mile from the village, which had no pub. The site was still there years after the war ended in 1945, its scanner confronting the weather.

Fairwood also took years to fade away. The control tower was left open (or the locks had been smashed), the ground floor littered with weather maps and signal books. Upstairs were big curved windows overlooking the runways; birds nested on the balcony. This was 1948. There was still life on the site. The YMCA canteen remained open in a hut near the road, as though standing by in case the war started again. In the meantime it sold sandwiches to walkers and motorists. The man behind the counter said they still had aircraft land there. 'A lady' sometimes came over from Llanelly in her private plane; she had usually been drinking and would emerge clutching a bottle of brandy. Her family were brewers. He told me their name in a whisper.

In 1943 American troops came, getting ready for the invasion of Europe. Their camps were all over Swansea and Gower – in Singleton Park, in the grounds of Oystermouth Castle, on the road to Rhossili at Scurlage, at Penclawdd and at Penrice Castle, where men were in tents across the parkland. Their officers were inside, living at the top of the house; rooms were partitioned for them, and electricity reached the attics for the first time. Lady Blythswood, fond of animals, was already host to ninety dogs, acquired when Swansea Dogs' Home closed for the duration. Military manoeuvres went on all over the peninsula, most excitingly when men stormed beaches. Boys made the most of all that. It was possible to watch if you got near the dunes at Oxwich, where you were not supposed to be, and see landing craft, smoke, men running, men shooting, and umpires deciding who was dead.

At the beginning of June 1944, there were suddenly more ships than usual in Swansea Bay, leaving the docks fully laden and

then anchoring. Others entered the bay from the Channel. On Sunday June 4, sixty or so ships were there, facing east into the tide as it ebbed. When it turned, in the middle of the morning, the ships turned with it, slowly, on their anchor chains, as though taking part in a marine display, to face the flood-tide coming up from the west.

That afternoon, or perhaps the day before, two of us went to the end of the Mumbles pier, within earshot of a coasting vessel where black American soldiers were lying on deck in the sun, playing Glen Miller music on a gramophone. 'American Patrol' and 'Chatanooga Choo-choo' came over the water. We hoped they were something to do with invading Europe. By Monday morning the approximate ship-count reached thirty-five freighters and troopships, thirty coasting vessels, half a dozen oil tankers, a few landing craft and a hospital ship. Such a fleet had never been in the bay before, and never will be again.

Swansea Bay from Mumbles, morning of June 5, 1944
(drawn by Rod Cooper from a contemporary note)

Early in the afternoon about half of them sailed, and next morning, Tuesday June 6, the invasion of Europe began. Our ships – people felt proprietorial – couldn't have reached Normandy yet, and the other half had not even left, and didn't until later on Tuesday. The troops, or some of them, were from the American 2nd infantry division, which went ashore at Omaha Beach soon after. They were not part of the initial assault; they were lucky.

American veterans who trained in South Wales before D–Day, or just passed through, still post comments and questions on the net. 'Your message from the fellow in the Headquarters Company, 3rd Battalion, 289th Regiment of the 75th Division who wanted the name of the Welsh village where we trained – I believe the name of the village is PENCLAUDE. They had a particularly great pub there as I recall. My first experience with fish and chips and warm beer.' Another, also at Penclawdd, quotes from his diary. '13 November 1943. C.O. left with basketball team for Gowerton to play an exhibition game for townsfolk.' Already these are memories on the edge of memory.

The Lambs

An old Gower myth or rumour about biological warfare experiments, supposed to have taken place on the northern marshes, has persisted for years. An artillery test-range for 'proving' gun barrels and shells was established at Crofty, near Penclawdd, and for years, big guns fired daily, red flags flew, explosive and non-explosive shells thumped into sand or mud, and the cockle-women had to restrict their hours for cockling. Military sites were supposed to be secret, and false rumours could have sprung up alongside the conventional work of the firing ranges. But the biological-warfare story turns out to be true. The usual test-site for such experiments was the island of Gruinard, known for security reasons as 'X-base,' off north-western Scotland. In 1942 the Burry Estuary – despite the string of adjacent villages on the south side, in Gower, and an industrial town, Llanelly, on the north - was used for an experiment with an anthrax bomb. Just the one, as far as available information goes.

The anthrax organism is not easily destroyed. When the bacteria meet unfavourable conditions (cold and dry rather than warm and moist) they go into a kind of hibernation and become spores. If their situation improves – say, when breathed into an animal or human lung – they become bacteria again. This adaptability makes anthrax ideal for munitions. In extremis, Britain would have used it in shells and bombs. Test results were shared with Canada and the United States, and the latter planned to manufacture anthrax on an industrial scale. But the war ended first.

Extensive tests were needed at Gruinard to see how the weapons performed in different circumstances. In one experiment, an anthrax bomb was dropped from an aircraft. It fell on a marshy surface, and the controlling scientists from Porton Down, the government's experimental station in Wiltshire, needed to know what happened when anthrax bombs hit something firmer. The wide sands of the north Gower coast, swept by strong tides that would disperse and destroy the spores, supplied suitable conditions.

At five in the afternoon of October 28 1942, exactly at sunset, an old-fashioned Blenheim IV bomber flew over the Burry Estuary at 182 m.p.h., height 4950 feet, and dropped a modest (30-lb, 13.5 kilogram) bomb, containing anthrax spores, aimed at sixty sheep, tethered on the sands that lie beyond the marshes. It's not possible to identify the exact dropping point, but it was 'near the mouth of the estuary.' The nearest Gower village was either Llanmadoc, or more likely Landimore, just over two miles to the south. Llanelly, population twenty thousand, was about three and a half miles to the north-east. The wind, very light, was south-east.

The aircraft's course is undisclosed, but its likely approach would have been south-west over Llanelly, where shaded lights were coming on in the wartime 'blackout.' The town would have been highly visible, with its docks and smoking workshops, on the edge of the water. Less than a minute later the bomb-aimer pressed the button. On the sands, the sheep, 'yearling lambs of the Welsh hill type,' were drawn up in two lines. The large number of animals was to counteract 'chance factors.' Attention to detail went so far as to include, among unpredictable events, the possibility that a sheep would hold its breath, presumably aware that something nasty was going on.

The bomb fell twenty yards from the aiming point, an acceptable degree of error. The explosive charge was small, a pop rather than a bang, although one sheep was killed by a bomb splinter. Days later two sheep died of anthrax. All were slaughtered. The experiment was considered 'very satisfactory,' and 'The successful results previously obtained with bombs functioned at rest [on Gruinard] have now been confirmed with a bomb dropped by an aircraft flying at operational height.' Sheep could be fatally infected by such a bomb, and it was deduced that 'deaths in personnel' would have occurred if an enemy unit had been up to 200 yards downwind.

The tide ensured that 'the whole area was [...] effectively decontaminated.' Low water had been two hours earlier, and the sea reached the sands not long after 5 o'clock. There would have been frantic activity, in the dusk, to clear the site and move the animals. There is no evidence that the experiment was repeated in the estuary, although no one is sure what happened on the sands during the war. It is possible that among the conventional shells fired by the guns as part of the weapon-proving process were some that contained unconventional material. A former scientist at Porton says that it is impossible, sixty years later, to know what was going on. It is conceivable that an anthrax simulant was used in other experiments with shells. But there are no files, or if they exist, their existence is not on record.

The official account of the Burry Estuary experiment concludes that 'Further trials to compare directly the width of [anthrax-bearing] cloud produced from bombs dropped and functioned at rest are in progress.' It doesn't say where. Trials are known to have continued at Gruinard in 1943. Unassociated chemical-warfare tests could have taken place in the Burry Estuary, using, for example shells containing mustard gas. Such shells have been found in the area; no one seems to know where they came from. Even the experiment of October 1942 may not have been quite what it seems. The official report blamed marshy ground at Gruinard for making a new test necessary. If that was the reason, why not find a non-marshy bit of Gruinard? Why go to an estuary in Wales and then drop the bomb on sand?

By October 1942, military planners were thinking about the invasion of Europe. The unfortunate raid on Dieppe, two months earlier, had given a foretaste of problems to come. Someone may have considered the possibility that when the invasion took place, a year or two hence, one side or the other would provoke the use of biological weapons. In that case, it would do no harm to see what happened when an anthrax bomb hit a beach.

As for the lambs expended in the trial, they were buried deep, 'at the seaward edge of the marshland area,' and their skeletons must still be there.

CHAPTER 15

'OMIT GOWER'

THE ARTILLERY TESTING RANGE in north Gower worked uneventfully during the war, apart from being a nuisance to the cockle-women, and occasionally killing or maiming one of them. The army camp, and the site where guns and munitions were brought to be test-fired, was at Crofty, on the tongue of land near Penclawdd that ends in Salthouse Point. This north-eastern edge of the peninsula was the only part of Gower served by a railway, necessary to bring in the weapons and munitions. In wartime a government can build whatever it likes wherever it's needed, but in any case the north Gower marshes were not accorded the same respect as the 'golden sands' and 'majestic cliffs' of southern Gower. Wetscapes like the estuary's are more popular now than they were then.

In practice, military establishments where things go bang are usually built in places with little potential for protest. West Wales was useful in that respect. Pendine, across Carmarthen Bay and beyond Laugharne, still has a weapons-testing range. Pembrey, next to Llanelli, had an isolated munitions factory near the beach, built in World War 1, still busy in World War 2. Maps didn't show it; now a country park is there.

In Penclawdd during the war, Army and residents seem to have got on with one another. The guns fired to the west, across four or five miles of mud and sand, the stretch of tidal ground where the unrelated anthrax bomb was dropped. Red flags warned the cocklers, a bold breed of women, when to stay away. If firing finished earlier than expected, the officer in charge phoned the post-mistress, who told the cockle women. Even so, there were accidents. Unexploded shells were not always collected. A cockler with horse and cart was returning from the sands at night, along a track she thought was safe, when the animal trod on a shell, which exploded. The horse was killed; she was unhurt. There are still warning signs in the estuary area. Now and then a rusty shell turns up.

A local band played for the weekly church-hall dance. Girls, coming from miles around, had to queue to get in. The army organised its own concerts. One of the performers was a Private Frank Howard, an unsoldierly soldier who worked as a clerk in the admin office at Crofty, and wanted to be a professional comedian; he used to take a notebook to the Swansea Empire, where old-style music hall was still staged, and write down jokes. The locals took to him. They all heard that he was gay ('queer' would have been the word), and that he was known in his unit as 'Daphne.'

Long after the war, when he was famous and had changed Howard to 'Howerd,' I was writing an article about comedians, and went to meet him in Weymouth, where he was appearing in a variety show. After lunch we took a stroll on the cliffs. It was a warm day, and when we paused and sat down to admire the English Channel, we fell asleep. Waking, both of us faintly embarrassed, we restarted the interview, and he said the sea made him think of the village he spent the war in, a remote army camp in Wales at somewhere called Crofty. 'Nice place,' he said gently, 'very odd,' and left it at that.

The war ended, the establishment closed in 1946, Salthouse Point was no longer behind barbed wire, and the cocklers had no red flags to contend with. Some of the buildings were still there, seven years later, when a car or two turned up, bringing strangers who wandered about making notes. Behind the scenes, Crofty was being reassessed, this time for economic as much as military reasons. The cold war between East and West was under way. America was rearming and wanted to buy British ammunition, and we were stockpiling it as well. The American contract would earn $150 million, at a time when dollars were badly needed in a nation recovering from the economic effects of a long war; in 1953 some foods were still rationed. 'Stringent testing' and 'a tight time-table' made the prompt reopening of Crofty 'imperative.'

A Whitehall document headed SPECIAL URGENCY began, 'The Ministry of Supply require to re-open part of the wartime Proof Range at Penclawdd. The site [...] has an area of roughly 7300 acres [...] The range will be used for proving ammunition, the types to be restricted mainly to the 20 pdr. [pounder] and 25 pdr. guns, i.e. of much smaller calibre than some of the natures [sic] fired when the range was last in operation.' Every effort, it was said, would be made 'to enable the local cockling industry to operate with as little interference as possible [...] it is extremely unlikely that any fixed time-table can be established, but the Ministry will endeavour to achieve a satisfactory working arrangement with the cocklers through friendly cooperation and liaison.'

They were trying. The range would be reopened for only two or three years, and it would keep civilised hours, Monday to Friday, 8 to 5, and Saturdays till noon. There would be jobs for a hundred and twenty people.

Early signs favoured the Ministry. The Nature Conservancy (then only two years old) apparently had no objection. Nor did Gower Rural District Council (R.D.C.). The motto on its Coat of Arms was 'Gloria Ruris Divina,' roughly 'The glory of the countryside is God's.' It saw nothing wrong with reopening the range, as long as the sewage outfall at Salthouse was not interfered with.

The Council for the Preservation of Rural Wales (C.P.R.W.) was told about the proposal at the end of June, and given ten days to respond. It felt it should do something, and on July 1 the

Secretary wrote to the Gower Society, asking for advice. The society had existed since December 1947, a small group at first, bristling with enthusiasm. The status of Gower, and of other 'scenic' areas, changed after the war, as people became more sensitive to the natural scene. Every year brought more cars to remote places. The idea of the 'beauty-spot' as common property to be conserved wasn't new, but its enlistment as political policy was a novelty, not always popular.

The society had already won a skirmish or two. Its chairman and driving force was a bluff, occasionally menacing Swansea doctor ('emotional totalitarianism' was a phrase someone used), Gwent Jones. The letter went to him. Three days later, after talking to colleagues, he wrote a thousand-word reply to the C.P.R.W., aimed at the Ministry. It was a masterpiece of rhetoric. The doctor's defence of cockling dwelt on the work-force – among them eighty women and a number of former coal-miners, their lungs damaged by silicosis – who between them, he said, raked up hundreds of tons a year of food rich in protein. By mentioning the nourishment in cockles he touched on memories of wartime stringency and people's awareness that they still lived in exacting times. Train-loads of cockles left Penclawdd throughout the year, said the doctor. The Romans had cockled there; it was Britain's most historic shell fishery.

What of the growing tourist industry? Where else but Gower could families from the Welsh coalfields go to relax? There was the bird-life question, especially wild-fowl, and of course the noise question and the blast-damage question; there were the unexploded shells and there was the Welsh language. Dr Gwent was a passionate defender of Welsh and Welshness. Early in the war he had been accused of painting 'Wales wants Home Rule, not war,' on a wall not far from where he lived. The case was, of course, dismissed by the local magistrates. Now, in his letter, he managed to turn Penclawdd – its cockles and its Welshness

– into a rallying call for any fellow-countrymen who might be that way inclined, but essentially for the benefit of the men at the Ministry, out of their depth in these matters. If there was a touch of bamboozlement about the doctor's argument, they weren't going to know.

> The size and strength of the Gower Society is only one expression of the affection and esteem which is held by the people of South Wales for the Gower Peninsula, and especially for the remarkable village of Penclawdd, which has been the centre of important sociological and linguistic studies – it is the only Welsh-speaking part of the Gower Peninsula. It is certain that the whole of Wales would be concerned if these proposals affecting Penclawdd were made public.

But it was the cocklers ('hardy and independent') who were the heart of the matter. Even during the war, said Dr Gwent, there were times when they had to defy the rules in order to survive.

A copy of the letter survives in the Ministry of Supply file. The civil servants dealing with the matter had seen trouble coming. In a hand-written minute dated June 27 1953, before Gwent Jones knew anything about reopening the range, an unidentified official asked his unidentified superior, 'I take it there is no objection to sending copy of proposal, with map, to the Gower Society.' On June 29 the recipient sent it back with a scribble in the margin, 'Omit Gower Society.' That was why the letter reached Dr Gwent indirectly, via the C.P.R.W.

When the Ministry realised the strength of feeling, it fell back on 'local consultation.' A semi-private 'conference' was held on the site, in what had been the canteen, at two in the afternoon of July 16. A dozen officials from Supply and other ministries were there. Waiting to speak their mind were representatives of thirteen local interests, among them councils, fisheries, Llanelly Harbour Trust and wild fowlers. The Gower Society was there in the shape of the militant doctor. The list of participants who signed-in has 'Gwent Jones, Chairman, the Gower Society, Royal Institution, Swansea,' in red ink, not blue or black like the other signatories.

In the chair was a Mr Jerman of the Welsh Office, at the time Whitehall's outpost in the west, in Cardiff. It was an informal inquiry, he said, not a public one. There were no journalists, so 'everyone could speak their minds quite freely.' They did just that. A seven-page summary, written for private circulation, shows stubbornness on both sides. A Mr Collier explained the problem. The Ministry of Supply, he said, had three test ranges, which was too few, thanks to rearmament and the American orders for ammunition. Firing-times at Pendine had been increased, but they still needed Crofty 'for a temporary period of about three years.'

Collier, trying to calm fears of unexploded shells, said that those found since the war had probably landed in the sea and drifted in. They used to fire about ten thousand a week, and they couldn't recover them all. He added that when firing was not in progress, the public could access the range area, but 'entirely at their own risk. They should not touch any stray objects which they may find.' The only disturbance, he added, would be to sheep. As for the amenity side of things, the range was 'right away on the less attractive side of the peninsula,' and would not affect Gower as a whole.

A Brigadier Dobbs, 'chief superintendent of ranges,' pointed out that there was a lot more noise at Woolwich Arsenal, where they fired 15-inch guns. He admitted that occasional damage was caused by firing ranges; this, he kindly explained, was because blast could not be controlled. (The brigadier also said, in passing, that 'certain secret experiments' had to be undertaken, a remark that might have raised eyebrows if the meeting had known about the anthrax bomb). A Mr Ferguson said there was no time to waste because it would cost half a million pounds of taxpayers' money if they went anywhere else. A Major Tughill said that the guns used by wild-fowlers upset the wild fowl more than the artillery, though this could have been a joke.

None of the arguments went down well. Gower R.D.C.,

perhaps nervous about disagreeing with Gwent Jones, had changed its mind and was now standing up for cocklers. The man from Llanelly R.D.C. spoke of damage to property and nervous tension among the inhabitants, declaring that it was 'not nice for his wife to suffer the daily "bang-bang" from the range.' Glyn Samuel, the Llanelly Harbour Collector, who more or less ran the moribund port, said that during the war, shells went astray, hit buoys and sank them. Were fishing boats safe?

What about cockles? Gwent Jones was ready with the facts, though he didn't confine himself to fish. He began by saying that the Ministry's case was 'full of "If this" and "We think that".' He then read a long statement. It was so long that he was still speaking when the chairman had to leave to catch his train to London. The doctor overshadowed proceedings. At one point the clerk to the local Llanrhidian council was called on to speak. Gwent Jones pounced. Who, exactly, did this person represent? It turned out that he worked for the Ministry of Supply as 'range warden.' Implicitly, he was employed by the enemy. So he was not allowed to join in, and had to withdraw from the meeting.

The Ministry's 'special urgency' was not enough to save the project. Two months later, in September 1953, the Ministry's Mr Collier telephoned to say it had been decided 'not to proceed for the time being with the proposal.' It was not heard of again. Only some 'Danger' signs are left.

CHAPTER 16

TERRITORY

THE GOWER SOCIETY was founded by optimists at a time, after the war, when the public mood about life in general lay somewhere between hope and resignation. Few were clamouring for an amenity group with high aims. Gower had managed perfectly well in the past. It was a decent place for bathing and walking. You could build a house there if you had the money, or pay the farmer a few pounds and put a caravan in his field for the summer. Only optimists could have seen a future for a society devoted to Swansea's backyard. There were not even guaranteed supplies of paper to print a journal, which was an essential part of the plan, if you could call it a plan.

The prime mover was the suburban-Swansea doctor, Gwent Jones, who was to outflank the armed forces a few years later, in the gun-range affair of 1953. Soon after the war ended in 1945 he was thinking of a local-history society and a journal to go with it. Two students from Swansea who had an interest in Gower history came into his orbit. They were both called Rees, though unrelated. J.E. Rees, a young historian, was just down from Oxford University. The other Rees, David, was at the local university, in Singleton Park. He was keen on archaeology, and at Swansea Grammar School he and I had started an archaeological society. David is the Rees I know about. One afternoon c. 1945 the members (we totalled about six) dug inexpertly into what we hoped was a Bronze Age tumulus on common-land near Cilibion. Two feet down we found a cigarette packet. We all laughed hysterically, except David. We were tickled; he was upset.

He lived in the western suburb of Sketty, and had already met a professional archaeologist with a Gower background, Audrey Williams (she supervised the hasty excavation of Bronze Age mounds on Fairwood Common in 1940, before they disappeared under a runway for ever). She suggested he talk to Gwent, whom he knew already, because Gwent Jones was (I believe) his family doctor, as he was mine.

David was a strange and talented boy, better read and informed than I and most of his peers, fond of girls and Glen Miller and American films but dogged by a social clumsiness that lasted all his life. He tended towards hypochondria – with good reason, as it turned out – and sometimes carried a faint aroma of TCP antiseptic. Perhaps his visits to the doctor, who was interested in the psychological origins of illness, had already made Gwent aware of his abilities.

The doctor's practice extended into the peninsula, and David sometimes went with him on visits to patients, when they would stop at historical sites and take photographs. J.E. Rees was already involved. At one point they thought of calling their group 'The Gowermen.' 'Then,' wrote David later, 'one evening, sitting in Gwent's car on Tycoch Road, the three of us decided to form ourselves into the Gower Society.' At the time I knew nothing of this, and would not have been interested if I had.

The venue has a hint of the clandestine. They feared that an organisation founded by two students and a doctor might not sound weighty enough. Sitting in the car and inventing the society, Gwent said they should invite Ernest Morgan, the former Swansea Borough Architect, to be chairman; they needed endorsement. It was formally set up on December 23 1947. David became less involved than he hoped because as the idea took shape he was diagnosed with tuberculosis in a mass X-ray screening at the university, and disappeared to a sanatorium for two years. Eventually he became a writer, and most of his life was spent in London, though he was often back in Swansea and Gower. In 1962, when Dr Gwent died, aged fifty-two, he wrote in the society's journal, '[I]f Gower has so far been preserved from the schemes of the unspeakable bureaucrat, the predatory developer and the other Goths who infest our society, it is above all to Gwent that we must be grateful.'

The first public meeting was at the Royal Institution ('the Museum') in Swansea in January 1948, when an audience of one hundred and twenty-five turned up. It has flourished ever since, a focus of public and private interest. So has its journal, *Gower*, published yearly, a cumulative record of history and reminiscence that is required reading for anyone who cares about the place. The society was a local, self-generated effort to achieve what soon became a national policy, to save the British countryside, or some of it, from the Goths. The idea of creating 'National Parks' had been around since at least the 1930s. A report published in 1945, immediately after the war in Europe ended, proposed ten National Parks and thirty-four 'amenity areas,' one of which was Gower. (Did the Gowermen already know this when they invented the society?) A fuller report two years later refined the plan, but it was 1956 before Gower became an 'AONB,' a row of civil-service initials that stood for 'Area of Outstanding Natural Beauty.' Gwent was said to have privately persuaded a National Park commissioner.

Well before that, the society was in business, opposing the forces of darkness (or, if you were a developer or a builder, the march of progress). In the society's second summer, 1949, mild panic broke out over rumours that someone wanted to create a holiday camp in the sand-dunes at the Llangennith end of Rhossili Bay. The society prepared to fight ('vandalism, monstrosity'), but if there ever was a serious developer, he retreated; people liked to say, 'Billy Butlin found Gower too hot for him,' though no evidence was ever produced to show that Butlins were involved.

The following year the enemy was more visible. The satisfying ruin of Oxwich Castle, then the responsibility of the Government's Office of Works, was said to be in dangerous condition, and it was soon to be demolished. A working farmhouse was alongside the castle, and the farmer seems to have been keen to get rid of it. Society members, making an 'excursion' to the ruin, were threatened by 'an Alsatian dog and a bull.' When farm and castle were offered for sale, Lady Blythswood of Penrice Castle, just up the hill from Oxwich, was persuaded to persuade an English relative, Lady Apsley, to buy it for £5,000. Again, Gwent Jones was involved. The Office of Works changed its mind about demolition, and all was peaceful, except that Lady Apsley, having become a local landowner, announced that Oxwich woods, which came with the castle, had no public footpaths, and walkers were banned. After negotiation, she conceded that Gower Society members could walk there if they wore a badge. Somebody, probably Gwent, persuaded her not to be silly.

The society prospered, addressing issues great and small. Egg-stealing on the Worms Head became a police matter, with the chief constable promising to stamp it out; a progress report in 1949 said that 'despite keen watch, no one had been apprehended.' Red double-decker buses were being used as chicken sheds. Car-racing was proposed on the abandoned Fairwood airfield (1953). The theoretically hard-up Methuen-Campbells at Penrice were said to be thinking (in 1956) of leasing foreshore rights in Oxwich Bay to the Gower Beauty Parks Development Co., which had interests in fun-fairs. The minutes record that the syndicate 'took its interest elsewhere ... all we can wish is god-speed on their journey from Gower.'

Fairwood and the Oxwich foreshore were left alone, perhaps because of the society, perhaps not. But the society had a cumulative effect. Many of the issues were minor. A stile was blocked, a hedge needed watching. 'Travelling salesmen' were on the beaches in a heat-wave (1949). Cars were parking on cliff-tops. They were driving on to the sands at Llangennith. The stranded *Cleveland* was still on the beach there in 1959, and some of the steel, which no one seemed to want any more, had been buried on the spot. The War Office yearned for an ammunition dump on the Mumbles Head. Someone had gone to seek out the bones of Paviland's Red Lady and found them (1950) in a cupboard in Oxford; they ought to come back, thought the society, but didn't have much hope.

At Rhossili, in 1959, some bounder planned to build a road around the base of the hill and set up a tea-room in an old outhouse; he was a coal-merchant as well as being from London, which made it worse. Rumours suggested that the Penrice estate was involved. Christopher Methuen-Campbell issued a pained denial. Rhossili's 'grandeur and unique beauty' were untouchable; nothing would change. Attention to detail seems overdone at times. As working parties in the field complained (1951), 'some activity more exciting than picking broken glass from dead grass would appeal more.' But the society felt it needed to be rigorous in all directions, and no doubt it was right.

New houses had to be kept an eye on. Many were 'at shocking variance' with the landscape (1950). When council houses were being built at Nicholaston, the society said, recklessly, that they ought not to have roads or pavements (1951). The peninsula was being 'suburbanised,' which of course was what most people wanted. I knew a resident in the 1950s, a retired man short of funds which he needed to repair and improve his own, seriously old property in a village, who sold off an adjoining field that he owned, which made life easier for him and his family. He would have rejected the idea that he was rapacious, or uncaring about a village his forbears had lived in; he was just provident. A small estate went up in the field and is still there, hardly 'suburban' but hardly 'rural' either.

Caravans were the unsolvable problem, as they still are. Complaints in the 1950s that they were 'insanitary' may have been a way of condemning them without actually saying that they were a blot on the landscape and should be thrown in the sea, as some would have liked. They could be controlled, that was all. Gower R.D.C. let Port Eynon have fifteen more in 1960, as if they were rationed, after which there were forty-two. Where would it all end? It is still said, in the Gower Society, that at least one large, sprawling site by the sea might have been nipped in the bud in 1960, when the Caravan Act gave local authorities the power to object to existing sites, and Gower R.D.C. did nothing till it was too late. Perhaps it weighed up both sides and decided on masterly inactivity.

Over the years the society has sometimes had an uneasy relationship with the local authority, or, more exactly, with councillors rather than council officials. Gower R.D.C. is long gone, and the City and County of Swansea now rules in the peninsula as well. Until recently (it is said, in Gower) there used to be a feeling among the city's elected representatives, who were likely to lean to the Left, that people living west of the Mumbles could look after themselves, presumably unlike the downtrodden city-dwellers. A trace survives of the days when Swansea's western suburbs – half-way to Gower – were seen as snobbish by those on the east side. Sketty, where I was born, was mocked in the ancient aphorism, 'All fur coat and no knickers.' By 2008, local-authority antipathy, or indifference, to Gower was said to be in decline. For the moment, peace reigned between east and west.

Small dramas are played out. A hypothetical farmer might have a tiny caravan tucked away in a field for years, long enough to become a fixture. Then he swaps it for a large caravan. If he sells it, he can make a small fortune. Planning law on caravans is complex. A surveyor is said to go from place to place, advising.

The society knows it is unpopular with people who are not allowed to have a caravan on a headland or a house with funny chimneys. It is not the Gower Society that has stopped them; all the society can do is inform, advise and publicise. But it has a reputation for exerting influence that it doesn't go out of its way to deny.

The Prince and the Stone

In 1998 the society had its fiftieth anniversary, which it celebrated with outings, expeditions and lectures. A loan of the Red Lady's bones from Oxford was sought but refused. The lord mayor of Swansea gave a reception. And the heir to the throne, who was going to be in Wales briefly during the summer, agreed to perform a ceremony in the peninsula. On a Sunday morning he would be at Cefn Bryn to inaugurate a footpath. A five-ton chunk of stone with a plaque had been set up near the eastern end of the hill, above Penmaen. He would unveil it. One Prince, one good cause. There was nothing to go wrong.

The Society had conceived the idea of a path called 'The Gower Way,' to run the length of both the Gowers, peninsula and upland, from Rhossili at one end to Penlle'r Castell thirty-five miles away at the other. It was a concept, not a physical project. The paths were there already, although some local clearing and signposting were needed. Where the route has to pass under the M4 motorway, it is briefly the main road. But in general it reminds people that there are two Gowers and that you can walk from one to the other. The route east from Rhossili crosses Cefn Bryn, and the hill is conveniently close to Penrice Castle, where royal visitor and Gower Society committee were to go for lunch.

The night before the Prince was due at the Stone, another (and rougher) Gower – a place where things go wrong, and in time get turned into stories – made itself felt. This particular story was hushed up. Only a few people ever knew, and they have kept quiet. The journalists who were there – a couple of newspaper reporters, a camera crew making a film about Prince Charles for Canadian television – saw nothing. There was nothing to see: that was the point. Around eight o'clock in the morning, which was damp and windy, a man who was staying at the King Arthur in Reynoldston went for an exercise-run by himself, on one of his usual routes, south-east across the hill to the 'reservoir,' an underground storage facility near the eastern end of the ridge above Penmaen. The path through the bracken is part of the Gower Way. The runner, who was my son, J., knew vaguely about the Stone and the Prince's visit. When he reached the end of the crest, he saw that it had moved since the day before. It was fifteen yards downhill, in the bracken, accompanied by tractor marks.

J. knew that one of the Gower Society's officers lived nearby, Edward Harris. His house was below the ridge, at Penmaen. J. proceeded downhill and banged on the door, but E.H. was away and visitors were staying. They let him in and he got E.H. on the phone. The society had about three hours. Its chairman, Malcolm Ridge, who also lives at Penmaen, organised the labour

and a tractor to have the Stone dragged uphill and put back on its plinth. In due course J. returned, this time with his two sons, aged five, ready to see the Prince perform. 'You got it back pretty quick,' he said to the Gower Society principals. 'Got what back?' they said. It had not happened. The Stone had not moved. No one was willing to breach security by saying thank you.

Soon the Prince arrived in a 4x4 from Fairwood airport, a police vehicle in attendance. By now the Stone was draped in the society's flag, fishing weights sewn along the edges so it wouldn't blow away. The ceremony consisted of Prince removing flag from Stone. People clapped. As the 4x4 drove off, down to Penrice and a jolly lunch, he waved. J. says he thought he was going to be knighted on the spot. But the visitor was waving to one of my grandsons, perched on his father's shoulder.

Long afterwards, when I spoke about the incident to the equable Malcolm Ridge, whom I didn't know in 1998, he said, 'How on earth did you hear about that? We clamped the lid on that very, very tightly.'

A motive for Stone-shifting is hard to find. It must have been a few Saturday-night drunks, thinking, what a laugh, take a tractor up there, it'll be on the telly, 'I say, you cheps, show a bit of respect.' Perhaps. Or does a trace of antipathy to 'incomers' survive, an ancient resistance to those who act in the interests of outsiders, who think that the raw and awkward and primitive have gone for ever?

There is still a core of people who have Gower in their blood. Mansel/Talbot genes remain in place at Penrice Castle, but they are not the only family to remember a long past. A Lucas was there till recently, and may be again. The Gibbs family hovers nearby, at Gowerton, in the shape of Michael Gibbs. They have been in the area at least since 1417; a family tale says they arrived in a rowing boat, perhaps from north Devon, unless it was south Pembrokeshire, or Kidwelly on Carmarthen Bay. They were at the Oxwich affray of 1557 (the Battle of the Figs). A Gibbs wielded a spade at Paviland cave.

The current Michael Gibbs, whose benign presence can be felt throughout this book, lives outside Gower, though not by choice. 'Of course people resent things,' he says. 'My grandfather moved out of Horton and went to Swansea in 1900. My father couldn't afford to move back there. Neither can I. But I am proud to have brought up my sons to be *of* Gower. We shall get back there one day. It's where we belong.'

Gower's far past was full of invading strangers. Territory matters. Years after the night of the tractor, the Stone, long since concreted into the plinth, had its gunmetal plaque attacked. This time it was a person with a hammer. A metalworker was commissioned to replace it. He said he counted one hundred and seven blows.

NOTES

Introduction

10   The Viking legend: J.D. Davies tells it twice, Vol. 3, p. 26, and Vol. 1, p. 20, where he gives Lady Wilkinson as the source. She was a Gower woman married to Sir Gardner Wilkinson, an Egyptologist, who later wrote about Gower antiquities. They lived at Brynfield, Reynoldston. Jason Thompson and Robert Lucas, 'Sir Gardner Wilkinson in Gower,' *Gower* 46 (1995).

1   Origins

12ff   St Madoc's church: G.R. Orrin, *The Gower Churches*, p. 44.

14   New Year's Day, 1136: Gerald of Wales mentions the incident in *The Journey Through Wales,* Ch. 9.

14-15   Davies at Llanmadoc: F.G. Cowley, 'Revd. John David Davies: Anglo-Catholic Pioneer, Woodcarver and Local Antiquary,' *Morgannwg* (journal of Glamorgan History Society) Vol. XXXVIII (1994). 'Popery' protests: R.L.T. Lucas, *Gower* 33 (1982), 'Llanmadoc and "The Scarlet Woman".'

15   Davies's ghost: see Ch. 12.

16   'hovel': the Radnorshire diarist, the Rev. Francis Kilvert, visited Davies on April 16 1872. 'He took us into the Churchyard, but let us find our own way into the Church, which was beautifully finished and adorned but fitted up in the high ritualistic style. The Vicar said that when he came to the place the church was meaner than the meanest hovel in the village.' *Kilvert's Diary* (1960 edition), Vol. 2.

16-17   Christopher Lewis's story: Davies, Vol. 2, p. 3.

17   The 'Advectus' stone: Davies, Vol. 2. He wrote (pp. 76-7): '[Initially] I thought the first line of the inscription was one word – VICARIVS – and the first word of the second line, SWAN, and supposed that this was a sepulchral stone to the memory of a former incumbent named Swan, of whom there remained no other record [...] [T]hat it had been so read in former days I have very little doubt, hence the origin of the name of a small meadow – "Swan's Meadow" – near the Church, where in all probability the stone was originally found, and where most likely it had stood for many ages before it was taken and used as a quoin stone in the parsonage house.' There is no agreed translation of the words on the stone; see www.ucl.ac.uk/archaeology.

18   Man in chimney: Davies, Vol. 2, p. 61.

18-19   The six-bedroom rectory: Peter and Sally Lyne, the present occupants, who possess Davies correspondence and other papers, have uncovered a small mystery. When Kilvert visited Llanmadoc (p. 16, above), he noted the 'bare unfinished ugly barracks of a Rectory.' This is assumed to have been Davies's new residence in the making. But it was another four years before he applied to 'the Governors of Queen Anne's Bounty' for an £800 loan 'to rebuild the Parsonage House of Llanmadoc, which has got into such a decayed and ruinous state that I cannot with any comfort or safety reside in it much longer.' The letter is dated January 21 1876.

20-21   St Cennydd legend: Davies, Vol. 3, pp. 11-25.

21   'College Farm' etc: F.G. Cowley, 'Llangenydd and its priory,' *Glamorgan Historian*, Vol. 5 (1968).

21-2   Burry Holms service: Canon Williams, pers. communication.

22   Reasons to be there: I was born and brought up in Swansea, and lived there till January 1953, when I moved to London. In December 1953 I married Gloria Moreton, elder daughter of the Gower doctor, W.E. Moreton, though the marriage was later dissolved. The Moretons' family house was Brynfield, in Reynoldston. Gloria and I stayed there often; both our children were born in the house.

2   Hanged Man

23   John Mansel, 1201: Joanna Martin, pers. communication, 19.9.2007.

24-37   William Cragh's story: A.T. Bannister, *The Cathedral Church of Hereford, its History and Constitution*, 1924; Jussi Hanska, 'The hanging of William Cragh: anatomy of a miracle,' *Journal of Medieval History* 27, 2001, pp. 121-138; Robert Bartlett, *The Hanged Man. A story of miracle, memory, and colonialism in the Middle Ages*, 2004. The primary source of their material – and mine, via them – is the Vatican archive which contains (in Latin) the testimony of witnesses given in London and Hereford.

24   de Breos origins: the name is from Braose, near Falaise, in Normandy. William the Conqueror was born there.

25   'I had a girl': Hywel ab Owain Gwynedd (c. 1140-1170), 'In Praise of Fair Women,' Joseph P. Clancy (ed.), *Medieval Welsh Poems*, pp. 137-8.

25   'I saw savage troops': Cynddelw Brydydd Mawr (fl. 1155-1200), 'In praise of Owain Gwynedd,' Clancy, op. cit., p. 148. Owain Gwynedd was the ruler who did the blinding and emasculating.

26   Red Book of Hergest: A Welsh manuscript book of prose and poetry, bound in red leather, dating from the late 14th century, although the contents are thought to be older. It is at the Bodleian Library.

27   Pennard manorial court: David Leighton, 'Some aspects of life and economy in medieval Pennard,' *Gower* 55 (2004), pp. 34-5.

27   November 1290: The year is unproven, but is the likeliest. The month is almost certainly correct.

27   Swansea Castle: First mentioned in 1116, when it was still an earth-and-timber structure, not on the same site. The stone castle, built by the de

Breoses, had probably replaced it by 1290. In the 18th-19th centuries it was used variously as a town hall and a prison. A newspaper office was built into it in the 20th century and the *South Wales Evening Post* was still being edited and printed there in the 1950s; when the presses were in action, the building trembled. In 1957 there were plans to demolish it. The castle survived and is still there, a rather small ruin. W.H. Jones, *History of Swansea and of the Lordship of Gower*, Vol. 1 (1870), pp. 267ff; Edith Evans, *Swansea Castle and the medieval town* (1983); pers. knowledge.

27 de Breos Jnr, the unsavoury son: W.H. Jones, op. cit., p. 279. '[He] proved to be the worst of all the De Breos type, fraudulent and deceitful in disposition... hated and feared by all about him.'

29 'The Round School' was built in 1932. It is semi-circular, but from below, the crescent creates the illusion.

33 Seventeen miracles: Bannister, op. cit. pp. 167ff. Among them were several women cured of paralysis, four drowned children who came back to life, and another hanged person, a woman. Her body was given to the family, who revived her with warm beer.

33 silver ships, wax men: Bannister, op. cit.

36-37 who saved Cragh? Bannister's 1924 account says the evidence shows 'with quite sufficient clearness' that there was 'a plan arranged to save the man's life, a plan in which Lady Mary [...] herself took part.' Bannister assumes that her motive was simply that she felt 'sorry for the man.'

36 de Breoses related to Canteloups: Bartlett, op. cit., p. 115; 'Our Folk' Website, www.renderplus.com; Wikipedia.

36 'Black William': even by de Breos standards he came to a distressing end. He made an alliance with the leading Welsh prince of the day, Llewelyn the Great, but at Easter 1230 he was caught in Llewelyn's bedroom with the latter's wife, Joan, daughter of the English King John (she had been made to marry Llewelyn twenty-five years earlier, when she was aged ten and he was thirty-two). Next day Llewelyn hanged him in public at Aber, North Wales. There is a vague tradition that he was buried in Gower. The Welsh writer Saunders Lewis's sympathetic play *Siwan* (Welsh for Joan) is based on the affair. There are many accounts. The story is retold succinctly by Gary Gregor, 'The Welsh dramatist, the English Princess and the Norman knight,' *Gower* 56 (2005).

37 death of de Breos senior: Hanska, op. cit., p. 135 cites an order of Edward I, dated January 6 1291, which refers to 'the lands late of William de Breus.' Hanska adds, 'There is no possibility of error since there are two other royal documents on the same matter.'

3 Red Lady

39 knowledge of bones: Buckland, *Reliquiae Diluvianae*, p. 82.

39 Gower's first doctor: Davies, Vol. 3, p. 120. 'The first resident medical

practitioner was Mr Daniel Davies, Surgeon, of Reynoldston, who died at a very advanced age a few years ago, and who came into this district about the year 1816.'

39   Prospect Cottage: *Cambrian*, June 26 1823, records the marriage of Mr Davies, surgeon, of Prospect Cottage, Reynoldston, to Sarah Bristow of Sussex.

39   Unrelated Davieses: some accounts say they were brothers; they were not. Davies's family history is well documented. Also he mentions them both in the same sentence (Vol. 3, p. 228). If they were related he would have said so.

40ff   Buckland and his work: Professor Jim Kennedy, Director, Oxford University Museum of Natural History, pers. communication. The museum has an informative website. The Red Lady has generated a vast literature. For clarity and insight, see a 1942 paper by F. J. North of the National Museum of Wales: *Annals of Science* Vol. 5, No. 2, pp. 91-128.

40   The king's heart: Nicolaas A. Rupke, *The great chain of history. Wm Buckland & the English School of Geology (1814-1849)* (1983), p.255.

40   Rev. John Davies Snr. and the Talbots: Diary of L.W. Dillwyn, September 23 1818: 'Sir Chr. Cole & Revd. Mr Davis [sic] of Porteynon came to Dinner, after a hard days convass in Landilo tal y bont.'

In 1818 Cole, a former naval officer, was the head of the Talbot household. T.M. Talbot had died in 1813, and his widow, Mary, married Captain Cole two years later. Cole, who had political ambitions, contested and won the Glamorganshire seat at the 1818 General Election. Richard Morris has the diaries of Dillwyn, leading Swansea industrialist (and naturalist) of his day, at present unpublished.

40-1   Talbots and natural history: Joanna Martin, *Wives and Daughters. Women and children in the Georgian country house* (2004), Ch. 11. Dr Martin, a Talbot descendant, is the family chronicler.

41   Crawley Rocks: Buckland, *Reliquiae Diluvianae*, pp. 80-1.

41   Buckland to Miss Talbot, 26.11.1821: National Museum of Wales, NMW 84.20G.D162. Buckland letters at the museum are in the De la Beche Archive, Department of Geology.

41-2   flowers on pottery: D.J. Harris, 'The rise and decline of the Swansea ceramics industry,' *Gower* 37 (1986). Jonathan Gray, pers. communication.

42   Sir H. Davy, 1778-1829, chemist, inventor of the safety lamp for miners: Dillwyn diary, 1.3.1822. W.H. Wollaston, 1766-1828, pioneering physicist: 27.10.1819. Sir J. Banks, 1743-1820, botanist and explorer: 5.12.1819. British Museum: 4.11.1822.

42   'Penllergare': this version has been in use since the early 1800s, and is shown thus on the seal of the estate office. Richard Morris, pers. communication.

42   Sir Christopher Cole: see Note to p. 40. Although he married the owner's widow, a Talbot trust kept control of the estate, and Capt. Cole had to pay rent to live at the castle: Martin, op. cit., p. 337.

42   Buckland to Lady Mary, Christmas Eve 1822: NMW 84.20G.D165.

43   J. M. Traherne: John Montgomery Traherne, 1788-1860, had a brief career as a practising clergyman, then came into money and settled down to collect old books and manuscripts. In 1830 he married one of the Talbot daughters, Charlotte.

43   acknowledging a tooth. NMW 84.20G.D166.

43-4   'went immediately': *Reliquiae Diluvianae*, p.83.

44ff   tides at Paviland. Predicted times of low water 1823: Jan 18, 03.15, 15.41. Jan 19, 03.54, 16.24. Jan 20, 04.41, 17.15. Jan 21, 05.43, 18.27. Jan 22, 07.08, 19.56. The predictions are for the Mumbles, but there is no significant time-difference. Source: UK Hydrographic Office. The cave is accessible for about two and a half hours either side of low water.

44   John Dillwyn's letter: Richard Morris, unpublished ms.

44-5   frosty roads: Dillwyn's diary, Jan. 22, 'The Frost continues unusually severe.'

47   Buckland to Lady Mary: 15.2.1823, NMW 84.20G.D167.

48   grave explosion: Oxford University Museum of Natural History website.

48-9   a very old Red Lady: Stephen Aldhouse-Green, *British Archaeology*, October 2001, '[When the Red Lady was unearthed, he] was not only the first such burial to be found but also the first human fossil to have been recovered anywhere in the world.'

       Aldhouse-Green edited the comprehensive *Paviland Cave and the 'Red Lady'. A definitive report* (2000).

49   Redating the skeleton: R.M. Jacobi and T.F.G. Higham, 'The "Red Lady" ages gracefully: New ultrafiltration AMS determinations from Paviland.' *Journal of Human Evolution* 55 (2008), pp. 898-907.

4   Bay

51   Port Eynon's prayer: Michael Gibbs, pers. communication.

51-2   'immense crowd': R.L.T. Lucas, 'The Lucases at Rhossili rectory,' *Gower* 25 (1974).

52   invasion obstacles: pers. knowledge

53   copper keel: Jack Bevan, B.B.C. radio, 'Country Magazine' No. 149 (1948).

53ff   *City of Bristol*: Gary Gregor, 'The "City of Bristol" Shipwreck,' *Gower* 49 (1972) is one of many accounts. Wrecking and inquest reports are in the *Cambrian*, November 20 and 27 1840.

56   William Poole and the caul: Jonathan Hill, a descendant, on the 'welcome to gower' website.

          - a caul in Gower: pers. knowledge.

58   *Handbook for Travellers*: John Murray, London, pp. 38-9.

59-60   Blue Pool gold: Davies Vol. 3, p. 147.

60   Norman doorway: G.R. Orrin, op. cit., p. 77.

60-1   earlier Rhossili church: L.A. Toft, 'The twin settlements of medieval Rhossili,' *Gower* 36 (1985).

61   Llanelli pilots: pers. knowledge.

61   Southey's nephew: R. Lucas, *Rhossili* (2004) p. 42.

          - Southey at Port Eynon: Michael Gibbs, pers. communication.

61   'old & ratty rectory': Dylan Thomas, *Collected Letters* (2000 edition), to Idris Davies, 16.2.1953.

62   Dylan Thomas and Gower: Evelyn Burman Jones ('rude bathing' etc.): Ferris, *Dylan Thomas*, Y Lolfa edition, pp. 95-6.

62   'dirty weekend' letter: *Collected Letters*, op. cit., May 27 1934.

64   a day at The Garth: Gwen Watkins: *Dylan Thomas: portrait of a friend* (1983, 2005).

5   Estuary

65   stepping stones: Davies, Vol. 2, p. 46.

65   Pembrey and Llangennith: Davies, ibid; National Library of Wales, Ashburnham 1 and 2. My informant: Sally Lyne of Llanmadoc.

66   'green meadow': Davies, Vol. 2, p. 55.

66   favoured nations: Rupke, op. cit., pp. 264-5, quotes a summary of a Buckland speech in 1839, where he suggested that the 'immeasurable beds' of iron-ore, coal and limestone near Birmingham were not there by accident, but expressed the 'clear design of Providence' to make Britain 'the most powerful and the richest nation on earth.'

67   'this peculiar advantage': Llanelly Tide Table, 1831.

67   Anne Lewis: she is named in Davies's will.

67-8   man without a hat and the disaster: Davies Vol. 2, pp. 63-4. *Cambrian* 24.1.1868 and (inquest) 31.1.1868.

68   'natural order of things': the January 24 *Cambrian* that reported the 'fearful disaster' at Broughton had a brief report of an incident a week earlier, when the *Albion*, a brig, was seen to be stranded on a sandbank in the Burry Estuary, after which seven bodies were washed up. They were presumably trying to escape the wreck.

69-70   Ossie Roberts, last of the Llanelli pilots: interview, 10.1.86.

70 landing craft at Llanelli: *Gower* 56 (2005), p. 30; pers. knowledge.

71 novel of the sixties: *The Destroyer* (1965). In the book they got her off.

6 The People

72 Bacon Hole: Christopher Stringer, 'Evidence of climatic change and human occupation during the last interglacial at Bacon Hole cave, Gower,' *Gower* 28 (1977).

72 Park-le-Breos cairn: www.whitedragon.org.uk

72-3 Arthurs Stone: Kate Bosse-Griffiths, 'The secret of Arthurs stone,' *Gower* 8 (1955). T.R. Owen, 'Further thoughts on Arthurs stone,' *Gower* 16 (1963).

73 Minchin Hole: Gerald Gabb, *Swansea and its history*, Vol. 1, pp. 287-92.

73 coins at Southgate: ibid, pp. 262-3.

73 farm bailiff: pers. knowledge.

74 Danish vessels: Davies, Vol.1, p. 20.

74 The Wilkinsons and Brynfield: Jason Thompson and Robert Lucas, 'Sir Gardner Wilkinson in Gower,' *Gower* 46 (1995). 'Formerly called Shepherd's Lodge, it became dilapidated towards the end of the eighteenth century, and in 1800 it was let to the Rev. James Edwards, Rector of Reynoldston, who rebuilt the house and named it Brynfield. [Wilkinson realised that the house] was on a dwelling site of great antiquity. In the grounds [...] is a circular bank and ditch probably dating back to the pre-Roman period. [During renovations Wilkinson found traces of an old window and fragments of painted glass, dated to c. 1400]. Caroline Wilkinson suggested that this was once the site of a religious house of the sisterhood of St Clare, but there is no known evidence to support her supposition.'

74 'a bloody battle': Davies, Vol. 1, p. 21.

75-6 the 'Doolamurs': Edward A. Martin speculates that they are Sir John Penrice (d. 1410) and his wife, not de la Mares. 'The Doolamur and the Dolly Mare: two medieval effigies,' *Gower* 30 (1979).

76 'From time immemorial': Davies, Vol. 4, p. 123.

76 drowned Knight: ibid, p. 124.

76-7 'Memorial at Oxwich': *Gower* 23 (1972).

77-8 Timothy's diary: 'The diary of John Timothy – 1864,' Introduction by R.O. Roberts, *Gower* 29 (1978).

78 'Honored Sirs': Michael Gibbs, 'The Gibbs Family,' *Gower* 27 (1976).

79-80 Harriet's family: Michael Gibbs, '"Dear Stay-at-Home",' *Gower* 34 (1983).

80 Collins on gin at Oxwich: *Gower* 22 (1971), p. 26.

81   Mr Leyshon's remedy: Davies, Vol. 3, pp. 122-3.

81   Mary Bennett's inventory: R.L.T. Lucas, 'Reflections on some Gower wills,' *Gower* 35 (1984).

82   Llanrhidian trades and population: R.N. Cooper, *Higher and Lower*, pp. 121, 123.

82   'great famine': Davies, Vol. 2, p. 103.

82   cow dung: Davies, Vol. 4, p. 139.

82-3   land ownership and David Williams: M.E. Chamberlain, 'The Gower farm labourer: vintage 1893,' *Gower* 25 (1974).

83   children kept from school: W.J.M. Gilchrist, 'Unwillingly to school,' *Gower* 27 (1976)

83   'doomed to a life of toil': source uncertain; probably *Gower Church Magazine*.

84-5   Richard John goes to school: Iorwerth Hughes Jones, 'Another chapter in the story of the John family of Ty'r Coed,' *Gower* 21 (1970).

84   the railway, 1866; the cockle trains: Cooper, op. cit., p. 96; also Cooper, *A dark and pagan place*, also p. 96.

85   photograph in cottages: Jack Bremmell, 'Change – though not decay,' *Gower* 3 (1958). Michael Gibbs, pers. communication.

86   Sollas photograph: Gabb, op. cit., p. 206.

86   Collins' diary: quoted in Robert Lucas, 'John Collins of Oxwich,' *Gower* 38 (1987).

86   Talbot support: F.G. Cowley, 'Revd John Davies: Anglo-Catholic Pioneer [etc],' *Morgannwg* XXXVIII (1994).

86-7   Talbot gifts: Robert Lucas, *Gower* 38, op. cit.

87   noisy children: Orrin, op. cit., p. 17.

87   'my joy': R.N. Cooper, *Higher and Lower*, p. 74.

87   'What a cheek!': Mrs Mary Morgan.

88   Sunday school outing: O. Tregelles Williams, 'Outing to Worms Head, 1854,' reprint of a radio talk, *Gower* 14 (1961).

88   Florentia marries William: R.L.T. Lucas, 'A Gower wedding in 1870: the Woods and Crawshays,' *Gower* 32 (1981).

89   bell-ringers at Cowbridge: Joanna Methuen-Campbell, 'Life at Penrice castle, c. 1800,' *Gower* 25 (1974).

89   'Horse's Head': Michael Gibbs, 'Old Christmas customs of Gower,' *Gower Gazette* No. 4. Davies, Vol. 2, p. 84. 'The custom of going about with the Horse's Head at Christmas time is not peculiar to Wales, and answers to what in Kent is called "Hodening," the Welsh call it Mary Llwyd.'

89   St George: Davies, Vol. 2, p. 85.

89   The Mabsant: Davies, Vol. 3, pp. 104-6. Michael Gibbs was once given 'whitepot' by his aunt; it was 'really dreary.'

89   William Griffiths: Robert Lucas, *Rhossili*, p. 36.

90   'a very pretty smart girl': Thomas Lloyd, 'The diary of a visitor to Swansea and Gower in 1821,' *Gower* 34 (1983).

91   Russell Davies paper: '"In a broken dream": Some aspects of sexual behaviour and the dilemmas of the unmarried mother in south west Wales, 1897-1914,' *Llafur* III, 4 (1983).

92   traction engines: J.D. Davies, Vol. 4, p. 44.

92   Patti on the phone: *South Wales Evening Post*, 18.8.1954, article about 'old Swansea,' citing an 1893 publication.

93   British Association: Margaret Walker, 'The British Association in Swansea in 1848,' *Gower* 22 (1971).

93   on strike, 1892: Gerald Gabb, 'Some cracks in the fabric of Victorian Swansea,' *Gower* 44 (1993).

93-4   T.U.C. 1901: 'Congress Souvenir. The Authorised Official Guide.' The poem runs to about seventy lines. The poet, (Sir) Lewis Morris, wanted healthier dwellings and better wages. He also hoped that workers' lives would become 'sober, provident, pure.'

94   wreath of sand: Davies, Vol. 2, p. 120. The spirit of a woman farmer who had cheated her customers was exorcised by a clergyman, who condemned her 'to make ropes of sand on Llanmadoc burrows.'

7   Race Relations

95-6   Robert Craven and the Star Chamber: *A catalogue of Star Chamber proceedings relating to Wales* [in the Tudor period], compiled by Ifan ab Owen Edwards (1929), p. 43.

96   'vitriolic letters': Alan Davies, Llandrindod, to the *Western Mail*, 12.7.2008.

96   'land of two peoples': Rees Davies, 'The identity of "Wales" in the thirteenth century,' in R.R. Davies and Geraint H. Jenkins (eds.), *From medieval to modern Wales* (2004).

97   Rhys Gryg's attack: *Brut y Tywysogyon* or 'The chronicle of the princes,' in the 'Red Book of Hergest' version, tr. Thomas Jones (1955). The Brut, an ancient history of Wales, is itself a translation of lost documents, covering a period from the 7th to the 13th centuries. No doubt written by monks, it blames the many troubles of the Welsh on their sinful behaviour.

98   'an end to English speech': O. Morien Morgan, *The Battles of Wales. The unconquered country of the empire* (1920).

98   Swansea castle accounts; Owen Glyndourdy: W.H. Jones, *The history of*

Swansea and of the lordship of Gower Vol. 2 (1992), pp. 38ff.

98   Glyndwr and the prophecy: Diane M. Williams, *A guide to ancient and historic monuments on* [sic] *the Gower peninsula* (Cadw, 1988), p. 20.

98-9   'Old Boney': Phoebe Simons, 'From the horse's mouth – I,' *Gower* 6, p. 3.

99   Gower worth £100: William Rees, *South Wales and the March 1284-1415. A social and agrarian study* (1924) p. 277.

99   dubious report: Davies, Vol. 1, p. 27.

99   'Welsh Border': *The Bread of Truth* (1963). It is not in Thomas's *Collected Poems*.

100   1823 Guide: quoted in Robert Penhallurick, *Gowerland and its language* (n.d.) (publisher Peter Lang, Germany).

100   A.G. Bradley: quoted in David Rees (ed.) *A Gower anthology* (1977), p. 41.

100-1   Gerald of Wales: Lewis Thorpe, intro. and tr., *Gerald of Wales, The journey through Wales and The description of Wales* (Penguin Classics edition, 2004). Lynn H. Nelson, *The Normans in South Wales, 1070-1171* (1966), p. 175.

102   'Kilvrough' v. 'Cilfrwch': David Rees, 'Map making in Gower,' *Gower* 21 (1970).

102-3   'Ffosfelin': Michael Gibbs, pers. communication. The earliest spelling is equivocal. 'It could have been "felin" for mill or "felyn" for yellow. I know that if you dig down two feet in Gowerton the water turns yellow.'

8   Family Affairs

105-6   The Phillipe Mansel story: Dr Joanna Martin, a Methuen-Campbell, says, 'I think that [he] is mythical. The Penrice Mansels probably descended from a John Mansel, who was a witness to a deed concerning land at Walterston in Gower between William de Barri and John de la Mare in 1201 – well over a century after.' Interview, 22.2.2008.

106   Mansels and de Penrice: Joanna Martin, 'Penrice Castle Farm,' *Gower* 27 (1976), p.6.

106-7   rise of the Mansels: Glanmor Williams, 'The Herberts, the Mansells and Oxwich Castle,' in *Castles in Wales and the Marches. Essays in honour of D.J. Cathcart King*, eds. Kenyon and Avent (1987).

106   Oxwich Castle: Diane M. Williams, 1998 Cadw guide, op. cit., pp. 24-6.

106-7   Mansel and Margam Abbey: Glanmor Williams, 'Rice Mansell of Oxwich and Margam (1487-1559)', *Morgannwg* VI (1962); Cadw guide, op. cit.

107ff   the affray at Oxwich: Davies, Vol. 4, pp. 164-195; Glanmor Williams in
          Kenyon and Avent, op. cit.; Glanmor Williams, 'The affair of Oxwich
          castle,' *Gower* 2 (1958).

          -Mrs Mansel nee Daubridgecourt: Mansel pedigree *in* Joanna Methuen-
          Campbell, 'Penrice castle farm,' *Gower* 27 (1976), p. 13. Papers relating
          to the Star Chamber hearings are in the National Archives, and are being
          transcribed for the Gower Society.

111   the lost brooch: it came to light in 1968, when repair work was in
          progress. In one version of the story, a workman on a ladder saw a
          chicken scratch up something that glinted. The inquest on the brooch
          had to decide how it got there in the first place. If it had been hidden
          inside the castle, it was treasure trove, property of the Crown. If it had
          been lost, it belonged to the owners of the castle, the Bathurst family.
          'In hurrying out of the hall,' their solicitor suggested, 'Lady Mansel
          [he meant Aunt Anne] put the brooch into some niche for safety.
          Sir George's men were beaten off.' So (in theory) no one ever hid
          it deliberately, and the coroner decided it was not treasure trove. Dr
          M. Redknap, the curator at the National Museum in Cardiff whose
          department now holds the brooch, has his doubts. There has also been
          speculation about how the brooch came into the Mansels' possession
          in the first place. J.M. Lewis in *Jewellery Studies* Vol. 2, 1985, thought
          it 'too fine an object to have originated with the Mansels or any other
          Gower family of the fourteenth century.' He suggested that it might
          have formed part of Edward II's treasure, known to have been lost in
          South Wales when he was on the run in 1326, some of which ended
          up at Swansea Castle and was never seen again. After the 1968 find,
          Cadw – the body that safeguards Welsh historical monuments and their
          contents – bought the ring brooch for a modest sum and gave it to the
          National Museum in Cardiff. Swansea gnashed its teeth, as usual.

113   the 'bad omen' story: Davies, Vol. 4, p. 163.

113   Edward Mansel: Michael Gibbs, 'Yesterday and the day before,' *Gower*
          22 (1971), p. 57.

113-14   J.W.'s story: J.D. Davies, 'Henllys in the parish of Llandewy,' *Gower
          Church Magazine*, n.d. It is not clear where Davies is paraphrasing or
          quoting, and the text here has been slightly edited.

114ff   Mansel and Talbot genealogy: John Vivian Hughes in Wales and Joanna
          Martin in England did their best to instruct me.

115   Twenty-three cases: John Vivian Hughes, 'Thomas Mansel Talbot of
          Margam & Penrice (1747-1813),' *Gower* 26 (1975).

115-16   Mary Strangways: Joanna Martin, *Wives and Daughters* op. cit., pp. 55ff.

116   Sydney Smith: Joanna Methuen-Campbell, 'Life at Penrice castle, circa
          1800,' *Gower* 25 (1974).

116   Margam and Penrice: J. V.Hughes, *Margam Castle* (1998); Joanna
          Methuen-Campbell, *Gower* 25, op. cit.; J. V. Hughes, *Gower* 26, op. cit.

9   Dynasty

118ff   C.R.M. Talbot: J.V. Hughes, *The wealthiest commoner: C.R.M. Talbot* (1977); Thomas Methuen-Campbell (C.R.M.'s great-grandson), 'C.R.M. Talbot: A Welsh landowner in politics and industry,' *Morgannwg* XLIV (2000).

119   Talbot and the pirates: Davies, Vol. 4, pp. 45-6; and 'oak woods,' ibid, p. 47.

120-1   Talbot and railways: Arthur Rees, 'C.R.M. Talbot and the Great Western Railway' (pamphlet, n.d.).

120   C.R.M. Talbot's obituary: *Cambrian* 25.1.1890.

120-1   Railway to Port Eynon: P.R. Reynolds, 'Schemes for a Gower light railway,' *Gower* 30 (1979).

121   Worms Head lamb: J.V. Hughes, interview.

121   Brunel story: *The wealthiest commoner*, op. cit., p. 27.

121   17 illegitimate children: J.V. Hughes, interview.

122   in Malta: *The wealthiest commoner*, op. cit., p. 22.

122   Theodore comes of age: ibid., pp. 29-30.

122   'saint-like': A. Leslie Evans, *Margam Abbey* (1958), p. 137.

122   'Bando': J.V. Hughes.

122-3   Theodore's life and death: Dr Muriel Chamberlain, 'Theodore Mansel Talbot and his times,' 5th annual lecture to the Friends of Margam Abbey (1985); *The wealthiest commoner*, op.cit.; J.V. Hughes.

123   'vacant blank': C.R.M. Talbot to Hussey Vivian, 20.7.1897, *The wealthiest commoner,* op.cit.

123ff   'richest heiress' and other detail: J.V. Hughes, 'Emily Charlotte Talbot (1840-1918),' *Transactions* of Port Talbot Historical Society (1974).

124   turf on Cefn Bryn: Isobel Thomas, 'Memories of Gower in the 1920s and 1930s' *Gower* 56 (2005).

124   shooting Miss Talbot's agent: *Cambrian* 28.6.1893 and 2.8.1893. Harry had formerly worked for Miss Talbot; the dispute was about money, but he also felt slighted. When the jury couldn't agree on whether his intention was to do grievous bodily harm, the judge said they would remain locked up until they had a verdict. So they decided to give Harry the benefit of the doubt.

125   closing the Ship: Robert Lucas, *Rhossili* (2004), p.4.

125   Evelyn on her pony: R.L.T. Lucas, 'Parson Davies,' *Gower* 38 (1977).

126   bailing out Capt. Fletcher: J.V. Hughes.

126   'furious motoring': John Fletcher (the Captain's son), *Coming to Terms with Destiny*, Vol. 1, 1991.

126   sale details: J.V. Hughes, *Margam Castle*, op. cit., pp. 69-71.

126-7   decaying Margam: ibid.

127ff   the Ken Matthews story: the Matthews' website, www.smokescreen.org;
         telephone interviews with Penny Matthews, Feb 2008 and March 4, 5,
         and 12 2008.

128   John Fletcher's memoirs: *Coming to Terms with Destiny*, op. cit. Fletcher's
         interests included travel, music and mysticism, and he was an admirer
         of Rudolf Steiner (1861-1925). The book consists almost entirely of his
         diaries, which sound as if they are being written by a thoughtful child.
         '9 January 1936. Margam Castle. Norah and I came here for my second
         lecture on Bali with a musical introduction. I gave it to the Women's
         Institute in the Drill Hall at Margam Village. Dad did not come, but
         Mum came for the first half.' There was no Vol. 2.

10   The Estate

131   30,000 acres: J. Mansel Thomas, *Yesterday's Gower* (1982), quoting C.
         Methuen-Campbell, p. 228.

132   tins of polish: Oona Methuen-Campbell, interview, 19.7.2007.

132   estate subsidised: *Yesterday's Gower*, op. cit., p. 230.

132   marriage rumour: *Time*, 28.5.1923.

133-5   Oona Methuen-Campbell: interview, op. cit.

134   *Evening Post* article: by Betty Hughes, 11.7.1969.

135   Lucinda Methuen-Campbell: interviews, 2007, 2008.

136   *The Pencil of Nature*: Fox Talbot (1800-1877) was a founder of modern
         photography. The book appeared in instalments, 1844 to 1846, which
         had to be bound (if at all) by the purchaser. The photographs were
         described as 'sun pictures' produced 'by the agency of Light alone.'

136   Allan Ramsay painting: John Vivian Hughes; Elizabeth Einberg, *National
         Art Collection Fund Review* (1989).

137   'completely archaic': C. Methuen-Campbell, *Yesterday's Gower*, op. cit.,
         p. 231.

137   Thomas Methuen-Campbell: interview, 11.10.2007.

138-9   David Methuen-Campbell: interview, 20.11.2007.

11   Crimes and Punishments

140   Walterston woman: David Rees, 'Walterston: an old Gower settlement,'
         Gower 35 (1984).

140   Johnny Hatchet: Michael Gibbs, 'Yesterday and the day before,' *Gower*
         22 (1971).

141   *La Jeune Emma*: pers. knowledge, research notes for a radio script, *The
         Silent River*, broadcast 8.1.1954. The vessel was returning to France

from the West Indies. The girl, Adeline Coquelin, was with her father, a colonel. Their grave is in the churchyard at Pembrey: 'Niece to Josephine, Consort of that renowned Individual NAPOLEON BUONAPARTE.' The Adeline Guest House is just across the road.

141   George Holland's diary: David Lewis George (ed.) *Gower* 18 (1967).

142   Cartersford toll gate: E.W. Nield, 'Ilston – a village in history,' *Gower* 32 (1981).

142   fighting etc.: Wendy Cope, 'Oystermouth in the late seventeenth century,' *Gower* 53 (2002). Hedges and mangy horse: R.N. Cooper, *Higher and Lower*, op. cit., p. 45.

142   joint of beef: Gary Lyle, 'First months at Kittle Hill. From a reconstruction of the missing diary of John Griffith Hancorne,' *Gower* 33 (1982).

142   Prosecuting Felons: D.H. Hey, 'Gower United Association for the Prosecution of Felons, 1810-1892,' *Gower* 13 (1960).

142-3   P.C. Jones: 'Diary of a Swansea Police Officer,' www.south-wales. police.org.uk.

143   last contraband: Davies, Vol. 2, p. 50.

143   a hundred kegs: Davies, Vol. 3, p. 209.

144   Hounds Hole brandy: ibid.

144   Highway: Michael Gibbs, 'Brandy for the parson,' *Gower* 24 (1973). Same author: 'Mr Arthur's profession,' *Gower Life* (winter 2001).

144-5   looking out for press gangs: Davies, Vol. 2, p. 129.

145   The *Caesar*: W.N. Jenkins, 'The last hours of the "Caesar",' *Gower* 26 (1975).

146   brandy at Weobley: *Gower Life*, op. cit.

146   the Brandy House: Davies, Vol. 2, p. 196.

146   Thomas Prance: R.N. Cooper, *Higher and Lower* op. cit., pp. 86-9; R.N. Cooper, *A Dark and Pagan Place,* op. cit., pp. 70-71.

147-8   Penrice murder stone: Davies ms at West Glamorgan Archives. He gives the wrong date for the murder, October 5 instead of 3.

148   Cadoxton and Felindre stones: E.L. Reynolds, 'Murder Stones,' *Gower* 14 (1961).

149-58   Mamie and Georgie: pers. knowledge. In the 1960s I interviewed Supt. Tom Williams, who had been the investigating officer when Mamie Stuart's skeleton was found in 1961. Years later I wrote a novel based on the case, *Infidelity* (1999), using South Wales Police files, and newspaper reports from 1920, the year that she disappeared and Shotton was gaoled for bigamy.

150   *Marriage Before and After*: A. Dennison Light (editor of *Health and Vim*), price one shilling. n.d., p. 34.

150   Annie Danks: the other Mamie was involved in a lawsuit involving a threatre in Buenos Aires in 1907, where she refused to sing suggestive songs and take her skirt off. In *Sex and the British* (1994) I managed to confuse the two Mamies (paperback edition, p. 50).

154   the Caswell sisters: Prys Morgan, 'Caswell – the making of a landscape,' *Gower* 32 (1981).

154   literary traveller: Henry Wigstead, *Remarks on a tour to North and South Wales in the year 1797* (1800).

154   broken hedges: Gerald Gabb, *Swansea and its history*, op. cit., pp. 309-10.

158   'hundreds of bathers': *Swansea and Mumbles. The official guide*, n.d., but c. 1931.

12   History Man

159   E.W. Nield: 'Ilston - a village in history,' *Gower* 32 (1981).

159   Capgrave's account: Davies, Vol. 3, pp. 11ff.

159   Worms Head cavern: Davies, Vol. 3, pp. 202-3.

159-160 The Helwicks: ibid, pp. 209-12.

160   the 'Mansion House' beams: Davies, Vol. 2, p. 47.

160   floods of 1607: E.A. Bryant and S.K. Haslett, 'Was the AD 1607 coastal flooding event in the Severn estuary and Bristol Channel (UK) due to a tsunami?' *Archaeology in the Severn Estuary* 13 (2002).

        A government website (2007) does not dismiss the possibility of a Bristol Channel tsunami, and discussed a tsunami-like event of 1755 whose effects were most severe at Swansea, 'where waters were agitated, beached vessels were floated and some were turned onto the river bank.' www.defra.gov.uk/environment.

161-2   the white horse: Davies, Vol. 4, pp. 158-9.

162   exorcising a ghost: Davies, Vol. 2, p. 120.

162-3   the grey ghost: *Gower Church Magazine*, September 1900.

163-4   midsummer roses: Davies, Vol. 4, p. 32.

164   Davies letter, 8.6.1901: Jeff Towns, Dylans Book Store, private collection.

165-6   the Lucas forgeries: Robert Lucas, 'Stouthall and the Lucas family,' *Gower* 23 (1972); 'The pirates of Porteynon,' *Gower* 31 (1980).

166   fortified Salthouse: Robert Lucas, *A Gower Family. The Lucases of Stouthall and Rhossili Rectory* (Appendix to 2005 edition). 'Musket balls': *Independent*.

166   Davies and Llanmadoc Church: F.G. Cowley, *Morgannwg* XXXVI.

166-7   Kilvert's visit, 1872: *Kilvert's Diary* (1960 edition), Vol. 2, April 16.

167   picnic at Langland: *Kilvert*, Vol. 3., 16.10.1878.

168   Davies's burial place: Cowley, *Morgannwg* XXXVIII, op. cit.

13   Hill Country

170 where Gower ends: David Rees, 'The Gower estates of Sir Rhys ap Thomas,' *Gower* 43 (1992).

171 *East Gower.* W. Ll. Morgan, Lt. Col., late R.E., *An antiquarian survey of East Gower, Glamorganshire,* 1899. Morgan wrote in his Preface: 'In treating of East Gower I have been careful not to encroach upon the sphere of influence of the learned historian of West Gower.'

172 Penlle'r Castell and the Welsh: J. Beverley Smith, 'Penlle'r Castell,' *Morgannwg* IX (1965).

  -An inventory of the ancient monuments in Glamorgan Vol. 3, Part 1b, Royal Commission on the Ancient and Historical Monuments of Wales (2000).

173 radio telephone link: www.frenchaymuseumarchives.co.uk.

173 bankrupt, 1914: www.winterbourne.freeuk.com.

174ff Air Ministry file: National Archives, AIR 5/179. Treasury file T1/11857.

174 Pen ponds trial: E.H.G. Barwell, *The Death Ray Man* n.d., but c.1941. Barwell cites E.E. Fournier D'Albe, *The Moon Element* (about selenium and its properties).

175 Hammond experiments: *New York Times,* 16.12.1911.

176 post-war reports: Wikipedia; other websites have Press citations.

177 raising money: 'Brief outline of Mr Grindell-Matthews' Invention and Draft Particulars of Private Company proposed to be formed to acquire same.' Initially the company wanted to raise £20,000. 'At present,' promised the document, 'at 64 feet Mr Matthews, by the application of the electric energy alone, is able to stop the functioning of a petrol motor by causing a short circuit in the magneto windings, the insulation being penetrated [...] he has already set fire to his work bench and blown all the fuses in the building [...] It is thought possible that either the electric energy or the beam of light, or the two in combination may have therapeutical powers, and this is being investigated by Mr Matthews in collaboration with an eminent surgeon...' National Archives, AIR 5/179, op. cit.

178 death rays and radar: R.V. Jones *Most Secret War. British scientific intelligence 1939-1945,* Coronet Books, 1979, pp. 42-3.

178 to S. Wales, 1934: Wikipedia.

179 dressed for dinner: Dr Lindsay Morgan, son of Dr Gwynne.

179 Colonel Etherton: Barwell, op. cit., pp. 130-31.

180 goings-on: 'Y Dyn Ar Y Mynydd' ('The Man on the Hountain'), S4C, the Welsh-language TV channel, 1999. Interviews with elderly residents were included.

180-1 Madam Walska: sundry websites. The diamond: www.famousdiamonds. tripod.com/walskadiamond. Lotusland: lotusland.org.

181   Walska letter: Barwell, op.cit., p.163.

14   War and Memory

182   Dr Moreton and Brynfield: pers. knowledge.

182-3   local defences: pers. knowledge.

183   Swansea and A.R.P.: J.R. Alban, 'Preparations for air raid precautions in Swansea, 1935-9,' *Morgannwg* XXVIII (1984); pers. knowledge.

183   German war directive, and Swansea air raids in general: J.R. Alban, *The Three Nights' Blitz* (1994).

184   Dornier off Port Eynon: R.T. Pearce, *Operation Wasservogel*, 'The story of the South Buckham Farm bomber crash in Dorset and the final raid on Swansea' (1977), p. 61.

184   September 1940 raid: Alban, op. cit., p. 4.

184   Thomas to Watkins: Dylan Thomas, *Collected Letters* (2000), p 525.

184   'stirring times': *Gower Church Magazine*, n.d.

185   police on the beach: B.D.J., 'Life at Nicholaston – 1937-1957,' *Gower* 14 (1961).

185   Vernon Watkins: Gwen Watkins, 'Taliesin in Gower: Vernon Watkins – a retrospect,' *Gower* 48 (1997).

185   beached at Southend: pers. knowledge.

185-7   R.A.F. Fairwood Common: Nigel Arthur, *Swansea at war* (1988), pp. 107ff. Richard E. Roberts, 'Four degrees west: The W.A.A.F. presence at Fairwood aerodrome,' *Minerva* 2 (1994).

185   Bronze Age mounds: Gerald Gabb, *Swansea and its history* op. cit., pp. 164-5.

185   slagheaps: the poisoned tips at the lower end of the Swansea Valley, covering hundreds of acres, were the result of two centuries of heavy industry. The metal and chemical residues showed up as greens and purples after rain, like malevolent rainbows. German reconnaissance photographs of this wasteland were said to have been used by the enemy as propaganda, showing damage supposedly caused by bombing. The area was finally cleaned up in the 1960s. Pers. knowledge.

185   shooters at Penrice: Thomas Methuen-Campbell, 'Game shooting on the Penrice estate before 1950,' Part 1, *Gower* 47 (1966).

186   two-thirds of a man: 'Four degrees west,' *Minerva* 2, op. cit., p. 16.

186   practice camp: *Swansea at War*, op. cit., p. 108.

186-7   James Farrar: Bernard Lloyd, 'Halcyon days in Gower', *Gower* 28 (1977). Farrar, b. 1923, was killed when he tried to intercept a 'flying bomb.' A collection of his prose and poetry, *The Unreturning Spring*, was published in 1950.

187   radar station: pers. knowledge.

187   Fairwood airfield: pers. knowledge. 'Fairwood's idle drome and deserted control tower,' *South Wales Evening Post*, 17.7.1948.

188ff   Americans in Gower: Nigel Arthur, *Swansea at War* op. cit. Pers. knowledge.

188   wartime Penrice Castle: Thomas Methuen-Campbell, *Gower* 47, op. cit. Officers in attics: Oona Methuen-Campbell.

188-90 ships in the bay: from a 'shipping log' I kept as a schoolboy. U.S. 2nd Infantry Division: Nigel Arthur, op. cit.

191ff   biological warfare and the Burry estuary: National Archives, DEFE55/120. G.B. Carter, pers. communication. G.B. Carter, *Chemical and biological defence at Porton Down 1916-2000* (2000), pp. 63-4. Qinetiq archive department. Robert Harris and Jeremy Paxman, *A Higher Form of Killing. The secret story of gas and germ warfare* (1982). 'Llanelli History' website, 'Gerald Grant's Tales of Seaside [...] The Burry Estuary. Chemical & Biological Warfare Weapons, Germ Warfare [etc.].' The late Mr Grant's account, which cites only the Paxman and Harris book as a source, is not reliable.

193-4 the 'D Day' theory: author's speculation.

15   'Omit Gower'

196   post-mistress, dead horse etc: Ann Roberts, *Estuary People. Penclawdd 1900 to 1970* (2001), pp. 209ff.

196   Frankie Howerd: Ann Roberts, ibid, pp. 207-8. 'Comedians': *Observer* magazine, 5.10.1969.

196ff   the proving ranges affair: National Archives, Ministry of Supply, BD28/90, AB/43/4/. Ministry of Housing and Local Government (Welsh Office), P228/1200B/1/.

197   Coat of Arms: Elis Jenkins, 'The Gower Rural District's Coat of Arms,' *Gower* 22 (1971).

198   'emotional totalitarianism [...] no matter what the cost in personal relations': David Rees, 'The Gwent Jones I knew,' *Gower* 15 (1962).

198   Dr Gwent and Home Rule: pers. knowledge. The local newspaper report of the incident has not been traced. Nor does the family have any record. But they are aware it happened.

16   Territory

202ff   founding the Gower Society: Gwent Jones, 'A history of the Gower Society' part 1, *Gower* 12 (1959); part 2, *Gower* 14 (1961). David Rees, 'The Gowermen' *Gower* 49 (1998). Jim Rees, 'Go Albilidger, Boy!', *Gower* 49 (1998). ('Albilidger' is explained as old Gower dialect for 'all be leisure,' i.e. 'take it easy').

204   National Parks and the A.O.N.B.: Malcolm Ridge, pers. communication.

204-5   Butlins rumours: Gower Society minutes ('*GS mins*'). These are informal summaries made by Ruth Ridge, the society's archivist. The rumours were widely reported.

205   saving Oxwich castle: Bernard Morris, 'Oxwich castle,' *Gower* 25 (1974); Bernard Morris, 'Oxwich castle: which came first, the farmhouse or the hall?', *Gower* 43 (1992); the Ridges, interview 25.3.2008. *GS mins*, 1949, 1950. Lady Apsley and the woods: the Ridges.

205-6   issues great and small: *GS mins;* the Ridges.

208   50th anniversary: Malcolm Ridge, 'That was a year that was...!', *Gower* 49 (1998).

208ff   Prince Charles episode: pers. knowledge.

209   Edward Harris: solicitor, Swansea. His grandfather acted for George Shotton, the bigamist who got away with the Caswell murder.

210   motive for stone shifting: local gossip names an individual who still lives in peninsula Gower.

211   107 blows: the Ridges.

BOOKS CONSULTED

J.R. Alban, Swansea 1184-1984 (Swansea City Council and the *South Wales Evening Post* 1984).

– The Three Nights' Blitz. Select contemporary reports relating to Swansea's air raids (City of Swansea 1994).

Stephen Aldhouse-Green (ed.), Paviland Cave and the 'Red Lady'. A definitive report (Western Academic & Specialist Press 2000).

Nigel Arthur, Swansea at War (Archive Publications Manchester 1988).

W.G.V. Balchin (ed.), Swansea and its Region (University College of Swansea 1971).

A.T. Bannister, The Cathedral Church of Hereford, its History and Constitution (SPCK 1924).

Robert Bartlett, The Hanged Man. A story of Miracle, memory and colonialism in the Middle Ages (Princeton University Press Oxford 2004).

E.H.G. Barwell, The Death Ray Man. The biography of Grindell Matthews inventor and pioneer (Hutchinson n.d., but c. 1941).

Black's Guide to South Wales (1910).

William Buckland, Reliquiae Diluvianae (John Murray 1823).

Joseph P. Clancy (tr.), Medieval Welsh Poems (Four Courts Press Dublin 2003).

R.N. Cooper, 'A Dark and Pagan Place' [Penclawdd history] (D. Brown & Sons Cowbridge 1986).

– Higher and Lower [Llanrhidian history] (Subboscus 1998).

James A. Davies (ed.), A Swansea Anthology (Seren n.d.).

J.D. Davies, A History of West Gower. (Four volumes; only Vol. 1 has this title), (1877, 1879, 1885, 1894).

Russell Davies, Hope and Heartbreak. A social history of Wales and the Welsh, 1776-1871 (University of Wales Press 2005).

Lewis W. Dillwyn, Contributions Towards a History of Swansea (1840).

Ifan ab Owen Edwards, A Catalogue of Star Chamber Proceedings Relating to Wales (University Press Board, Cardiff 1929).

A. Leslie Evans, Margam Abbey (1996).

Edith Evans, Swansea castle and the medieval town (Swansea City Council 1983).

Paul Ferris, Dylan Thomas. The Biography (Hodder 1977 – Y Lolfa 2006).

(ed.) Dylan Thomas. The Collected Letters (Dent 1985, 2000).

J.T.T. Fletcher, Coming to Terms with Destiny. The memoirs of John Theodore Talbot Fletcher, Vol. 1 (Mercury Arts Publications 1991).

Barbara Freese, Coal. A human history (Perseus n.d.).

Gerald Gabb, Swansea and its History Vol. 1 (2006).

Gerald of Wales (Giraldus Cambrensis), tr. Lewis Thorpe, The Journey through Wales and The Description of Wales (Penguin Books 2004).

Robert Harris and Jeremy Paxman, A Higher Form of Killing. The secret story of gas and germ warfare (Chatto and Windus 1982).

J.V. Hughes, The Wealthiest Commoner. C.R.M. Talbot (West Glamorgan County Council 1980).

W.J. Hughes, Wales and the Welsh in English Literature (Wrexham, Hughes & Son 1924).

Alun R. Jones and Gwyn Thomas (eds.), Presenting Saunders Lewis (University of Wales Press 1983).

R.V. Jones, Most Secret War. British scientific intelligence 1939-1945 (Coronet Books 1979).

W.H. Jones, History of Swansea and of the Lordship of Gower Vol. 1 (1920).

- Vol. 2 (Royal Institution of South Wales Swansea 1992).

Francis Kilvert, Kilvert's Diary, ed. William Plomer. Vols. 2 and 3 (Cape 1960).

John Edward Lloyd, The Welsh Chronicles (Sir John Rhys memorial lecture, British Academy 1928).

Robert Lucas, A Gower Family. The Lucases of Stouthall and Rhossili rectory (Cross Publishing 2005).

- Reynoldston (1998).

- Rhossili. A Village Background (Gower Society 2004).

Joanna Martin, Wives and Daughters. Women and children in the Georgian country house (Hambledon and London 2004).

O. Morien Morgan, The Battles of Wales. The unconquered country of the Empire (D. Salesbury Hughes Liverpool 1920).

W. Ll Morgan, An antiquarian survey of East Gower, Glamorganshire (Chas. J. Clark 1899).

- The Town and Manor of Swansea (W. Spurrell & Son Carmarthen 1924).

Kari Maund, The Welsh Kings (Tempus n.d.).

A. Morris, Glamorgan (John E. Southall, Newport 1907).

Murray's Handbook for Travellers in South Wales (John Murray 1870).

National Union of Teachers handbook 1897 conference Swansea.

Lynn H. Nelson, The Normans in South Wales, 1070-1171 (University of Texas 1966).

Lewis D. Nicholl, The Normans in Glamorgan (Cardiff 1936).

Geoffrey R. Orrin, The Gower Churches (Rural Deanery of West Gower 1979).

David Painting, Amy Dillwyn (University of Wales Press 1987).

R.T. Pearce, Operation Wasservogel. The story of [...] the final raid on Swansea (Hamblin Books 1997).

Robert Penhallurick, Gowerland and its Language. A history of the English speech of the Gower Peninsula, South Wales (Peter Lang, Frankfurt am Main n.d.).

Port of Llanelly Official Handbook (early 20C.).

Pryor's Gower Guide 4th edn. (?1950s).

David Rees (ed.), A Gower Anthology (Christopher Davies Swansea 1977).

–   The Son of Prophecy. Henry Tudor's road to Bosworth (Black Raven Press 1985).

William Rees, South Wales and the March 1294-1415. A social and agrarian study (OUP Humphrey Milford 1924).

Ann Roberts, Estuary People. Penclawdd 1900 to 1970 (2001).

–   Service with a Smile. Jobs of bygone days (2005).

Nigel A Robins, Eye of the Eagle. The Luftwaffe aerial photographs of Swansea (Tawe History Publishing 1993).

Nicolaas A. Rupke, The Great Chain of History. William Buckland and the English School of Geology, 1814-1849 (1983).

South Wales Coast Resorts Association Official Handbook (c. 1931).

Swansea City Council, Lower Swansea Valley – legacy and future (n.d., c. 1975).

J. Mansel Thomas, Yesterday's Gower (Gomer Press 1982).

Lewis Thorpe (tr.), Gerald of Wales. The Journey through Wales and the Description of Wales (Penguin Books 2004).

Trades Union Congress 'Souvenir' (Swansea 1901).

David Walker, The Norman Conquerors (Christopher Davies Swansea 1977).

C.S. Ward and M.J.B. Baddeley, Through Guide to South Wales (Dulau & Co. 1901).

Gwen Watkins, Portrait of a Friend (Y Lolfa 2005).

A. Leslie Williams, Margam Abbey (1958).

Stewart Williams (ed.), Glamorgan Historian, Vol. 4 (D. Brown Cowbridge 1967).

Swansea & Mumbles Official Guides (early 1930s).

Trades' Union Congress Swansea 1901 Souvenir.

INDEX